TRY TO
SEE IT
MY WAY

TRY TO
SEE IT
MY WAY

*Being Fair in Love
and Marriage*

B. Janet Hibbs, Ph.D.

WITH KAREN J. GETZEN, PH.D.

AVERY

a member of Penguin Group (USA) Inc.

New York

Published by the Penguin Group
Penguin Group (USA) Inc., 375 Hudson Street, New York, New York 10014, USA • Penguin Group (Canada),
90 Eglinton Avenue East, Suite 700, Toronto, Ontario M4P 2Y3, Canada (a division of Pearson Canada Inc.) •
Penguin Books Ltd, 80 Strand, London WC2R 0RL, England • Penguin Ireland, 25 St Stephen's Green, Dublin 2, Ireland
(a division of Penguin Books Ltd) • Penguin Group (Australia), 250 Camberwell Road, Camberwell, Victoria 3124,
Australia (a division of Pearson Australia Group Pty Ltd) • Penguin Books India Pvt Ltd, 11 Community Centre,
Panchsheel Park, New Delhi–110 017, India • Penguin Group (NZ), 67 Apollo Drive, Rosedale, North Shore 0632,
New Zealand (a division of Pearson New Zealand Ltd) • Penguin Books (South Africa) (Pty) Ltd,
24 Sturdee Avenue, Rosebank, Johannesburg 2196, South Africa

Penguin Books Ltd, Registered Offices:
80 Strand, London WC2R 0RL, England

My thanks to Dr. John Gottman, for his permission to reprint an exercise from the
Gottman Institute's *Clinical Manual for Marital Therapy*, 2005.

Most Avery books are available at special quantity discounts for bulk purchase for sales promotions, premiums,
fund-raising, and educational needs. Special books or book excerpts also can be created to fit specific needs.
For details, write Penguin Group (USA) Inc. Special Markets, 375 Hudson Street, New York, NY 10014.

Library of Congress Cataloging-in-Publication Data

Hibbs, B. Janet.
Try to see it my way : being fair in love and marriage / B. Janet Hibbs with Karen J. Getzen.
p.   cm.
Includes bibliographical references and index.
ISBN 978-1-58333-332-7
1. Interpersonal relations.   2. Love—social spects.   3. Couples.   4. Fairness.   1. Getzen, Karen J.   II. Title.
HM1106.H53   2009   2008046232
646.7'8—dc22

Printed in the United States of America
1   3   5   7   9   10   8   6   4   2

Book design by Meighan Cavanaugh

For Earl, Jared, and William—

life's meaning is time with you

ACKNOWLEDGMENTS

Nothing in my life quite prepared me for the undertaking of writing a book. Fortunately, everything in my life pointed the direction, and along the way key people lent encouragement, wisdom, and love. *Try to See It My Way* was in the gestational stage for twenty-five years, following my clinical training in contextual family theory. I owe a profound debt of thanks to the brilliant author of contextual theory, my teacher, the late Iván Böszörményi-Nagy. His elegant theory gave me a new professional direction and paradigm to live by. I also had the great fortune of studying with his colleagues, Barbara Krasner, the very spirit of contextual theory, who was my mentor, and Margaret Cotroneo, who shared my love for the pragmatic and first encouraged my research in this field. Another important influence was the late Emmy Pepitone, at Bryn Mawr College, who urged me to continue my writing. These great thinkers trained, befriended, and inspirited me over many years.

As with other important things in my life, I did this process backward. I wrote the book first and then sought a publisher. First, Barbara Cullen, then Liz Widdicombe, friends in the academic publishing world, reviewed a chapter, made suggestions, and then assisted me in finding an agent. Through Liz, Bruce Nichols, and the seven degrees of separation in the world, an early draft arrived on the desk of my agent, Priscilla Gilman. Priscilla took a big chance representing a first-time author.

An embracing thanks to Priscilla, who tirelessly and astutely edited early drafts of the book, saved me from inelegant writing, then guided me through the publication world, until the book found a good home. Richard Prud'homme deserves tremendous credit for his keen suggestions on the all-important proposal, which aided me in transforming the ghost of an outline into a compelling read.

Lucia Watson was a dream editor, par excellence at the Penguin Group, Avery/Viking Studio. Lucia rescued me from repetitiveness and other flaws with her extraordinary editing. Her finely tuned ear for the nuances of language, and well-honed vision for the book's cohesiveness, made this a much finer and more accessible book. Many thanks, Lucia, for your professional wisdom, personal grace, and kindness, too.

My trusted friend Karen Getzen turned the solitary pursuit of writing a book into a dialogic process. Karen responded to every word I wrote (and rewrote), striking an artful balance between challenging and deferring, while making valuable contributions. Karen, thank you for this process, along with the gift of your steadfast patience.

My sister, Gwenn Hibbs, generously took on, at the eleventh hour, a final polishing of that same crucial proposal. She also kindly read and made most insightful comments on the last draft of the manuscript. Gwenn was exceptionally helpful. My close colleague Suzanne Brennan responded to my earliest formulation of the book. My dear friend Jane Buhl contributed the concept of the well of trust. Other talented friends: Jamie Lilley drew the book's charming line illustrations, and Weaver Lilley created and updated my Web site. My thanks to my colleagues—Drs. Susan LaDuca, Andrea Bloomgarden, Arlene Houldin, Steve Levick, Paul Schaefer, Caroline Mac-Moran, and Jan Filing, who shared my excitement about the project. For quotable comments, my thanks to Jim Bradberry, Claire Robinson, Dr. Jim Hoyme, Weaver Lilley, Diane Luckman, Mark Sivrine, and Ted Loder. My deepest appreciation to family and good friends who were "there for me" while life inconveniently happened at the same time.

My goal in writing this book was to make a complex body of work as simple as possible, but no simpler. There is a long learning curve before you can write in an uncomplicated way about the concepts of relational ethics. Along that curve, my family therapy graduate students taught me to make abstract concepts comprehensible. A large part of the curve was learning from my patients. Their lives have enriched mine, and the lessons I've gained will now benefit the lives of others.

Most crucially, I learned to practice what I preach in my own family. I thank my parents, in memory of Max and in honor of Jeannette Hibbs, who blessed me by having dreams and aspirations for me, that I could have them for myself. They lovingly embraced all the challenges I posed for them in my life as a family therapist. My in-laws, Ruth and Earl Marsh, graciously supported my writing in many ways, allowing me time to write when we visited, spending time with the kids, and baking the world's best cookies. Thank you for the love you have brought to us all.

To my children, Jared and William, I thank you for the great joys you've given, and the humility that parenthood brings. They patiently indulged my constant refrain "I'll just be a few more minutes" during the many hours I wrote.

Above all, I owe the deepest gratitude to my husband, Earl. It would have been impossible to write a book about fairness for couples if I hadn't experienced it first-hand. Earl has a great generosity of spirit to which I aspire. His resolute support, unflagging belief in me, and good humor ("the book is done again") made this undertaking not only possible but also a treasured gift of love. Earl, I thank you with all my heart, now and always.

—B. Hibbs

I want to thank B. Hibbs for coming to me five years ago and asking me to contribute to a book on fairness. Through that time I've had the pleasure of learning more about her vision and her deep desire and ability to share that vision with others. In the early stage of the development of *Try to See It My Way*, my friends and fellow writing group members, Annette Lareau and Erin McNamara Horvat, gave feedback that was helpful in making the book more focused. My colleagues in the English department at Chestnut Hill College in Philadelphia have been supportive and able to find humor in unlikely moments, and have welcomed me into their world. To all my close friends and family, especially my newborn granddaughter, Kayla, thank you.

—Karen Getzen

CONTENTS

Part Two

REPAIRING EVERYDAY INJUSTICES
AND BREACHES IN FAIRNESS

INTRODUCTION

Why Being Fair Will Make Your
Relationship Stronger

To be happy, one must be just.
—ARISTOTLE

L ife isn't fair. But relationships can be. Fairness is the key to solving problems and making love last. Despite the fact that most of us learned to tell
right from wrong at about age three, curiously, few partners have mastered
the art of what it takes to be fair to each other. And you can't solve this vexing
(and sometimes deadly) relationship problem simply by taking turns, or even
"fighting fair." Instead, you need a new way of understanding the intricacies
and intimacies of fairness. This new way recognizes that partners bring to
their relationships a host of deeply felt "truths" about fairness, based on their
own unique family experiences. When these differing "truths" collide, they
can prompt a downward spiral of unhappiness. In this context, you need to
learn to be fair in a whole new way. If you do, you'll have a more loving and
vital marriage. That is my conviction and the promise this book makes.

When most of my clients first hear this message, they look at me with disbelief and curiosity as if I must live in a fantasy world and certainly must be
clueless about their lives. Most couples don't think of fairness as their defining problem. Most reveal their troubles, as Michelle and Jim did, with a cross
fire of accusations. Though this was only their second therapy session, like

many couples in distress, it was easy to see that Michelle and Jim were having a recurring argument. They were stuck in their own private, hellish loop with no exit and no apparent solution.

Jim recounted his complaint for what sounded like the umpteenth time: "The spark is gone. I want passion and romance, someone who wants me. I want the woman I fell in love with. I've been unhappy for a long time. I don't think Michelle can meet my needs."

Michelle retorted: "I'm so sick of those two words, *passion* and *romance*. I think if I hear them again, I'll scream. We have two little kids. I feel like a cow, always breast-feeding, or changing diapers, wiping noses. Have you ever considered that helping me, like doing the dishes or cooking dinner, might be a form of foreplay? You're totally oblivious. You have no idea about what I go through every day. How could you treat me this way and think I'd have mad passion for you? I don't think you love me. I don't even think you like me, and I'm not sure I like you anymore, either." Michelle then broke down crying, as Jim stared blankly, at a loss for words.

I wondered if their marriage was in trouble simply because they were overwhelmed by the overload of child care demands. Was this yet another well-worn scene from the chore wars? Clearly, division of labor was a problem area, just as their sex life was. But my hunch was that there were other barriers to a loving relationship, or as Jim put it, romance and passion. In my experience, most problems in relationships, whether small or large, have issues of fairness at their core. Similarly, the resolution of conflict requires that partners feel fairly treated. Yet fairness goes beyond simply reassigning chores, communicating better, meeting each other's needs, or adding romance. Fairness is the silent working model that guides couples' expectations of each other and underlies every interaction between them. You need fairness to build trust, feel close, and make your marriage work. Yet, how do partners decide what's fair to give and to get, and who gets to decide?

I stopped their argument, and challenged each of them: "Jim, not having romance and passion is merely a symptom of something deeper going on. So instead of thinking this is simply Michelle's problem, let's look at what the problem is between the two of you. And Michelle, help me understand how you've asked Jim for help, because blaming him, or telling him he's oblivious, won't work. Tell me more about what you expect from each other, and where you learned those expectations. Tell me what you learned about love and fairness from your families growing up. Tell me when it broke down for the two of you."

Michelle began: "Fairness didn't matter in my family. My mother was a doormat, and my father was a bully. Sounds a lot like Jim and me. I have a hard time standing up for myself, with Jim or really with anyone. I know this comes from my growing up. But knowing it hasn't helped me. The only way I got around my father was by being pleasant and giving in. I did the same thing for years with Jim." Michelle addressed her next remarks to Jim: "I used to try so hard to please you. For years I went along because if I didn't, you'd get angry. Arguing with you is like being in a boxing match with a heavyweight champ. Even if I win, I'm beat up. Now I don't care what you want, I don't care about your so-called romance. I'm out of energy."

Once again, Jim sat stunned. He was used to her accusations. But he wasn't prepared for her hopelessness, or for her willingness to take some responsibility for her part of their problem. I prompted Jim to tell Michelle if he could see some truth in what she'd said. Finally, Jim spoke: "Michelle, you're right. I do have a really short fuse, but for me it blows over. I didn't know I had shut you down all these years. And maybe I have expected you to do more than your share." Then Jim turned to me: "Michelle isn't the first person who's told me that when I think I'm right, I don't budge. I'm used to being in charge—since I was a kid. Maybe that wasn't as good for me as I thought." He paused, and then turned back to Michelle: "Michelle, I'm really sorry I hassled you so much. I guess I knew it in some sense, but I hadn't put two and two together—about me and your dad."

Jim had begun to see Michelle more sympathetically. Then he asked Michelle to try to see it his way. "But you know, I feel rejected by you. How many hundreds of times can a guy hug his pillow instead of his wife without feeling hurt? I guess I turned my rejection into a demand and a put-down of you. I helped create my own rejection." Jim was beginning to realize how each fed into the cycle of unfair expectations, rejection, and hurt between them. Jim's expression of acknowledgment and remorse, and his own display of vulnerability moved Michelle. He added, "I hope it's not too late." She slowly smiled and took his hand. Now for the first time after months of tension, they felt more hopeful. The couple had begun the process of learning to be fair.

In this brief scene from a marriage, we glimpse how a couple's distinct disappointments are rooted in both past and present unfair patterns of relating that fuel their quarrels. Their imbalances of give-and-take created a withholding cycle between them, in which neither felt cared about. Like Michelle and Jim, most couples don't present their problems as fairness issues. Fairness problems come disguised in loyalty conflicts: *Why do we have to go to your parents for the holidays? Remember, I have a family, too. Why don't you take my side when your mother puts me on the spot? You choose your kids over me—but I didn't marry your kids.* Fairness conflicts also pop up in the everyday abuses in relating: *It was your turn to clean the kitchen. Why didn't you fill up, when you were the last one to use the car?* Fairness concerns also underlie the growing pains of life: *Why am I always the one getting up in the night with the baby? Why are you supervising what I spend money on? I earn money, too, you know.* And the lack of fairness is at the heart of the enduring injustices of a relationship, such as affairs, alcoholism, a secret life, financial infidelity, and other massive betrayals.

Yet couples don't intuitively think in terms of fairness. They say there's not enough love, or they say they're unhappy. They ask me, "What's fairness got to do with love?" When people first learned that I was writing a book about fairness in love and marriage, I got a variety of responses. "Is it fiction?" one joked. "Good luck," another quipped, "it must be a small book." But for many it struck a serious chord. "Absolutely, you can't have a loving relationship unless people are fair-minded." Several others agreed that "couples struggle with problems of fairness all the time." A mother of young children challenged, "Marriages with children can't be fair!" Others zeroed in on the core questions: How do you decide what's fair? And who gets to decide? This book shows you how love crucially depends on fair treatment. Fairness helps you resolve conflicts, enables you to give and to get what you deserve, and is the key to a healthy, happy marriage. *Try to See It My Way* offers a fresh way to understand fairness in the world of intimate relationships, while providing a road map for creating a more loving relationship because it is based on fair relating. Let's start by looking at the importance of fairness in sustaining love.

What's Fairness Got to Do with It (Love and Happiness, That Is)?

There are two conditions for enduring happiness. One of these is relatedness. We are wired from birth to respond and to engage in a primary relationship. Humans, second only to ants, are a hypersocial species. Relationships can make us feel happy and cared about over time. That's why couples still seek the secret of lasting love, hoping to defy the odds, even as more and more relationships fail. But it's not any kind of relationship that makes us happy. After all, an unharmonious relationship, the kind I treat in my clinical practice, is one of those noxious stressors that couples never get used to. Interpersonal conflict makes us unhappy. Not only are couples stressed by conflict, but those negative stressors can also contribute to heart disease, depression, and a lower rating on that elusive goal of "happiness." So what is the other condition for happiness? Fairness. Fairness is that enigmatic, critical component of an enduring, loving, happy relationship. Unromantic as it sounds, it takes fairness to sustain love. Your own understanding of fairness in the world of close relationships begins with the decisive first step of acknowledging that fairness is at the heart of all healthy relationships and that imbalances of fairness underlie many problems that ail relationships.

This book begins by asking you to explore your own "take" on the fairness issue. While everyone, even kids at the playground, thinks they know what's fair, have you ever bothered to thoughtfully state and then evaluate what you expect from your partner? Have you ever named what you expect from your marriage as a whole? Do you know what disappoints you? Do you know what you owe your spouse, and what you deserve? In other words: do you feel that you are treated fairly or unfairly? Some relationships feel fair. In others, partners are seething with resentment. And in many, there's a mixture of satisfied feelings and anger at unfairness. To see how fair relating can enhance and sustain your relationship, you must first understand your own expectations for give-and-take, and how they developed.

Fairness is so deeply felt that our guiding intuition about what's fair is impossible to ignore, though it's often hard to define, and at times even more challenging to agree upon. You only have to observe a few couples to conclude that partners often disagree, sometimes chronically and most unhappily, about what is fair. That's because fairness is a curious blend of universal rules mixed up with variations you learned in your family. I think of this blend as the two realms of fairness.

The first realm is universal. Everyone has access to it. This realm of fairness is made up of your gut feelings—telling you right from wrong, fair from unfair. You expect others to share these basic rules with their implications for intimate relationships: *It's not fair to cheat on your partner; it's wrong to take more than you give; it's right to take care of your children; it's important to treat each other with respect.* If everyone agreed on universal principles, there'd never be a divorce. But relationships aren't that neat. Sometimes even when spouses do agree in principle, they find themselves doing something that offends even their own moral sensibilities. They break their own fairness rules. That's where the second realm of fairness comes into play.

Complicating your innate, universal imperatives are fairness rules learned in your family growing up (your *family of origin*). Not only do families embody vast differences traversing culture, ethnicity, religion, behaviors, and traditions, but each partner also brings a unique experience of fair or unfair treatment from his own family. Each couple imports these differing and sometimes opposing directives from their families of origin into their intimate relationship. Those dictates might include: *Men take care of women, and women take care of kids; women take care of almost everything and get the deciding vote; marriage is monogamous; marriage is serial; marriage is unnecessary; family meals are eaten together; it's no big deal if we eat separately; partners should be co-parents; mothers are better at parenting; Sunday is a day of rest, so*

we go to church; Sunday is a day of rest, so I play golf; it's important to see ex-
tended family often; the fewer visits the better; parents can never do enough for
their children; pleasing your parents trumps what your partner wants. Some differences are merely preferences, but others feel like moral imperatives. You
have the task of negotiating your differences to arrive at what's fair between
you and your partner. This second realm of fairness, learned in your family,
is an idiosyncratic and messy blend of perceptions, assumptions, and expectations for give-and-take. It is this second ambiguous and crucial realm that *Try*
to See It My Way sets out to explore and map. Let's briefly survey these two
domains of fairness as we turn to the questions this book will answer: just
how important is fairness? How do you decide what's fair? Who decides
what's fair? When the relationship's not fair, how do you repair it?

Just How Important Is Fairness?

Fairness is recognized as part of ancient wisdom that reflects an innate aspect
of the moral code that makes us human. The universally shared motivation
for fair treatment is so elemental that even animals are capable of protesting
an unfair experience. In a recent study, chimps that were "stuck" with nonreciprocating chimps became so angry that they hurled their feces at their unfair partners. Fortunately, human couples are typically more sophisticated in
their responses to unfair treatment. But we are almost all instinctually sensitive to unfairness, even if we each act unfairly at times.

This innate sense of fairness exists in children as well as in adults. As a
result, fairness is an organizing principle of life and is the basis for trust
throughout our lives and in the world at large. Research proves that the biological indicator for our gut feelings about fair and unfair treatment is located
in the right prefrontal cortex of the brain. Neuroscientists have traced our intuition for fair dealing to an electromagnetic pattern. Some have even suggested from recent studies that there is a fairness "organ" in the brain—by
which they mean a strong system for tracking give-and-take. Because humans have lived in groups from the earliest times, the ability to track reci-

procity was likely a key to survival. Various studies confirm that participants will punish a group member who isn't playing a game in a cooperative manner—even when the punishment disadvantages the avenging player. But wherever scientists pinpoint the biological impulses guiding fairness, partners intuitively register and respond to fair and unfair behavior. And like the chimps, most of us feel a spontaneous rush of righteous indignation when our partner treats us unfairly.

At that moment of unfairness, you have a strong certainty that you're in the right, and protest, "That's not fair!" In day-to-day life, these fairness skirmishes for a couple might sound like this: *It was your turn to take out the trash; you owed me a call—you knew I had to take my dad to the hospital; I went out of my way for you this morning—the least you could do is help me now; we have two kinds of money—yours and ours; you never ask me how I am; the household and kids shouldn't just be my job; you put your family first—what about me?*

Emotional battles also erupt over major breaches of trust as well as patterns of unfairness: *I worked all day and came home to the kids hungry and you drunk; you forged my name and withdrew money; you treat me like dirt; when we argue, you throw in everything but the kitchen sink; our marriage is a cesspool after your affair.* As significant as these problems may be, they are only the oblique indicators, the *symptoms* of relationships that are out of balance because they are plagued by real or perceived unfairness. Our innate sense of fairness must be off-kilter when partners are more motivated to harm each other than to play fair. How did it go so wrong?

While our gut feelings about fairness instruct us in the moral code of not harming another, as the above violations of fairness indicate, those instinctive feelings take us only so far. That's where the second realm of learned fairness takes over. We each bring our unique familial "script" or model, full of unexpressed beliefs (reasonable or not) to our relationships. Your fairness model isn't formally taught but, more powerfully, is learned through growing up in your family. Family relationships forge expectations for give-and-take that are handed down over many generations. The understanding of what you owe your family is called *loyalty*. Loyalty is the payback system for how a child (over a lifetime) gives back to parents and family. Each partner brings familial loyalties to their marriage, and layers them onto the model of what a couple owes each other. Family loyalties, even more significantly, instruct an individual in the "who comes first" in a marriage. Does what you owe your parents trump what your spouse wants? Does spending time with your extended family create conflict with your partner? Do you expect a partner to mirror the give-and-take you learned in your family? Or, more subtly, do you have a distant or an estranged relationship from a parent, but expect your partner to make up for your losses? There are as many loyalty variations and expectations as there are families.

Your familial fairness model, of which loyalty is a part, is so deeply ingrained that by adulthood, your beliefs about fairness feel like objective truths that are automatically (often unconsciously) brought into all of your relationships. Yet fairness between partners can't be decided based on only one partner's understanding of fairness, no matter how good or fair a person he or she may be. When partners transfer their differing familial "truths" of fairness into their intimate relationships, conflict is inevitable. True fairness, then, is a process that is lived out and has to be discovered *between* partners, rather than a truth imposed by one on another. And although we may never consciously label or scrutinize our fairness creed, it rules our lives and shapes our patterns of relating in our most intimate relationships. *Try to See It My Way* helps you analyze the fairness models you "inherit" from your family and then bring to your marriage. But most important, this book shows you how you can apply this knowledge to create a new working model of fairness with your partner. Learning a new fairness model is the key to resolving everyday conflicts and loyalty clashes, and to repairing major violations of trust in order to make your marriage thrive.

How Do You Decide What's Fair?

Once you accept that fairness is at the heart of relationships, and that unfairness creates many problems for couples, you're still left with the dilemma of how to agree upon what's fair. Couples often arrive at my office in distress over money, bad communication, infidelity, in-laws, housework, parenting, and sex. These troubles are obvious and tangible, unlike fairness. Yet to resolve these problems, couples need to understand their direct link to being fair. Otherwise, couples may get temporary pain relief by focusing on the predicament at hand without a long-term cure for the underlying problem of unfair relating.

For example, a Band-Aid solution for Jim and Michelle, our opening couple, could have been a deal where Jim would do more housework and Michelle might feel a bit more amorous if she weren't so exhausted. They'd get short-term symptom relief without understanding their underlying fairness models at play. But the new fairness model we're building isn't a quid pro quo negotiation: *If you have sex with me twice a week, I'll do the dishes every night.* Such an arrangement feels stilted. It coldly reduces love to a business formula that substitutes rigid rules in place of basic trust and a commitment to become fairer. This tit-for-tat economy leads couples to keep score and focus their reactions on isolated, observable offenses, while overlooking the underlying and fundamental fairness models that motivate their behaviors and drive their problems. Instead, the new fairness we're constructing thoughtfully takes into account the familial learned realm of fairness that Jim and Michelle, like many couples, unknowingly replicate in their marriages.

Your learned fairness model reflects your inherited family script—a governing, but largely unexamined set of beliefs and possibly irrational expectations, which leads you to think that you're accurately judging what's fair. Your loyalty to your family's model gives your script an extra moral punch. That makes it difficult for partners to recognize that their host of perceptions reflects their family model, rather than an absolute objective truth about fairness. Fairness can be hard to agree on because while everyone has a strong, even moral take on fairness, it's not always the same take. So how do you come up with a practical way to decide what's fair when partners disagree? You begin by taking an honest look at your underlying assumptions and perceptions.

Since fairness isn't an objective truth, but the often-muddled mix of partners' views and expectations, you need a way to unpack those competing perceptions. The building blocks of your intuitive fairness "script" are the expectations for what you owe and deserve. You assume the job of an ethics expert when balancing your sense of obligation to another against both your sense of deserving from them and their sense of deserving from you. Partners often appeal to me: *Tell her she's being unreasonable! Tell him he only thinks of himself!* Yet in a loving relationship, no one person can dictate expectations or the terms for give-and-take, because fairness requires mutual care and consideration of another's point of view. You and your partner must each discover the familial fairness models (which feel like truths) that you bring into your relationship. Then you have to negotiate your differences and decide on the new governing values. Your decisions will shape the give-and-take between you and determine how the relationship *feels*. To illustrate this, let's take a look at the conflicting convictions a couple holds about what each owes the other, as they engage in a skirmish over an e-mail exchange.

Bill insists that Sandy, his wife of two years, stop e-mailing her former college boyfriend. Bill wants her to cease the contact and end the friendship. Sandy refuses, and feels mistrusted and controlled. As the exchange between Bill and Sandy heats up, Sandy defends her innocence, while Bill becomes more frustrated and demanding.

BILL: "I can't believe that you're still e-mailing your old boyfriend, even though I've asked you not to."

SANDY: "And I've told you it's nothing. He's *just* a friend. I married *you*. You have *nothing* to worry about."

BILL: "But when I've asked you to stop e-mailing him, you've just blown me off. You have to choose him or me."

SANDY: "You sound just like a child. Frankly, I'm insulted that you don't trust me."

BILL: "And I'm outraged that you'd put our marriage at risk."

SANDY: "It's not me putting it at risk—it's *you*, being so controlling."

BILL: "It's him or me—I mean it!"

SANDY: "That's your choice, then!"

Who Decides What's Fair?

If you're wondering who decides what's fair here, you're asking the right question. Individual perspectives are just the starting point for determining fairness. In our couple above, Bill and Sandy have competing perceptions and beliefs. Bill is sure that Sandy owes it to him to give up the e-mail exchange and all contact with her old boyfriend. Sandy is convinced that he's being unreasonable. Is it fair for Bill to insist? Is it fair for Sandy to refuse? Neither seems particularly aware of the fact that they are hurting the other person and the relationship, too. Both defend the right to their own positions.

Bill and Sandy are stuck in a circular argument rooted in their conflicting, but unrecognized models of fairness. Their ideas about their obligations and entitlements in the relationship are diametrically opposed. They are each burdening their relationship with rigid expectations, without knowing or examining the source of their differing values. Bill feels strongly that Sandy owes it to him to comply with his request. In his family, it was selfish to put your own needs ahead of those of someone you love. Bill's underlying belief is that if Sandy loved him enough she would simply stop this argument, and do what he needs.

How is Sandy's fairness model influencing her behavior? Her mother's domineering treatment wrote large parts of Sandy's fairness script. While Sandy is aware of her anger toward her mother, she is unaware of how this rules her actions and limits her capacity for fair and emotionally intimate relating now. She is quite reactive to what she interprets as Bill's attempts to control her. Sandy mistakes her unyielding stance for what she regards as her right to assert herself and oppose Bill's influence. Bill blindly idealizes and accepts his family's model, while Sandy treats Bill as if he were her mother. Both operate from learned fairness models whose biases are largely unknown to them, and certainly unknown to their partner. The result is an escalating argument.

This couple's lack of insight about their own blind spots as well as their inability to grasp the meaning of their partner's family legacy, results in their mutual, righteous indignation that each "knows" what's fair. At this point, neither is willing to negotiate. But alone, neither can define the truth of what's fair between them because fairness isn't an objective truth. True fairness is a fluid *process* of blending different legacies of owing and deserving from the mix that each person brings to the relationship. But before partners can thoughtfully negotiate fairness, they both must sort out their inherited model of expectations for what they owe and deserve. Without that insight, couples, like Bill and Sandy, may resort to power plays and threats.

You may be thinking, "But I'm not a philosopher, I don't have a *model* of fairness." Yes you do—it just operates at such a subconscious level that you're usually not aware of it. By adulthood, your personal style of fairness is so embedded that it becomes a default way for relating. As a result, you interact on autopilot, hostage to a set of powerful, unexamined assumptions and mistakes in fair relating. In this way, your "fairness philosophy" silently rules your life and your most intimate relationships. More often than not, unexamined fairness models lead to powerful and competing views between partners about what's fair—and who's right and who's wrong.

That's what we see in the exchange between Bill and Sandy—the unstated but controlling influence of their fairness models that handicaps their relationship. Both are unable to put themselves in the other person's shoes because each is imposing a "truth" about fairness onto the other. Because Bill and Sandy are unaware of their operating models, fairness is elusive.

Once you understand that your familial fairness model is not "the truth," then a new fairness—or way of relating—can emerge between you and your partner. The new fairness arises from thoughtfully reevaluating and revising your old model for what has counted as fair. The new fairness helps you resolve conflicts because you lose your old, self-righteous certainty that you know what's right. In its place, you gain an appreciation for the perspective of your partner. You lose your naiveté about the fairness style you've been relying on, but you gain a powerful understanding that will help you evaluate what you owe and what you deserve across all relationships, especially your most important relationships. A new understanding of fairness will lay the groundwork for a more compassionate and loving relationship based on trust, not power. In addition, you and your partner will feel closer as you experience the rewards of mutual fairness.

Try to See It My Way provides a framework for appraising your old model of fairness, teaching you a new model and guiding you through this process. In the first part of the book, I'll introduce the common beliefs confusing love and fairness as you learn to evaluate your own experiences of fair and unfair treatment across your relationships. You'll discover the tricky balance of give-and-take, and see how to right imbalances of fairness, with the help of true-to-life stories. You'll explore the consequences of your unfinished business while you learn how to identify and stop its negative impact. You'll also realize the crucial influence of family loyalty on your marriage.

The second half of the book vividly brings these themes into the realm of day-to-day life by focusing on the lives of couples experiencing four basic violations of fairness. Some violations of fairness are universally experienced, and others are devastating betrayals. In these pages you'll probably catch glimpses of your own relationship.

Four Basic Violations of Fairness

Fairness conflicts fall into four basic categories that often overlap. The first are **loyalty conflicts,** which involve competing obligations. Loyalty conflicts often appear as "choose-between" tugs-of-war: "Who comes first, your parents or me? Your kids or me? Your traditions or mine? Your family's values or mine?" You owe everybody something, yet can't please everyone—and sometimes can't please anyone. Loyalty conflicts are unique because they involve an entirely separate dynamic history between each partner and his or her set of parents and family of origin. Early in a couple's relationship, loyalty tensions can create crucial and sometimes enduring resentments that often underlie both the everyday infractions and the common dilemmas as marriages "grow up."

The second category of conflict is what my clients often call *"stupid" fights*. These are seemingly petty disagreements, the little aggravations of marriage that you can't shake. My clients often preface their remarks with, "We had a stupid fight, but I can't get over it." These everyday abuses of fairness include common irritants, lack of appreciation, and misunderstandings. Here the little things that seem like they shouldn't be a big deal—such as forgetting to pay a bill, cooking the eggs the wrong way, not taking a turn minding the kids, not being given the benefit of the doubt—can set off a torrent of feelings of injustice. Yet "stupid" fights, when understood in context, often represent meaningful patterns of relating that, when left unattended, can create serious cracks in a relationship.

Growing pains of a relationship consist of financial inequities, sexual tensions, career conflicts, and the chore wars. These are the common challenges that most couples face. After couples learn about their own models of fairness, they begin to see how conflicts around housework, parenting, money, and sex are fueled by old assumptions about give-and-take that can create unfair patterns of relating. The failure to resolve these growing pains means that the relationship stays stuck rather than grows up.

The last category we'll explore is that of **enduring injustice**, which threatens a marriage by an act of betrayal or a chronic climate of unfairness. These major violations of fairness include affairs, drug or alcohol abuse, broken promises, abusive relating, and financial duplicity. Often, one partner is the more deeply injured and deserves better treatment by far. But however you assign fault, both partners, even the one who has suffered the most, must develop a new and fairer way of relating. People are often surprised to know that when partners commit to repairing the damage, these marriages can become more vital than they ever were.

Repair is essential, because without it, the effects of unfairness can destroy a relationship over time. When conflicts emerge, as they inevitably will, you need the skills to rebalance fairness and heal the emotional distance between you. Simply finding another partner is seldom the answer. After all, wherever you go, there you are—taking your same issues with you into the next relationship. The incidence of multiple breakups and divorces suggests that people aren't learning from past relationship problems. While we don't have the statistics for the prevalence of split-ups outside of marriage, we do know that the rate of divorce for first marriages is 50 percent, and the rate of divorce for second marriages is more than 60 percent, and it's higher still for third and subsequent marriages.

Yet the rate of marital dissolution is the same today as it was a century ago. It's a surprising statistic, which makes sense when you consider that a hundred years ago the primary cause of marital dissolution was death; today it's divorce. Divorce has become a functional substitute for death. Since you can no longer count on your partner to die in order to resolve unfairness, it seems prudent to learn new skills.

Many of you reading this book might be separated or considering divorce. Am I saying divorce is bad? No more than I'm saying that a marriage without fairness is good. What I am saying is that couples sometimes resort to divorce because they don't have the survival skills to develop a fairer, more balanced relationship. While divorce always remains a viable option for getting out of a destructive situation, restoring fairness can salvage even some relationships that seem unfixable.

My own conviction that fairness guides and motivates behavior follows from my clinical experience of treating couples for thirty years. In my practice, I've found that most violations of fairness, even serious ones, can be resolved when partners learn to be fair and learn to heal injustices between them. This book and my clinical work draw on the body of contextual theory, developed by Dr. Iván Böszörményi-Nagy and his colleagues, which focuses on the ethical nature of family relationships. Contextual therapy looks at the past and present balances between what is owed and deserved between intimate partners, as well as among family members. Because all good therapists must practice what they preach, this book is also based on the transforming power of fairness I have experienced in my own relationships, as well as in my clinical practice.

The case studies I'll discuss in *Try to See It My Way* are true but composite in nature. They reflect my own work with couples and conversations with colleagues over many years. The stories are modified with changes in names and details of the situations in order to protect family members' privacy. Most of the people whom I've known, treated, learned from, and grown with will be relieved that these are composites. However, a few have joked, "Why aren't we in there? Could you make me taller and wittier? We want our story in print." I owe a debt of thanks to these individuals, couples, and families who have deepened my understanding and appreciation of fairness. It has been a privilege to be part of their lives.

The stories I'll share include a broad spectrum of issues between couples and will help you identify the struggles you deal with in your own relationship. Then you'll apply the lessons you learn. You'll see that it takes the same skill set to rework fairness issues whatever the magnitude of the injustice. I'll also show you how to account for feelings, but not use them as an endpoint. Feelings have validity. They offer important clues to the pain of injustice between partners. Yet feelings can change and soften as you gain a greater understanding of your partner's side. Feelings can shift as partners learn to value fairness.

Who Is This Book For?

Try to See It My Way is for anyone who wants to understand the key to a more harmonious, trusting, and loving relationship. But what if you're the only one who's trying? It's not uncommon for a relationship to improve because one brave partner begins the change—one person sees the need first, and starts the work of becoming fairer. That person—you—can be a catalyst for change and a beacon for your partner. Because fairness is a process *between* partners, this book provides the tools for individuals as well as couples to learn a new way of looking at relationships. Since fairness is blind to marital status, the lessons learned in this book apply equally to all intimate relationships. All romantic relationships with future hopes and dreams, shared history and commitment, bump into many of the same challenges of negotiating fairness. This includes married and cohabitating couples, whether the same or opposite sex. This book helps when:

- You feel like love and trust are gone.
- Daily fights are threatening your marriage.
- You and your partner have grown distant.
- You want to stop repeating unfair patterns.
- You don't know what's fair to give or to get in relationships.

Because fairness is the core value of this book, it may require some changes in your behavior. Be prepared—becoming fairer takes courage. You may be faced with risks and transformations in your relationships as you leave behind some old and unhelpful ways of thinking and relating. The payoff for those changes can be great, however—a relationship that becomes more loving because it is fairer.

My goal in writing this book is to take you beyond theory, beyond intuition, and even beyond your own beliefs about fairness, and offer a practical guide to the crucial lesson that you can make your relationships stronger when you *learn* to be fair. You'll learn when fairness issues exist, how to sort out the baggage you bring, how to negotiate competing points of view, and how to restore trust. While you can't change the facts of what has happened in your relationship, I strongly believe that the vital negotiation of fairness for healing is possible. So whether you've been together for thirty years, are contemplating the possibilities of life with a new partner, or are entangled in an unhealthy pattern of relating, this book proposes a radically hopeful way of rebuilding, renewing, and strengthening your love. From it, you'll learn how you and your partner can decide what's fair for each of you and *between* you. Take a chance—risk learning to make love fair.

Part One

UNDERSTANDING FAIRNESS

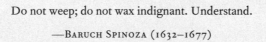

Do not weep; do not wax indignant. Understand.
—BARUCH SPINOZA (1632–1677)

RECOGNIZING YOUR BLIND SPOTS
AND FALSE ASSUMPTIONS

"We're both trying our best. It's just that we're using different currencies. You think that if I really loved you, you shouldn't have to tell me to buy you flowers—but I'm not a mind reader. I take care of so much, but you still don't feel loved. I'm worn out." *(Al, thirty-two, married to Ginny for two years)*

"I thought that loving my husband meant putting my needs second. As I look back, I feel short-changed. I gave and he took. Now I'm angry at myself and at him." *(Jean, thirty-six, married sixteen years)*

The people above are in relationships that they just don't feel are fair. But most of us have blind spots when it comes to accurately gauging what expectations are fair in marriages and romance. Take Al, for example—he takes care of a lot of things, and thinks that his wife should know he loves her. But Ginny sees things differently. She believes that if Al really loved her, she wouldn't have to clue him in to the little things that matter to her, such as buying her flowers or making a reservation for a romantic dinner on their anniversary. She doesn't want to have to ask, because then she thinks he's doing something out of obligation rather than true love. When he fails to deliver, Ginny tallies another point against him. She doesn't give Al much credit for what he has done, but rather counts what he hasn't done. Her misguided belief about love tilts the balance. Then there's Jean, who thought it was selfish to put her needs first. After putting her needs second, third, and last for many years, now she resents her husband. Her husband is caught like a deer in the headlights facing the oncoming traffic of Jean's pent-up anger. Yet both of them had assumed for all those years that her sacrifices were a normal part of love.

These two couples, like most of us, learned their complex beliefs and assumptions about love and about what's fair to expect from their families. Then they brought their assumptions into their intimate relationships, with problematic results. Because your beliefs (and misconceptions) about love and fairness are so much a part of who you are, you're often unaware of your embedded biases. This lack of awareness makes change that much harder. After all, your beliefs seem "normal" until you allow yourself to explore them—or until, like Jean's husband, you're forced to. Fortunately, you can learn to reassess your ideas about what's fair, and then decide how well they serve you and your relationship. The first step involves identifying these sometimes mistaken beliefs, and then challenging them. Let's take a look at the most commonly held but questionable beliefs that govern many people's expectations for love and fairness.

Belief #1:
If I am loved "enough," my partner will meet my needs and will be fair automatically.

Let's return to Al and Ginny to untangle Ginny's belief about love. "Al's a great guy, but I'm very frustrated with him. He keeps telling me that I have to tell him what I want rather than expecting him to know. But if he really loved me, then he'd know. It spoils it if I have to tell him what I need. If I have to tell him to buy me flowers, then I don't want them."

Ginny's underlying assumption: "If he loves me, he'll automatically meet my needs." In my work with clients, I have heard variations of this theme thousands of times. In its simplest reduction, this belief implies that you won't have to voice or even identify your own needs. But the belief that your needs will automatically be met simply because you love or are loved by another is a distortion. Automatic thoughts and accompanying distorted beliefs such as these have been well studied by cognitive therapists. It's both unrealistic and unfair to expect your partner to act in an unconditionally loving, sacrificial, and even omniscient way, as if he'll know what you need or want even better than you do. The fact is, love doesn't teach you mind reading or bestow that magical power upon your partner.

Why do people equate mind reading with love? One reason is that it's a childhood longing that we carry into adulthood. From a child's perspective, a mother or father often meets needs for nurturing, care, and love without any prompting. Being so well known that you don't have to identify your needs is a treasured experience (indeed a basic need) of infancy and childhood. However, you'll be disappointed if you carry this expectation into marriage.

However, there's another important reason that individuals want their partners to mind read—to protect themselves. Fill in the blank: "If you really loved me, you'd _____." The blank usually means "You'd know me so well that I wouldn't have to make myself vulnerable by telling you what's fair to me. If I have to resort to asking for my needs to be met, then I run the risk that you might say no. By not disclosing what I want, I don't risk rejection." This defense has its roots in childhood experiences, too. Parents have the enormous job of imagining (and guessing) what it's like to be you, and then responding sensitively. That might have included comforting you and not dismissing your distress over a small disappointment. It might have meant demonstrating sympathy when you wanted to quit an activity, rather than berating you for "being a quitter." It might have been taking your opinion into account, rather than having a "do it because I say so" relationship.

But if your parents didn't encourage you to ask for what you needed, if they didn't sensitively respond to your needs, you may feel too vulnerable to explicitly state what you need now. Most of us, after all, feel vulnerable at some level, simply because no parent perfectly imagines and meets a child's needs for fair consideration all the time. If you're lucky, you had what noted child psychiatrist D. W. Winnicott called "the good enough parent," who, like the weatherman, got it right about half the time. I say this not only as a clinician but also as a parent humbled by the job.

Despite love, no one can read your mind, and no one can compensate for earlier lapses in fairness, whether by parents or former partners. You handicap your spouse and your marriage when you don't make your needs explicit. Otherwise your spouse can neither know whether he's done what you want nor whether he's done enough. Instead, you must take a risk to be vulnerable and make your needs known.

Belief #2:
Love conquers all.

You may be thinking to yourself, but if you love someone, love should compensate for lapses in fairness. Shouldn't it? Doesn't love conquer all? Doesn't love mean never having to say you're sorry? Doesn't love make up for unfairness? Unfortunately, no. In intimate relationships, lasting love and happiness depend on being fair to each other.

A young woman married only a few years called me, asking for individual treatment for depression. It was easy to see that her depression was rooted in her feeling trapped by her husband's poor financial decisions—all made without her knowledge. When she discovered a new debt or financial problem, he'd justify his actions instead of offering any apology or promise of change. She tried making more money to pay off the debts, only to have him make more bad financial decisions. Her depression was a symptom of the toll his irresponsible behavior had taken. She had gotten worn out. Despite the love she knew was there between them, love wasn't enough. She needed her husband to be fair by taking responsibility for his actions.

Love is absolutely necessary for a strong relationship, of course, but you can only feel love for so long without fairness. Fairness is a tonic, an aphrodisiac, and a vital part of long-term relationships. Abiding love, trust, happiness, stability, and longevity of relationships are made possible by mutual give-and-take. As much as you wish it would, you can't rely on the power of love to establish fair relating. I see many couples in distress who love each other, but they're depleted and exasperated from failures to treat each other fairly. You have to let go of the misconception that love alone will solve every problem in your relationship.

Belief #3:
What's fair is intuitively obvious.

Everyone instinctively knows when "It's not fair!" People mistakenly assume that they know what's fair because they can *feel* it. But feelings aren't always right. What's fair to me may not *feel* like what's fair to you. For example: Is it fair for me to ask you to cut down your drinking when you think I'm over-reacting? Is it fair to you if we spend more time with my family than we spend with yours? Is it fair to me to have more household and child care responsibilities than you despite the fact that we both work full-time? Is it fair to you if I don't want your children (from your first marriage) to spend much time with us because they aren't warm to me? Is it fair for me to ask for sex more often than you're interested? Is it fair to you if I more routinely say no to your overtures?

Because feelings seem so natural, people don't recognize the blind spots of their unexamined yet deeply held assumptions about fairness that trigger their feelings. So while feelings are clues to deciding fairness, they may yield a distorted view. Though virtually anyone would *feel* that it's unfair for their partner to have an affair or commit flagrant violations of trust, there are many other situations where you can't rely solely on feelings to guide the process. Each person's feelings have some merit, which makes it impossible for feelings to be the definitive guide for determining fairness. Besides, if we judge fairness on feelings alone, then who gets to decide whose feelings are more valid when partners disagree, or when both feel hurt? Feelings count, but they're too subject to distortion and too changeable to be the authoritative principle. For these reasons, sometimes what's fair isn't intuitively obvious.

Belief #4:
It isn't fair for me to put my needs
ahead of those of someone I love.

Asking for fair consideration can feel like a selfish demand. Many of us are taught the Golden Rule: "Do unto others as you would have others do unto you." It's a practical ethic derived from many religions, and mandates a concern for the fair treatment of the other person. But responsibly considering the needs of another is only half of the equation. The other half of love is being free to ask for fair treatment for yourself. Hillel, an ancient religious scholar of the first century BCE, summed it up best:

> If I am not for myself, who will be?
> If I am only for myself, what am I?
> And if not now, when?

It's healthy to balance concern for self *and* others. While being selfish isn't good for you or your relationships, neither is being selfless. Linda Thompson, a noted sociologist, talks about how to be responsible to both yourself and others without being a doormat:

> Responsibility is the activity of receiving and responding to another. Family members strive to meet everyone's needs, prevent harm, and take positive action to protect and promote each other's welfare. . . . Responsibility does not mean family members must be servile or self-sacrificing to be sensitive to the needs of others. Striving to meet everyone's needs includes both one's own and other's needs.

Balancing your own needs while taking into account your partner's needs requires more vulnerability, risk, and trust than devoting yourself exclusively to meeting another's needs. Jean, whom we met at the beginning of the chapter, learned this lesson the hard way: "For so long I put everyone else's needs ahead of mine. If my husband wanted dinner at six on the dot, I'd scramble to have it ready. If a friend needed me to babysit, I'd drop everything. If my children wanted my undivided attention, my plans would come last. Even becoming a teacher was partially because the schedule was convenient for everyone else. No wonder I was so worn out—and I'm still trying to recover."

Because of her misconception that love meant being sacrificial, Jean had been unable to see the difference between caring *for* someone (until she was depleted), and caring *about* someone. She slowly realized that she could care about her husband, children, or friends without always taking care of them, and without feeling selfish for taking her own needs into account, too. In my office one spring day, Jean laughed about how buying okra now represented her newfound balance of fairness. "In the past, I would allow myself to buy okra once, maybe twice a year, because no one else liked it. In fact, they made fun of me because I loved this slimy vegetable." But after challenging her old notion that love meant selflessness, she started to buy okra on a regular basis. "At first, it seemed so revolutionary buying and serving okra to my family—imagine that!" She laughed again at the near-absurdity of it. Jean had changed her governing assumption that she should do for others, but not do for herself. After years spent relating this way, Jean got her husband and the kids to help out more, and stopped exhausting herself trying to accommodate everyone else. "What I understand now is that it's fair to have a life in which I get something for myself, too, instead of a life of only giving to others. In fact, my family appreciates me more now. We even laugh together about the okra—bite by delicious bite." Jean learned, quite painfully after years of selflessness, that "asking for what we want can be as caring an act as responding to someone else's apparent need."

Belief #5:
Since I am a good person,
my "take" on things is usually fair.

Most of us have a vested interest in seeing ourselves as good people. But even truly scrupulous, earnest, and wonderful people are unfair at times. If you consider yourself to be a good person, you may find it disturbing to think that you've been unjust. This isn't to suggest that there's no such thing as a good person—only that everyone has times when they're unfair. To think that a person can be all good and always fair-minded is simply to miss the many facets of who that person is. Jerome Kagan, a well-respected psychologist and author, writes: "Humans are selfish and generous, aloof and empathic, hateful and loving, dishonest and honest, disloyal and loyal, cruel and kind, arrogant and humble." I would add to that list, unfair and fair.

Being unfair occasionally is a universal experience. Who hasn't been thoughtless sometime? Perhaps it was the time he left the laundry in the washing machine for days, leaving you to deal with mildewed clothes; or when you left dirty dishes on the counter overnight, knowing that drives him crazy; maybe it was the incident when you "lost it" because he forgot to mail something that was important to you; or when you charged more on credit over the holidays than you'd agreed to. These are lapses, moments of inadvertent unfairness, human error, which most people manage without retaliation.

Beyond such momentary slips, despite love and being a good person, your "take" on things may not be fair. Why is this? As we learned from Jean, your upbringing conditions your expectations for what counts for being a good spouse. Many partners are certain that they alone have the inside track on fairness. One husband whose wife had separated from him, reflected on how critical he'd been toward his wife and children, and explained it this way: "I thought telling my wife how she could improve herself was normal. I thought I was helping her. My family was very big on offering tips for self-improvement. I thought I was a good guy. Now I know I took her for granted. And of course, I had such a big blind spot about this. When she'd call me on my criticism, I'd tell her she was being too sensitive. Now I realize I picked on her for twenty years. She felt I was really unfair, even mean. I guess I was."

Belief #6:
The past is the past, and has nothing to do with how fair my relationship is now.

Everybody brings baggage to their relationships. But many individuals believe that their marital troubles are here-and-now problems, unshaped by prior experiences. In reality, the past shapes fairness issues in two major ways. First, there's the pattern of give-and-take you learned from your parent-child relationships. What parents give and what they in turn expect may be fair or unfair, but children are unable to recognize this—they have no other yardstick to measure by, other than the one their parents gave them. Yet an imbalanced family model can skew your future sense of what you owe to or deserve from a partner.

The second way that past experiences shape fairness is through the "hot button" topics that parents install and partners push. Hot buttons reflect negatively charged childhood experiences. This extra emotional charge could stem from specific factual hardships such as a family's financial difficulties or a parent's early death. Hot buttons might also result from ongoing conflict, poor boundaries, unmet needs for security or affirmation, or a physically or emotionally unsafe home environment. The power of a hot-button charge occurs in direct proportion to its painful link to the past. Bill, a middle-aged man, described his hot button: "My father's business went broke when I was ten. We had our cars repossessed and had to move from our house to an apartment over a mom-and-pop grocery store. I've worked from age ten on. Now when my wife goes over our budget, I get crazed. We've argued over this for years. She tells me I'm unreasonable, and she's right. The stupid thing is we have enough money."

Hot buttons can't tell time for all practical purposes—the past *is* the present. When current injustices carry an extra charge from the past, the injury won't *be* the same as in childhood, but it will *feel* the same. One spouse described it this way: "When you've had salt poured on a wound, even salt air stings." The result is an exaggerated reaction, like the one Audrey had to her husband, Will.

One Saturday afternoon, Audrey took the kids to the park to play. Later that evening, Audrey berated Will for spending time at work instead of with the family. This was a familiar feeling to Audrey, who described her father as a workaholic. In fact, it was rare for Will to work on the weekends. Yet Audrey *felt* perfectly justified in her complaints. Audrey didn't see that the strength of her response belonged to her past, not her present. This was the unfinished business that she brought to the marriage. Because your past is such an integral part of you, it's important to challenge the misconception that "the past is the past." Otherwise, you're stuck repeating it.

Belief #7:
You can only have a fair relationship if the other person changes.

Most commonly, people want their partners to change. But many partners resist change with "the Popeye defense": "I y'am what I y'am" (and I'm the same person you married—so stop trying to change me). Waiting for your partner to change is at best frustrating, and can create a tendency toward blame and a feeling of helplessness. You've tried talking, but that was useless. You've tried the silent treatment and that went nowhere. You've tried screaming, but that only got you a sore throat. So here you are in a stalemate—stuck and waiting for your partner to change. The wish for your partner to change his behavior is quite understandable, but it's out of your control. James Hollis, a noted Jungian analyst, put the dilemma this way: "If we forever see our life as a problem caused by others, a problem to be 'solved,' then no change will occur." Waiting for your partner to change sets the stage for ongoing disappointment.

Even without your partner's commitment to change it's more productive to identify how you can take charge of certain aspects of fair relating. Initially, you may find it easier to look at the wrongs you've sustained rather than the wrongs you've inflicted. That's true for most of us. However, taking responsibility can mean reassessing whether what you expect is reasonable and realistically based in the present, rather than on a past longing or emotional pain that you're carrying around with you. Ultimately, if you're willing to confront these issues you can potentially change the dynamic in your relationship. You can decide to relate in a new, more constructive way, as Amika did.

Amika met with me without her husband—he didn't believe in therapy. After eight years of marriage and two young children, she'd had it. Amika described her husband as a milder version of her father—a screamer and a scolder. It had rubbed off on her—now she was a screamer, too. Yet Amika didn't want to leave her marriage—when times were good, they still loved each other. And then there were the kids to consider. While Amika understandably wanted her husband to stop his yelling and put-downs, I suggested that what was under her control was changing her way of relating. She could be fair even if he wasn't. We worked on how she could stay "glued together," rather than engage in their usual screaming matches. She learned to stand her ground constructively. She learned to ask for what she wanted directly, rather than criticizing her husband. She learned to disengage when he was unreasonable. As she changed, her husband learned from her how to remain calmer in an argument—and their relationship improved. One day toward the end of our therapy together, Amika proudly announced, "We saved my marriage— you and me! But the best part is, now I know I can stand my ground and do what's right for me, regardless of how my husband responds."

Amika learned that when one partner changes her own thinking and behavior, her spouse may change in response. Moreover, focusing on what you can change is a more satisfying and empowering way of relating. So don't make your personal growth dependent upon another's change—that's a Catch-22 that binds you to an unproductive cycle of relating. It's a grown-up version of holding your breath until you turn blue in the face. Instead of protesting helplessly, you can expand your options through insight.

Belief #8:
Insight just excuses bad behavior.

Some clients ask me, "What good is insight? Isn't it just another tiresome way of excusing a partner's bad behavior or a more sophisticated way of blaming your problems on your parents? After all, that ship has sailed." I'm the first to admit that all the insight in the world can never change the past, but what it *can* change is the future. If you lack the perspective of insight, you're likely to play out the past without realizing it. Without insight, you may unfairly shift responsibility to another, and justify your own behavior, or alternately you may settle for too little and be unfair to yourself. Individual insight provides a more complex and compassionate way of understanding your own struggles in your relationship, and helps you take your partner's behavior less personally.

Individual insight is a first step. But insight alone can't restore fairness and trust *between* people. Insight alone can leave you with the sad satisfaction of understanding why you feel hurt, or mutate into a smug superiority that you "know better" than your partner. Worse still, insight may lead you to conclude that a relationship is hopeless—that there's no possibility for change. Insight under these circumstances can be downright depressing and even destructive. For the biggest growth potential, you must share insights to promote compassion and understanding between you. Beyond insight, personal and relationship growth also requires endurance and an active commitment to become fairer.

Overlapping Beliefs

It may be apparent that these commonly held but unproductive beliefs are often overlapping rather than distinct. To help you see this more clearly, let's meet Celeste. Her deeply held beliefs about love and fairness aren't serving her well. For her own sake, as well as for her marriage, she needs to challenge the beliefs embedded in her old model of fairness. Celeste started therapy with me with a cherished but shattered belief about love and a crucial question about fairness.

Celeste was an attractive thirty-four-year-old dental hygienist and mother of two young children. She began that initial session tearfully reporting, "All of my relationships are a mess now. My husband had an out-of-town affair last year. I learned about it a month ago when I found a love note in a zippered compartment of his luggage. Jeremy says he loves me and wants to save our marriage. I've tried to forgive him, but I'm pretty devastated. I used to think that love conquered all, and that if you put others first, then you'd get what you deserved in return. I loved him, and I thought he loved me, but now I don't know what to believe about him, or us, or love. Jeremy begged me not to end the marriage. That's why I called for couples therapy. And to make it worse, now I'm in the middle between my sister, Liz, and my husband, and I don't know what to do. I confided in my sister—she's the only one who knows. She's been my rock since I was a kid. But now she hates Jeremy for what he's done to me. She thinks I should leave. I don't know what to think, or what to do." Celeste's beliefs about love and fairness were splintered.

Four months into couples therapy Celeste and Jeremy were each working hard to learn why Jeremy had betrayed her, and why their marriage had been vulnerable to such a major violation of trust. Celeste, though still in pain, was reassured by the fact that she and Jeremy were both working on their marriage. She didn't know how things would turn out, but they were becoming closer. She felt better and dared to be hopeful. But now a family holiday posed a threat to the couple's delicate balance.

Liz invited Celeste and her kids (Jay, age six, and Dana, age one) to share their traditional Christmas Eve dinner with Liz's family. But Liz excluded Jeremy, stating that she didn't want to expose herself or her children to the emotional turmoil she anticipated she would feel in Jeremy's presence. Though Liz could see that Celeste was intent on reconciling with Jeremy, she remained furious with him for hurting her "little sister." Celeste was keenly aware of Liz's disapproval of Jeremy and even of Celeste's decision to reconcile. "After all," Liz challenged, "how will you ever be able to trust him again?" While Jeremy had been unfair to Celeste, life had been unfair to Liz, whose husband had suffered a massive stroke that spring. Liz declared to Celeste that she would never cheat on her husband, despite the fact that now he was a paraplegic.

Jeremy was dispirited. He worried that Celeste and her family would never really forgive him. He felt that with his sister-in-law's rebuff even his nieces and nephews, who had been quite fond of him, would be turned against him. And perhaps most painful to Jeremy was his feeling that he *deserved* to be an outcast. As for Celeste, she initially felt understanding of Liz's exclusion of Jeremy, but within days she felt powerless, shamed, and angry. As hurt and angry as Celeste was with Jeremy, she still loved him and was encouraged by Jeremy's renewed commitment to earn back her trust and repair their marriage. Celeste felt that Liz was asking her to choose between them. Because Liz was her closest sibling, it was very distressing to be in conflict with her. It felt like a no-win situation. Celeste wondered how to balance what she owed Jeremy, if anything, and what she owed Liz given her sister's support, as well as Liz's current challenging circumstances with her disabled husband. Celeste couldn't meet everyone's needs. Her decision was bound to hurt someone.

Celeste agonized about her choice, fearing that it might have long-lasting repercussions. If she based her decision on need, Celeste felt she should choose Liz. After all, Liz was still dealing with her own husband's recovery. And Liz had always had her best interests at heart, something Celeste couldn't say for Jeremy. But if Celeste based her decision on what Jeremy and Jay, their six-year-old son, wanted, she should choose Jeremy. If she based her decision on who would be hurt the most, or who would be the least understanding, it was a draw. Before we could move forward, we needed to learn why Celeste's own beliefs about love and fairness were no longer working for her, despite the hold they still had. What, I wondered to myself, were Celeste's misconceptions about fairness?

Until this crisis, Celeste thought she intuitively knew what was fair. She believed that being "strong" and putting the other person's needs ahead of her own was right. She thought that she understood what was fair because she considered herself a good and caring person. She had believed that love conquered all. Now she asked herself how Jeremy could have treated her this way, and how could Liz ask her to make such an impossible choice? Celeste had relied on the power of love. That had failed her. She had believed it was selfish to put her needs ahead of someone she loved. But the sacrifices she'd made for Jeremy now left her feeling used. Celeste no longer knew what was fair, much less what to do. She wished that either Liz or Jeremy would relieve her of this awful decision—why didn't they know what she needed? Celeste tried to base her decision for the holiday dinner on need. But whose need was greater? All of Celeste's guideposts for what counted as love or fairness now left her strangely disoriented. How would she decide?

I challenged Celeste to stop trying to decide based on need or competitive suffering. They were all suffering. How about thinking of what she truly wanted, about what would be fair to her, Celeste? Until that moment, she hadn't yet wondered what she owed herself. If she focused just on herself, Celeste clearly wanted to have a holiday dinner that included Jeremy. I suggested to Celeste that it would be fair to let Liz know how painful her exclusion of Jeremy was, particularly because Celeste wanted to reintegrate Jeremy into her family as part of the couple's healing process. "You can't control what your sister will ultimately decide," I cautioned, "but you can ask Liz to reconsider including Jeremy, not for Jeremy's sake, because she doesn't owe that to Jeremy, but because she does owe fair consideration to you, just as you owe it to her. Making a claim for what you need and want may change what's possible for her."

Celeste felt equally relieved and appalled by my suggestion that she deserved to ask for fairness for herself, despite her sister's wishes. Celeste asked, "Isn't the right thing to put my sister's needs ahead of mine? Isn't that what love is all about?" She persisted, "Why is fairness the core value? Why isn't the morally right thing putting Liz's needs ahead of my own? Shouldn't I make a choice based on not hurting her? After all, look at what she's been through with her husband." Celeste had elegantly summed up the premise of unconditional love. Isn't love about turning the other cheek, doing for others, denying your own needs and feelings? Isn't it about assuming that someone else's suffering is more deserving of consideration than your own? Isn't that the truest demonstration of love? I replied, "You can both acknowledge your understanding of your sister's position and also make a claim for her to care about you by considering your needs. In that way you are both giving and asking for consideration. You aren't dismissing your sister's request or her concern, but you are asking her to consider yours, too. That's different than a selfish demand."

I wondered aloud if Celeste's old beliefs about love and fairness were serving anyone well. Was it possible that she was both shortchanging herself by making a sacrifice that her sister didn't recognize, and underestimating her sister's capacity for fairness by depriving her of the opportunity to take Celeste's needs into account?

Celeste felt intrigued by the notion that she could both be sensitive to Liz's needs and strive to respect her own needs in a new negotiated process of arriving at fairness. That made sense to her. She wanted Liz to know how important it was to her to include Jeremy. Yet Celeste was quite concerned that Liz would regard her as selfish. Celeste had learned from her parents that selflessness was the true measure of love. Putting the other person first meant you were a good person. In her family's model of fairness the strong emphasis was on obligation and what you owed others. Celeste felt that she owed Liz too much to ask for what felt fair to her. So Celeste continued to invisibly repay Liz by sacrificing her own needs and desires.

As she reflected on her beliefs about love and fairness and the patterns of relating within her family, Celeste realized that Jeremy's constant complaint—that she always put her family ahead of him—probably had more than a glimmer of truth. But the truth was she put everyone ahead of herself. So while Celeste's model of fairness didn't work particularly well for her, not wanting to feel selfish still trumped being fair to herself. I challenged Celeste to stop thinking about it as putting her needs first, and start thinking about it as a responsibility each person had to state his or her needs in order to arrive at what would be fair between them.

This shift from selflessness to fairness was hard for Celeste because it didn't feel like love to her. Her emotional paralysis at this decisive moment was rooted in a habitual way of relating. It wasn't merely that she was unassertive. On her job she had little trouble standing up for herself. But in her efforts to demonstrate love, she forgot to value fairness. Like many of us, she showed love by attempting to protect the ones she loved from feeling hurt or feeling challenged. And like many people new to the idea of a negotiated fairness, Celeste was inclined to choose harmony over truth, sacrifice over self-interest, and safety over vulnerability. Celeste felt that it would be too hurtful to object to Liz's conditional invitation after all Liz had done to support her.

I have seen well-intended efforts that confuse beliefs about love and fairness backfire many times. In an attempt to avoid a collision between another's personal happiness and your own individual deserving, fairness gets abandoned. Even more problematically, if you don't ask for what is fair to you (as Celeste was doing), you deprive the other person of knowing what you need. No one, no matter how much they love you, can read your mind, and even if they could, they can't determine what is fair to you. They can try, but ultimately it's your responsibility to let them know. You don't automatically get fair treatment because you are loved. Fundamentally, if you don't ask for fairness, you've narrowed your choices to sacrificing your own needs and desires or using manipulation to indirectly get your needs met.

As you can see in Celeste's dilemma, there is no perfect answer, no objective truth or cookie-cutter stamp for fairness, only a relational process. Celeste loves both her sister and her husband, but she is caught in a situation that requires her to look beyond the obvious love she holds for them, to the issue of what is fair, not only to Liz and Jeremy and the children, but also to herself. Celeste could choose to comply with Liz's wishes, but be unfair to herself. Alternately, Celeste could let her sister know what she needs most, and risk Liz's disappointment, anger, and temporary loss of closeness. But if Celeste risked asking for a different reciprocity, she might be surprised to learn that the result is both individual empowerment and a subsequent gain in trust between herself and the people she most cherishes. It's counterintuitive but true that relationships can become even closer when each person risks negotiating fairness. Fair consideration of yourself and others are not mutually exclusive, but joined in healthy relationships.

That Christmas Eve, Celeste still felt powerless to act on the idea that fairness included a different kind of responsibility to herself and negotiation with her sister. At first she attempted to resolve the holiday impasse by accepting Liz's request that Jeremy not attend. This sacrificed Celeste's own true desire to include Jeremy, and was her old style skewed toward sacrifice. This decision depressed Jeremy, but he was much too deep in the doghouse to protest. However, Jay, their six-year-old, felt no such compunction. "Why isn't Daddy coming?" Jay protested, "If he doesn't go, I'm not going, either!" This only made Celeste feel more helpless. In the final analysis, she couldn't tolerate making a choice against her husband and ultimately against herself, her marriage, and her children. She felt that no matter what she chose she would hurt someone. In the end, Celeste couldn't bring herself to ask Liz to reconsider. Instead, she used her old coping style of ducking conflict by making a last-minute excuse to Liz that Dana, the baby, was sick. Fairness was avoided rather than served. But now Celeste had the insight that neither sacrifice nor white lies were the only choices she had. For her own sake, she had to revise her assumptions about fairness and learn a new way of relating in every relationship, including those with Jeremy and even Liz. Everyone would stand to gain a more loving and honest relationship if she could change her former ruling model of love being above fairness.

Celeste's model of fairness may seem the more benign one to contemplate. After all, it was Jeremy who had the affair. In a parallel manner, Jeremy devoted himself to understanding how his own beliefs and expectations about fairness had led him to act so destructively. In chapter 9, we'll fully explore the underlying fairness model for the partner who has an affair. But Celeste's situation is an important reminder that to enact true and lasting change, each partner must revisit his or her own beliefs and models of fairness, no matter how obviously in the wrong the other is.

It took another Christmas Eve before both families reunited. During that time, Celeste and Jeremy struggled with their earlier assumptions about love and fairness. Some of the questions they grappled with were:

- How can you treat someone you love that way?
- How did each partner's beliefs about love and fairness create problems?
- Can you be fair to yourself even if it offends or hurts someone you love?
- What do you owe yourself and what do you owe your partner and others?
- What actions are necessary to rebuild trust?

Like many couples, Celeste and Jeremy struggled with these important and difficult questions. Through a deliberate process of exploration full of pain, anger, and tears but also mutual honesty and respect, Celeste and Jeremy slowly fortified the remaining but fragile trust between them by their work on becoming fairer. Over the course of their counseling, each evaluated and revised the old and ultimately unproductive beliefs and expectations of the models of fairness they'd brought to the marriage. There wasn't an easy fifty-fifty split on accountability—Jeremy had done the most damage by far. But like many couples reeling from a partner's injustice, theirs wasn't a hundred/zero split, either, with one partner entirely the innocent party, and the other entirely to blame. And similar to most couples, Celeste and Jeremy needed to restore fairness through a process in which they were each proportionately responsible for healing.

By debunking the eight commonly held but questionable beliefs about love and fairness, you can clear space for new options for relating. The next chapters challenge you to stop reacting in ways that are unconsciously governed by your past model of fairness, in order to gain a new and more realistic perspective that is more rooted in what is *mutually* fair. With your new understanding of the misconceptions between love and fairness, let's sharpen your awareness further with several exercises. Then in chapter 2, an easy-to-take questionnaire provokes fresh thoughts and new possibilities for fair relating.

EXERCISES FOR CHAPTER 1

For this exercise and for all others in *Try to See It My Way*, you may want to keep a notebook. Your responses can help you see patterns that exist between your thoughts, beliefs, expectations, and actions, and identify trouble spots as well as areas of strength in your relationship.

The exercises are included to help you and your partner apply what you learn. If you'd prefer to continue reading, you can also come back to the exercises at any time—even after you've read the entire book.

EXERCISE 1: THE PAST: FORMING CHILDHOOD BELIEFS AND EXPECTATIONS

The purpose of this exercise is to gain an awareness of your beliefs about love and fairness in your relationship. I'm providing some "jumping off" sentences to guide your writing and help you see how your beliefs about love and fairness arise from your childhood experiences, fantasies, wishes, and dreams, and are at work today. Your beliefs may be working to keep your marriage strong and vibrant, or they may be working at cross-purposes to that goal. For most couples, it's a combination of both.

Complete the following sentences
1. When I was growing up, I thought/fantasized that my marriage would be:
2. In what way(s) is your marriage like that? (Try to give specific instances or examples.)
3. In what way(s) is it different? (Try to give specific instances or examples.)

4. As a child, I thought that love meant:
5. I learned some of this from seeing/hearing my parent(s):

EXERCISE 2: PAST MEETS PRESENT: HOT-BUTTON ISSUES

The purpose of this exercise is to identify your hot-button issues. Hot buttons carry an extra charge from painful childhood experiences that are still active today. You may know what yours are immediately—especially if they're related to traumatic events. Perhaps your parents' divorce heightened your fear of loss. Now, just the hint of your partner rejecting you sends you into a panic or attack mode. Or maybe when your father lost his job, you lost your childhood home, and now you take your partner's head off when your finances are wobbly. Maybe you're quite jealous as a result of suspecting that one parent cheated on the other. These are examples of the more obvious hot-button issues. But hot buttons can also develop from less traumatic experiences. Perhaps you struggled in school and grew up thinking you weren't as smart as other people. Now, whenever your spouse makes a simple correction, you *hear* them say, "You're not so smart, you know." Complete these sentences below to help identify your hot-button issues:

1. I know that my hot-button issues with my spouse are:
2. I get really angry/anxious/upset when my partner:
3. I "jump all over" my spouse when:
4. The one thing that was painful about my childhood was:
5. I had a very good childhood, but I could have used more (or less):

Now, think about your responses and see if you can identify whether there's a live wire from the past charging the present.

EXERCISE 3: THE PRESENT: CURRENT BELIEFS ABOUT LOVE AND FAIRNESS

Complete this quick checkoff list. If you're unsure of your answer, check the box that seems closest to your true thoughts and feelings. Don't spend much time thinking about your answer. There are no right or wrong answers, just your own thinking on this topic.

	USUALLY	NOT OFTEN
1. I want my partner to know what I need and want without my having to say so. It means they really care about me.		
2. I believe that ultimately love does conquer most things.		
3. I believe my "take" on things is more accurate and more legitimate than my partner's.		
4. I feel it's selfish to put my needs first.		
5. Mostly, I'm in the right.		
6. I believe the past is the past. It has little impact on my life today.		
7. To have fairness in my marriage, my spouse has to change.		
8. I feel that most insight is really an excuse to complain or not take responsibility.		
9. I wish my partner would put his/her needs first.		
10. I think my partner's "take" on things is more accurate than mine.		
11. I believe insight is the end point of relationship exploration.		
12. I believe that love means total acceptance of the other.		

How should you interpret your responses? If you checked "usually" for the majority of questions (seven or more), chances are you hold some powerful but unproductive beliefs about love and fairness that are likely getting in your way.

Try to spend some time thinking about what these exercises may have brought to light about the way fairness works in your relationship. Now you're ready to move from your beliefs about love and fairness, to take a closer look at fairness in your most important relationships—those with your partner, your parents, and your children or stepchildren. You're ready to go on to the Fairness Questionnaire in chapter 2.

HOW FAIR ARE YOU?
A QUESTIONNAIRE

"Yea, we have a give-and-take relationship: I give and he takes."

The injuries we sustain and those we inflict are
seldom weighted on the same scale.

—AESOP

Unfair patterns in intimate relationships seem obvious—when you're the observer. *He thinks he's always right. She's high maintenance. He walks all over her. She spends it as fast as he makes it. He's mean. She's so demanding. He never helps with the kids or around the house. She takes all he does for granted.* Likewise, you may notice or even envy how fair and balanced other relationships are. *They're so respectful of each other. She's thoughtful of him but she also takes care of herself. He loves to spend time with her. They argue but they seem to work it out.*

It's easier to observe other couples' behaviors than to accurately interpret your own. It's easier to point an accusatory finger at your partner than to hold yourself accountable. Why is this? In addition to our blame-game culture, we have our genes to thank. Rebuking another person's unfair behavior is an innate human impulse, which has its origins in stone throwing.

We have a predisposition to notice and punish inappropriate behavior that would threaten group harmony or even survival. No doubt this was a tremendous asset when we lived in small groups in caves. The dilemma now is that observing and reproaching others isn't a particularly useful relationship survival strategy, but we still have this impulse to do it. The tendency to finger-point goes hand in hand with shirking responsibility. Yet taking responsibility is a necessary skill for reaching a fair resolution. This chapter challenges you to turn your observations toward yourself and situations in your own life.

The following questionnaire sharpens and expands your awareness about fair give-and-take in your closest relationships. There are no right or wrong answers. The purpose of this questionnaire is to help you to identify fairness patterns.

FAIRNESS QUESTIONNAIRE: Don't spend a lot of time thinking about your answers. If the categories "usually true" and "usually false" seem too rigid for a particular question, try to answer it anyway. This questionnaire is meant to give you a rough idea of how fairly treated you feel. If any section doesn't apply to you, just skip ahead to the next one.

FAIRNESS QUESTIONNAIRE

General Fairness Questions		
QUESTION	USUALLY TRUE	USUALLY FALSE
1. I go out on a limb for other people but am disappointed that they rarely do the same for me.		
2. When I feel hurt, I harbor angry feelings.		
3. When I'm angry, I blame myself.		
4. I do things for people because I want them to like me more.		
5. When I feel hurt, I take it out on the person who hasn't lived up to my expectations.		
6. When I want something for myself, I feel selfish.		
7. I secretly "test" others by waiting to see if they'll do for me what I would do for them.		

(continued)

QUESTION	USUALLY TRUE	USUALLY FALSE
8. I do things when asked, just to avoid disappointing someone else.		
9. I usually avoid conflicts.		
10. I find myself excusing other people's behavior most of the time and then unexpectedly blowing up at small things.		
11. When I forgive someone, I feel it's because I'm the "better" person.		
12. I tend to apologize for many small things.		
13. I rarely apologize, even when it might be the right thing to do.		
14. When I'm angry, I sulk in silence.		
15. I take on too much responsibility compared to the people around me.		
16. I feel selfish if I don't make a sacrifice to help someone.		
17. In close relationships, I see it as my responsibility to make the other person happy.		
18. When some of my needs in a relationship aren't met, I figure they weren't very important anyway.		
19. When I'm angry, I tend to blow up at other people.		
20. I bury my feelings when I think they'll cause trouble in my close relationships.		
21. When I feel angry, my first response is to blame others.		
Fairness with Your Partner		
1. I rarely express my anger at my partner directly.		
2. When I disagree with my partner, I keep it to myself.		
3. I want my spouse to automatically know what I need.		

QUESTION	USUALLY TRUE	USUALLY FALSE
4. I often feel angry that my partner doesn't give me what I need or want.		
5. I feel like the victim in my relationship.		
6. I feel caught between my children and my partner.		
7. If I'm honest, I'd say I blame my partner for too much.		
8. I take on more than my spouse does.		
9. My partner never wants to talk about problems.		
10. I accept blame when something goes wrong, even if it's not my fault.		
11. My partner's needs are reasonable.		
12. I can't count on my spouse to tell me what they need or want.		
13. I tend to tell my partner "what they did wrong," instead of making a request for how it could go better.		
14. My spouse doesn't really seem to care about my day, my interests, how I *really* am.		
15. I tend to "simmer in silence" in my relationship.		
16. When faced with the thought of discussing a problem with my partner, I decide it's "not worth it," because little or nothing will really change.		
17. What I do is taken for granted.		
18. After a run-in, we seldom seem to work it out.		

Fairness with Your Parents
If your parent(s) is no longer alive, preface each question with, When I think about my parent(s), I recall that:

1. My mother doesn't seem to care what I want.		
2. When I have a problem with my parent(s), I typically keep it to myself.		

(continued)

QUESTION	USUALLY TRUE	USUALLY FALSE
3. No matter how much I do for them it's never enough.		
4. My mother is typically responsive to me.		
5. My father doesn't give me what I need or want.		
6. My parents don't ask about how I *really* am.		
7. I feel caught between my spouse and my parents on a regular basis.		
8. I relate to my parents out of obligation.		
9. I have a close, but not "open" relationship with my parents.		
10. Another sibling was favored by my mother or father.		
11. When I get angry with my parents, I "explode."		
12. When I was growing up there were things I should have been able to tell my parents, but couldn't.		
13. I can never repay my parents for all they've done for me.		
14. I can't count on my parents to be there for me.		
15. I'll always be my parents' "baby."		
16. When I get angry with my mother/father, I "implode."		
17. I was the child expected to take on a ton of responsibility.		
Fairness with Your Children (If you have stepchildren, you may want to take this portion of the questionnaire with them in mind.)		
1. I feel disappointed in my kids much of the time for their insensitivity toward me.		
2. If I feel offended in some way by my adult daughter or son, I think it's best to let it go.		

QUESTION	USUALLY TRUE	USUALLY FALSE
3. If my kids talk to me about the ways I hurt them, I mostly defend myself.		
4. I feel that my children don't have time for me.		
5. It feels bad that I did more for my parents than my kids do for me.		
6. My adult son or daughter rarely seems interested in my life.		
7. No matter what, it seems they favor their other parent over me.		
8. My children just don't seem to understand me.		
9. My adult son or daughter tends to blame me, despite all I've done.		
10. I keep my regrets about parenting to myself.		
11. I wish I had a better relationship with my kids.		
12. I'm always trying to balance what I do for one kid with what I do for another. It's exhausting.		
13. My adult children favor their in-laws over me.		

Scoring the Questionnaire

Scoring is simple. If you answered "usually true" to five or more of the questions in either of the first two sections (General Fairness and Fairness with Your Partner) or four or more "usually true" in either of the final two sections (Fairness with Your Parents and Fairness with Your Children), this indicates that you are shortchanging yourself (and possibly others) in resolving fairness issues. There are imbalances of give-and-take in your relationships.

Imbalances in Fairness

Although an imbalance of give-and-take can reflect healthy nurturing (such as between parent and child) and trust between spouses (particularly if it's a temporary imbalance), ongoing imbalances in reciprocity have important consequences, personally and interpersonally. The questionnaire reveals two major mistakes you can make: you can give too much and/or you can take too much. Let's look more closely at the questionnaire and the kinds of responses that indicate those tendencies.

You probably noticed that many of the questions have similar themes. For example, several questions reflect the tendency to squelch upsetting feelings, especially those of anger, regret, or disapproval. Here's a sample—one from each section of the questionnaire: *I usually avoid conflicts; I rarely express my anger at my partner directly; When I have a problem with my parent(s), I typically keep it to myself; I keep my regrets about parenting to myself.* If you answered "usually true," it suggests that you self-silence rather than express your true feelings. This tendency is often seen in those who overgive. Another theme in the questionnaire expresses the feeling of being "pulled between" the needs of others. Again, here's a question from each section: *I do things when asked just to avoid disappointing someone else; I feel caught between my children and my partner; I feel caught between my spouse and my parents on a regular basis; I'm always trying to balance what I do for one kid with what I do for another. It's exhausting.* Affirmative responses suggest that you feel torn between competing obligations (and the real people involved). Again, those who overgive are more likely to experience these feelings. The person who takes more than their fair share is less likely to concern themselves with the needs—real or perceived—of others.

A theme that is most indicative of taking too much is blame. People who tend to take advantage of others are likely to blame others rather than taking personal responsibility themselves. Here are questions from each section that, when answered "usually true," reflect a blaming stance: *When I feel angry, my first response is to blame others; If I'm honest, I'd say I blame my partner for too much; When I get angry with my parents, I "explode"; If my kids talk to me about the ways I hurt them, I mostly defend myself.* People who feel owed err on the side of blame and defensiveness.

It's unnecessary to analyze each question in all four sections of the questionnaire. What's important is to see if your scores indicate an imbalance in any one relationship area, or if they suggest an overall pattern. Take some time to review the results of your Fairness Questionnaire. Now ask yourself: in which relationships are there patterns of unfair behavior? For those that indicate an imbalance, look at the specific questions that you marked "usually true." What do these answers suggest? Do you see any apparent patterns in the "usually true" responses from one relationship to the next (partner, parents, children)? If your responses show no imbalance, great. Still, you might want to look at the "usually true" responses to learn more about yourself and your relationships.

What if all four sections indicate an imbalance? This is simply more information for you as you move forward in *Try to See It My Way*. Don't interpret your answers as if there were a right or wrong, good or bad—but do recognize that taking a look at fairness in your relationship is a step toward a more satisfying life. In the upcoming chapters, you'll learn how to tell when you're relating fairly to yourself and to others, when the imbalance is healthy and when it's seriously askew, and you'll discover the underlying causes of unfairness.

DEFINING THE NEW FAIRNESS

"Sometimes I think, 'We're different, it won't work.' Other times I think, 'We're different—that's great!' But mostly I worry that we don't know how to fairly resolve our differences when we're hurt." *(Nick, premarital jitters)*

"Chuck didn't know how to be a partner in our marriage. He just didn't get what was fair—he didn't get the give-and-take." *(Clara, married eight years, divorced two)*

"Angela is all about feelings and I'm all about facts. That's why it doesn't work. I get stuck on justice. If things aren't fair, I can't get over it."

(Jonathan, living together three years)

These remarks are snapshots of how fairness concerns register in couples. Nick, on the brink of marriage, puzzles about the age-old question of how to resolve differences when opposites attract. Clara concludes that her marriage ended because Chuck "didn't get" how to be fair in a relationship. Clara lost trust that Chuck would be fair. Perhaps Chuck felt the same way about Clara. Jonathan ponders the great gender divide between feelings and facts that often exist between women and men. With so many takes on fairness, not only between any two people, but also across relationships, how do you decide what's fair? The last chapters challenged several common misconceptions you may hold about love and fairness, and introduced many questions about how fairly treated you feel in your relationships. In this chapter I return to that fundamental question: "Who's to say what's fair and unfair?" Fairness is lost in a two-person standoff when it's my version of reality against yours. Unless partners are able to take a three-sided perspective—your point of view, my point of view, and a shared perspective that incorporates the validity of both sides—fairness is a chimera. In order to rescue fairness from this illusory realm, you need a working definition that establishes the ideal basis for balanced, mutually satisfying relationships. Then, you can put it to work.

A Working Definition of Fairness

The bedrock of fairness balances what you owe and what you deserve, what you've given your partner and what you've received from them. While you don't consciously track give-and-take (though you may resort to this when feeling unfairly treated), nonetheless, it does register. It's as if you have an invisible ledger, a fairness account, made up of acts and defining moments that you can point to when declaring whether your relationship feels fair. For example, Clara told me that her marriage didn't work because Chuck didn't do enough to help her. She said he dumped too many responsibilities on her for the household, the finances, and the children. I wondered if Chuck would say that Clara had tallied up their accounting accurately? As you've learned, however true your take on fairness *feels*, one partner's perspective can't decide fairness. That's because we've each cobbled together a learned, familial model of expectations for what counts as fair. And our models often have biases about what both men and women are supposed to do to be good partners. The new fairness requires you to clear up your distortions, assumptions, and unreasonable expectations. Your new model of fairness replaces the tacit, competing models partners bring into marriage. The new fairness is a dynamic process *between* partners that requires reevaluating old models, then revising them and negotiating what is to count as fair.

If there were any one truth about fairness, my job would be much simpler. I could give all of my clients a handout at their first session. "This is what is fair," it might read. But I can't, because each couple must uniquely interpret what is fair for them. After all, what's fair to one couple may not count as fair to another. One couple may decide it's fine to spend most of their holidays with the wife's family. Another may decide that holidays are reserved for the couple alone. One couple may opt for traditional roles and division of labor, another may decide on splitting things down the middle. And even what feels fair at one point in time to the same couple may not seem fair later on in their relationship.

At this point you may be wondering what help this can be, since one of your problems is that you don't see eye to eye. You were hoping I'd tell you that there is one truth about fairness (hopefully yours). Otherwise, you'll have one standoff after another. Right? Unfortunately, that is right, if you stick with your original model of fairness you each brought into your marriage. That's why the new fairness asks you to examine your old beliefs and assumptions, your old moral certainties about owing and deserving in preparation for a new balance of give-and-take *between* you.

In determining what you owe and deserve, you need to be aware of your history of love and care, as well as disappointment or lost trust, in any particular relationship and across relationships over time. What you owe also depends on the "deal" of the relationship. One twice-married man summed it up this way: "Marriage is a negotiation, and the deal keeps changing."

A couple's deal has to do with the stated and unstated expectations between giver and receiver. Let's say we get married, and I want children, but my husband doesn't. We marry, but I secretly hope he'll change his mind. Perhaps it's not so secret. Suppose I'm miserably unhappy with the deal. After all, it was on his terms. Whose expectations are reasonable and realistic here? How do you sort it out when one person feels deserving, but the other feels they don't owe you what you're expecting? How do you negotiate what's fair when the deal no longer works for one partner, both partners, or perhaps it never worked at all? Do you want or even need the relationship? Are you obliged to keep a relationship, even if it seems unfair? Can you make it fair, or cut a new deal?

A new deal replaces your old model of fairness with four key components for negotiating a new fairness with your partner: *reciprocity, acknowledgment,* and *claims*. When these are in balance, you'll feel more fairly treated and the fourth component, *trust*, is strengthened. Trust is an organic part of a healthy relationship, and both the by-product and the goal of fair relating. Trust is built up by mutual give-and-take, the recognition of efforts and acts of care and fair claims, which serve as corrective feedback. Though no relationship is always fair, your goal is to sustain balance over time while building trust. While trust has a vague, abstract feeling, fairness creates a specific road map for a generous spirit of cooperation between partners.

The Process of Becoming Fair: Four Key Elements

With fairness, the whole is more than the sum of its parts. Reciprocity, acknowledgment, claim, and trust are its interlocking elements. Let's review these vital parts that together make up the working definition of fairness.

RECIPROCITY

Reciprocity is the balance of mutual care and consideration. Reciprocity isn't altruism. In altruism you give with no expectation of return. Intimate relationships and marriage aren't altruistic. When you give, it's reasonable to expect that your partner will return your care, in some way, at some time. It's okay, it's not selfish, and in fact it's healthy for you to want a return. At any one moment in a couple's life, the scales of give-and-take may balance or they may tilt in favor of one partner. The balance isn't static, but dynamic—because we all have times when we need an extra helping of care, and other times when we need to provide it. Below are two examples of how reciprocity might look in an ideal relationship.

> *Debbie isn't feeling well. Over the weekend, Eric runs all the errands, cooks the meals, and takes the kids to their sporting events. Debbie thanks Eric for taking over. Eric feels good about what he did, and tells Debbie that now he really knows and appreciates how much she routinely does.*

To help out, Mark goes out of his way to take Jenny's car to the shop. That eve-ning, Jenny cooks Mark's favorite meal to show her appreciation.

Although no relationship operates in the ideal realm, it helps to have a generous model of reciprocity as your goal. In the first two scenes, one part-ner's contribution prompts the other to offer acknowledgment and then re-turn care. These couples demonstrate what Robert Trivers, theorist and biologist, calls "reciprocal altruism"—people taking turns being nice be-cause they know the other will return the favor when they can.

You might think of other circumstances where loved ones share or sacri-fice with no expectation of return. Consider the man who nurses his partner through a devastating terminal illness. Certainly he won't get a return in kind; likewise, parents who make sacrifices for their children. Evolutionary psychologists would tell us this is because our interests are yoked because our genes are linked. More commonly, we call this love. But I'd suggest that even in these more extreme instances of giving, reciprocity is at work. That's be-cause in deeply connected, lifelong relationships, the balance of giving and receiving registers not only in the moment, but also across a lifetime. When I make a deep sacrifice for my spouse, I make it out of love, perhaps from a sense of obligation, and probably because it makes me feel good to know that I've given in a time of need. I do get something meaningful back. That's the beauty of healthy relationships—you want to give. Let's now return to how partners establish this reciprocal willingness to give turns.

Reciprocity operates in a seesaw fashion. Imagine two people on a per-fectly balanced seesaw. Then it tilts as one partner gives and the other re-ceives. Picture this: a wife sponsors her husband for a day off from the kids and household chores to take a bike trip. As she gives and he receives, the seesaw is set in motion. Visualize the movement of the seesaw as it reflects giving and receiving. This is illustrated in Figure 1.

Here, the wife moves toward the bottom of the seesaw as she gives, and the husband moves up into the air as he receives. Metaphorically, he is being held up in the air on the seesaw due to his wife's work to keep him there. As the wife gives, she gets the benefit of feeling that she's doing something

THE SEESAW OF RECIPROCITY

GIVING...
GAINS LEVERAGE
and EARNS ENTITLEMENT

RECEIVING...
INCURS
INDEBTEDNESS

FIGURE 1

good, even meaningful, for her husband. Beyond a good feeling, the giver is also earning entitlement, or credit for care. *Earned entitlement* creates the future right to ask the receiver for care in return.

The person on the receiving end (here the man at the top of the seesaw) incurs *indebtedness*. Indebtedness obliges you to return care. On the seesaw, the giver is on the bottom (they've gained leverage by giving) and the receiver is in the air—now dependent upon the giver. In order to regain balance, the indebted partner eventually needs to give. But what do you give? Do you give the same as you were given? Do you owe back according to the giver's accounting, or your own?

Typically, you can't return care or consideration in exactly the same fashion as it was given. For example, the husband in our story can't repay his wife by giving her a day off to go bicycling, because that isn't what she wants. Perhaps she'd like time off to visit a good friend. Possibly there's nothing she needs or wants now, but she's earned credit and built trust that she'll get consideration when she needs it. Going forward, the couple will need to negotiate what's fair to each and both. They may reach agreement by actively talking about their needs, or simply assuming that they'll "do right" by each other. Instead of an exact accounting of who did what, they trust that the give-and-take of daily life will be mutual.

When trust between partners is lacking, reciprocity in a relationship resembles a business contract—"I'll meet your needs only if you precisely meet mine." One couple I saw illustrated how this exact accounting produced further estrangement. The husband wanted more sex in their relationship; the wife wanted a greater show of appreciation. She wanted her husband to take her out to dinner more often. His solution? For every week they had sex three times, he would take her out to dinner once. If they had genuinely and mutually agreed to this, I might have scratched my head but called it fair, since they both embraced his idea. However, the wife was reluctant, resentful, and understandably hurt by her husband's negotiation. It was a one-sided, business-like maneuver, which, far from creating a generous climate of loving consideration, made a calculus of romance and created emotional distance. Now the wife was wary about stating any of her needs, lest her husband respond with another contractual arrangement that was superficially reciprocal, but absent the spirit of true regard for her. Loving feelings are not promoted by either unilateral demands or a conditional formula.

In contrast, reciprocity in a trusting, healthy relationship allows give-and-take to play out with infinite variety. You can trust that when you need a turn, your partner will be there for you, whether through thoughtfulness or helping out in small ways or large. Healthy reciprocity lets you forgo the tedious accounting of who's done what: "Hey—I get you coffee every morning, could you at least wash the breakfast cups?" Partners are able to assume, without taking each other for granted, that their give-and-take will be mutual. When reciprocity is balanced over time, a relationship feels fair and loving.

While it's natural to compare your marriage to others, you have to remember that acts of reciprocity for one couple may not have the same meaning to another. For example, my spouse may cook a big meal to say, "I love you." Yours may hate to cook, but surprise you with flowers, or a foot rub, or tickets to a concert. Another might listen attentively to how your day was and ask how you're *really* doing, or undertake a task that only they are best suited for. Another might offer to take on a chore that both would rather not do. Spouses express and reciprocate care in different ways.

> *Exercise:* Start a list of the small ways that you as a couple express reciprocity. Now, identify one situation in which you could have (but didn't) offer reciprocity. Then identify one in which your spouse could have returned a favor but didn't. Last, identify behaviors that you'd ideally wish to add to this list.

In a couple's invisible but powerful relationship ledger, reciprocity is the balancing act, that seesaw between care given weighed against care received. Sometimes the balance is tipped because of too much giving, too little receiving, or harm done. Anyone who has spent time on a seesaw knows that too much time spent either on the ground or in the air is no fun for anyone. When partners are stuck in their positions without the alternating rhythm of reciprocity, one is giving too much and the other is taking too much. When a couple's reciprocity is tilted, there's a toll on fairness and trust. Failures of reciprocity lead to mistrust, resentment, and less energy to keep trying. One man compared reciprocity to an alternator charging a car's battery: "A good exchange, back and forth, produces energy, it charges both people and the relationship. But when the alternator isn't working properly, when things aren't fair, then we get stalled."

Giving or Taking Too Much

There are two basic imbalances that can happen in reciprocity—giving too much or taking too much. Let's take a quick overview of these mistakes as we return to the bicyclist's marriage. If the bicyclist's wife, who has earned the right to the next turn, keeps giving without getting back what she needs, her giving may eventually turn into her resentment. The giving has cost her too much. Lopsided giving isn't good for either partner or for their relationship. Another risk to a relationship is that too much time spent in the giving position can result in relating from power rather than trust: "I (over) gave and now you owe me." One wife understandably reached a furious tipping point after years of trying to scrimp and save, only to have their car repossessed to pay off her husband's bad debt. She finally demanded that he put their house and the remaining assets in her name. When he protested, she derided him with "Yeah, payback's a bitch." There was no trust left—only power, and now it had pivoted to her control.

Sometimes the giver may try to tilt the balance of giving in his favor with the somewhat compelling argument, "Since I did this for you, now you need to do that for me." This line of reasoning has at least three flaws. First, if I didn't tell you what I expected back, that's hardly fair. Second, what if I gave something without your asking me to? It's not really a gift if now I expect a return on my terms. Third, the meaning each person assigns to the giving and receiving may be different.

Other risks to reciprocity may arise if the giver voices no expectations. Perhaps you made sacrifices without recognizing the eventual downside for yourself (you're tired of giving so much). Possibly you didn't imagine that overgiving would create an unhealthy dependency on you by your partner or a bad example for your children to follow. Or maybe someone has given so much, it seems that no matter what you do, it's never enough. Then what do you owe and on whose terms do you repay? Do you reciprocate what you think is fair? Or what the giver expects? Expectations for return may be reasonable or they may be unrealistic. Partners' expectations are sometimes verbalized, but, even more powerfully, they are often unanalyzed and sometimes-unknown assumptions about how they'll be "repaid."

Recently in my office, a young couple sat alongside each other on the couch but avoided eye contact; such was their level of frustration and anger. Monique began, "This weekend there's an engagement party for the fiancée of one of Christopher's many cousins. I've met the girl exactly once—she came to the baby shower Christopher's parents gave us last month. We're arguing now because I told Christopher that I didn't feel up to going. I'm eight months pregnant, I still have work to do to get the nursery ready, and he won't be at home this weekend. Besides, I don't feel up to driving the forty-five minutes there by myself. When Christopher can't support me in my decision, I go off the deep end. I feel hopeless. Anyway, his family literally has a get-together every other week. It's always someone's birthday, baby or wedding shower, anniversary, or funeral! I can't see how missing one event can be that big of a deal."

Christopher replied, "I feel like Monique doesn't get who I am or what's meaningful to me about family. In my family, you go out of your way to show up. I feel like she just wants the part of me that she wants, that fits in with her idea of family, which is very independent. Her family doesn't see each other that often, or even keep in touch very much. But this party is important to me and to my family. Everyone will be there but us—my parents, my brothers and sisters, all the cousins. It shows respect. I'm from a big Italian family and you learn respect before you learn to walk or even crawl. It's not right to say 'Sorry, you were there for us but we can't be there for you.' Believe me, it's a *big* deal."

Christopher is making a case about the imbalance created when you take, but don't give a turn. Christopher believes that he and Monique need to repay his family (for all they've done) by attendance at this event. Monique thinks she's given enough. I'll return to Christopher and Monique just a bit later in the chapter to show how their different assumptions and expectations about reciprocity get sorted out. But as you can see from this brief scene, relationship harmony depends upon negotiating what counts as a reasonable and fair return.

When you get a turn, but don't give a turn when the opportunity arises, you may be wielding a destructive "right" to receive. This is called *destructive entitlement*. Typically this looks like a person who takes the other for granted, is demanding, or has childish and unreasonable expectations for what a partner will provide (or tolerate). One woman admitted after her divorce, "I took him for granted. I thought my job was more important, because he worked part-time and made less money. I never thanked him for running errands, making dinner, or making my life easier. I guess I had an entitled attitude. My family wasn't big on appreciation, either."

A destructively entitled partner expects life on his terms, which drains trust. Worse yet, when a destructive taker denies responsibility or shifts blame, it distorts the very reality of his partner. After all, reality is socially constructed, and, in intimate relationships, reality is constructed together—in the *between* space. When you have two very different versions of what's fair, it causes true emotional distress because you aren't sharing the same reality.

Some years ago, a young mother told me, "I'm here to find out whether I'm crazy or not. My husband thinks I'm overreacting. I worked full-time before the twins were born this year. I had saved up enough money to stay out on a longer maternity leave. But now I can't. We need the money. Soon after the kids were born, my husband informed me that he'd taken out a huge second mortgage to buy a piece of land. He says it's the opportunity of a lifetime, and I just don't have any vision. Am I missing something—because it doesn't make any sense to me?"

The woman wasn't crazy, but she was in the disorienting twilight zone of her husband's destructive spin of what he felt entitled to do. In order to reduce distress, one partner may initially absorb the imbalance. But chronic accommodation leads to anger, resentment, and sometimes the end of a relationship. In fact, when there's chronic unfairness, the healthiest thing to do for yourself may be to end the relationship or marriage. One woman, now in her second marriage, described why she ended her first marriage of four years.

"At first everything was great—we were madly in love, my folks liked him—it was the whole nine yards. But gradually Dannie went from being a recreational drug user—marijuana mostly—to pretty regular marijuana use. Even then things seemed okay, and he had a great job. Over time his drug use increased, though he hid it from me. And he started using coke, too. I only figured this out because a large amount of money was missing from our account. I fought with him about his drug abuse, but he denied it—told me I was paranoid. I finally went to a support group for the families of addicts—and from my group I got the strength to tell him it was the drugs or me. He chose the drugs. I left. That was the best decision I've ever made—and the hardest. I still loved him, or who he had been. And at first my family wanted me to try to save the marriage. There had never been a divorce in my family, and they really had no clue about what I was going through. But eventually they understood and supported my decision."

In the upcoming chapter I'll explore the times when you should get off the seesaw—when the balance between partners can't be righted. Despite these destructive risks to reciprocity, in healthy relationships there is no exact quid pro quo and no need for one. With reciprocity the goal is balance over time. When that occurs, the teetering between give-and-take is comfortable for both people. When you expect to take turns (based on trust from your past experience), you stay on the seesaw.

Now that you're familiar with how two partners balance reciprocity, we're going to jump to light speed. As you've probably observed in your own life, reciprocity between partners doesn't occur simply in a dyad. If only life were that easy. Reciprocity occurs in the context of other competing claims on your time, energy, and obligations. But the most significant competing demand on a couple's relationship arises from parent-child (filial) loyalties. That's because loyalty isn't just another time sap. As you recall, loyalty is the payback system by which a child (over a lifetime) gives back to parents. But when it comes to couples, filial loyalty can be a puzzling, deeply conflicted sense about what you owe your family, what you owe your partner, and what you owe yourself. For each partner, the need to return loyalty expectations to their parents and family of origin is an additional weight on their seesaw.

Dr. Iván Böszörményi-Nagy, psychiatrist and preeminent family theorist, first noted that loyalty dynamics shape the family's model of expectations and the give-and-take of relationships. Nagy's contextual theory proposes that the inherent nature of the parent-child bond explains a child's early and growing recognition of parental care and prompts a child to return care. Loyalty is the parent-child form of reciprocity, which is based on birth and the years of parenting. Loyalty expectations are passed down from parent to child and also across generations within a family. How we are connected to our family of origin, strongly or tenuously, agreeably or painfully, full of pride or shame, has implications for individual development and growth. For any couple, loyalty means there are two families to be connected to, and two sets of obligations to balance. To understand the immense power of loyalty, and how it relates to a couple's reciprocity, let's take a look at how parent-child loyalty develops.

Loyalty is the "glue" that maintains the family bond. Family loyalty takes the form of obligations that a child acquires from being on the receiving end of care from parents. Parents raise children (however imperfectly) and then set powerful spoken and unspoken expectations (sometimes fair, sometimes unfair) for what a child should return. These are loyalty expectations—the almost moral imperatives, understood across time and cultures—that parents owe a child care and that a child owes the parents some return.

Children return care by attempting to meet parental expectations, whether that means making a parent proud by doing well in school, or later choosing work that reflects family values or traditions. Loyalty returns may also be expressed emotionally through a son's or daughter's thoughtfulness, or their willingness to help out in a number of ways. Meeting loyalty expectations may include positive and healthy expressions of reciprocity, such as carrying on unique family traditions or religious values, or more ominously for couples (like Christopher and Monique), it may mean an unfair expectation that you'll put your family's terms for payback before your spouse's needs, and even be blinded to your own needs.

Just as there is no one truth about fairness, there is no one truth about what you owe parents. Not everyone got the same from their parents, so they won't give back in the same way. The justice aspect of loyalty fuels the dilemma of what and how much you return. But here's the hitch—on whose terms do you return care? Yours or your parents? What do you owe because they raised you? Who's to say what's fair and what's enough? Because giving back to parents is part of the ticket to truly growing up, resolving filial loyalties enables you to live your life freer of guilt-induced obligations, and keep your couple's seesaw balanced.

The problem for Christopher and Monique is a case in point. The message Christopher gets from his parents is that he hasn't done enough as a loyal son. Is that true? Are their expectations for Christopher based on what they were expected to do for their own families? Because Christopher hasn't sorted out what he reasonably owes his parents, he's often in the middle between his parents and Monique, who has a competing view of what he owes her (versus what he owes his parents). How can Christopher, or anyone, figure this out?

To sort this out, think back to our seesaw of reciprocity (**Figure 1**). For a relationship between partners to have energy (and not get stuck) it needs a dynamic balance of give-and-take. The same is true for a parent and child relationship. But because of the very long period of childhood dependency and the intergenerational nature of family relationships, expectations for reciprocity between parents and children evolve for decades. **Figure 2** illustrates

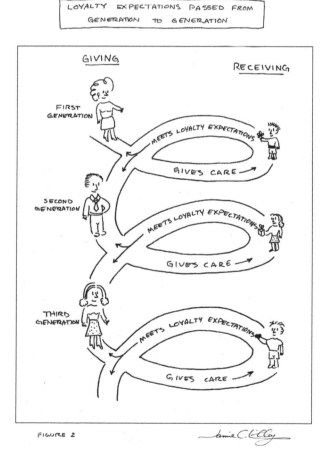

FIGURE 2

how loyalty works. Parents give (let's face it, toil and sacrifice for a child), and a child builds up a large debt on the receiving end of things. To grow up, that child needs to return care to "get out of the red." Children give back in many ways, but especially by meeting parental loyalty expectations that are transmitted generation to generation, parent to child.

But how do children, into adulthood, know what's fair to give back in order to meet parental loyalty obligations? They don't. Children (even as adults) often misjudge what's fair to return, one way or another. It's not like you can say, "Well you gave me birth, you raised me, but I gave you a painted macaroni bracelet when I was five, later got good grades in school, and made you proud—so now we're even." And it's not as if you get to decide what's fair all by yourself. Parents definitely have their own ideas about what you owe them, but they may misjudge what's fair return. Their ideas are often based on what they gave their own parents, the sacrifices they made on your behalf, as well as their own needs.

Families have wide variations between them about what's expected and what's a fair return. Each spouse then brings his own set of loyalty expectations to the marriage, and adds it to their reciprocity seesaw. But how can you be fair when what your parents and partner expect of you are on a collision course? Let's return to Christopher and Monique to see how Christopher's filial loyalty is getting in the way of his being fair to Monique.

As you recall, there's an engagement party for the fiancée of one of Christopher's cousins. In Christopher's large family, cousins feel like brothers. Christopher and Monique were invited, but Christopher can't attend—he'll be out of town. Christopher wants, even needs, Monique to go to fulfill an obligation, which for him represents the fact that they as a couple will continue to honor his family's expression of loyalty. In this situation, Christopher has unsuccessfully appealed to Monique to do what his family loyalty dictates. Next he tries guilt-tripping Monique for what he sees as her ungrateful attitude: "First, my family surprised you with an engagement party, and everybody came. Then they went all out for the wedding, even though they were the groom's family. And just a month ago, my family just gave you a baby shower, and a lot of people drove a distance for you. Now when you could show your appreciation by going to someone else's celebration, you don't *feel* like it." Christopher had barely finished when Monique protested. "That's not fair! You know that I didn't even want an engagement party. That was for them, not me. So I'm supposed to be so grateful even though I didn't ask for it? And don't you dare hint at putting my parents down about our wedding! You know my father was just getting over surgery. And your parents didn't just give *me* a shower—they gave the shower for our baby— you happen to be the father, you know."

I interrupted their deteriorating exchange, which was headed toward mutually assured destruction. They had each lost sight of their true goal— acknowledging the other's perspective as much as they could, and arriving at what would count as a fair resolution. I first addressed Christopher:

"Christopher, you're entitled to want to pay respects to your cousin and his fiancée in some way, but Monique doesn't owe it to you to go to this shower. She wrote the thank-yous for the baby shower your family gave, has bought your family gifts on most occasions, and in these ways she acknowledges her appreciation to them and their importance to you. She has valid reasons for not going, and is making a reasonable claim for you to accept her explanation. If you want to support your cousin and his fiancée, you could call to express your regrets that neither of you is able to attend. Alternately, you could send them a note or gift of congratulations, or even set up a time when just the four of you could get together for a belated celebration. You still have ways to wish your cousin well even if Monique doesn't go. You've gotten stuck in trying to respond to the letter of the invitation, rather than the spirit. You can respond on terms that work for you, and work for Monique, too."

Christopher slowly nodded and said, "You're right, I could do that. That would make me feel better." I could see out of the corner of my eye that Monique visibly relaxed. Christopher then insightfully reflected, "I think I feel a greater need to do things 'normally' and toe the family line since Monique and I got married in her church—it's Episcopal. That let my parents down." Christopher managed a laugh. "You know, my parents think the pope is like their best friend. They survived the wedding, but now I feel guilty. It's this argument inside my head. It's not that my parents really dis-approved." At this statement, Monique looked incredulous, and reminded Christopher that his mother had called them the night before the wedding and "jokingly" reminded them that their priest was free the next day—in case they changed their minds and wanted a Catholic wedding. Christopher went on. "Well that's true, they were upset, but mostly it's how we—sorry, I—disappointed them."

Christopher had made a major sacrifice to Monique by marrying outside his family's faith. The sacrifice wasn't so much his—he wasn't that religious—but a loyalty sacrifice of what he knew his parents expected of him. They had expected him to maintain their religion, their traditions. Those were their terms for repayment. Because the expression of loyalty is a way we repay our parents for all they've done for us, Christopher felt indebted and disloyal. His parents had given, and he hadn't returned what they wanted. He brought this extra loyalty tilt to his seesaw with Monique. His feeling of disloyalty took the form of his difficulty considering Monique's views and feelings as legitimate—even when the subject was something as seemingly minor as at-tendance at one of many family celebrations. Christopher had struggled to form his own values and traditions when they conflicted with those of his parents. Now he was asking Monique to make sacrifices for his lack of resolu-tion with his parents.

I explained to Christopher, "Look, your parents don't have to jump up and down and shout their disappointment for you to know what they'd pre-fer. You've lived with them for over two decades—the voice in your head is your acknowledgment that you do understand what they would want for you as a couple, and that you're straying from their values. You feel disloyal at the moment for not honoring your family's values and traditions, for not return-ing the favor when you have the chance. Right now you don't feel like you're doing what you need to do, to either pay your parents back for the baby shower or pay back by being a 'good, loyal son.' So in the short run, you want Monique to go to the engagement party—at least that would relieve some of your conflict. I encourage you to talk with your parents about your struggle, and your recognition that when you married outside their religion, you did something out of line with their values. You could make a claim for them to understand and even care about your decision, which is so different from what they wanted."

Christopher nodded, then looked at Monique, and said, "I'm sorry I put this on you." Monique smiled and added, "Babe, I know the wedding was upsetting for them. I'm grateful for what you did by getting married in my church—that meant a lot to my family and me. I didn't know that it had taken so much out of you, and left you feeling so responsible to somehow make it up to your parents. I hope that you can talk to them about it. And I'll try to be more understanding in the future. It's just that right now I don't have the energy to go to one more family get-together."

And what about Monique's notion of family reciprocity, her loyalties that seemed so slight in comparison to Christopher's? It was just as possible that she hadn't resolved her loyalty-based reciprocity with her own family. Perhaps she felt too little obligation, just as Christopher felt too much. It seemed that neither of them had sorted out the many reciprocities of what they owed each other, their families, and themselves. The couple would likely face many more of these negotiations until they settled their loyalty issues. Before the session ended, I pointed out to Monique that her comment about "going off the deep end" and feeling "hopeless" whenever Christopher couldn't support her decisions, would be worth exploring at a later date. After all, no one's decisions will—or should be—supported *all* of the time. I suspected that Monique's reaction predated her relationship with Christopher. For now, however, Christopher and Monique were relieved that they had righted their seesaw.

The two warring loyalty factions the couple carried internally had emerged to declare a truce. We'll return to loyalty in chapter 6, as we continue to explore its meaning and consequences for couples. Now let's move on to the second element in fairness: *acknowledgment.*

Acknowledgment: Doing Two Goods

Acknowledgment follows the imperative of giving credit where credit is due. Acknowledgment improves relationships in three ways: by verbally communicating credit, by affirming good intentions, and by validating a partner's perspective (their reality). When you acknowledge a partner's giving, the relationship scores two good deeds.

> *Jacob realizes after Anna's business trip just how very many responsibilities she has for her job as well as the household and the kids. He leaves her a loving message saying, "Wow, I'm exhausted from being Mom for a day! I don't know how you do it all. Thanks so much, I'll chip in more in the future."*

In the scene above, Jacob recognizes all that Anna usually does—he extends credit with his acknowledgment. No doubt his phone message helped Anna feel more appreciated. The appreciation of everyday acts is a meaningful balm to the many stressors of relationships. Those everyday acknowledgments might be as small as a thank-you for emptying the trash, an appreciation that your partner thought of the dinner menu, a verbalization of your awareness that your spouse took the kids to the dentist, a recognition that he walked the dog even though he was tired, too, an understanding of what it takes to plan a night out, a recognition of how hard she works, a caring question about how that meeting went that he was worried about. Some would argue, "But why do you have to make appreciation so clear? Shouldn't my spouse just know what I value? Do you mean I have to thank him every time he takes out the trash? Or thank her for making dinner? I figured if I'm not complaining, it's good enough." I tell those doubters just to try acknowledging the small things for a week and see the resulting goodwill.

Exercise: To amplify your awareness of the daily acts that deserve acknowledgment, think of these instances as if a friend had done them for you. After all, ideally, don't you want to treat your partner as well as you'd treat a friend? Begin by noticing what your partner is doing that helps you or the household. Don't define help only by what's important to you. Define help by things that need to get done. Define help, not by how you would do something, but that it was done. If your spouse took the kids to the doctor's, that means you didn't have to. If the household needed cash and your spouse made an extra trip to get it, that helped you, too. If the dishwasher was dirty in the morning but clean and emptied by day's end, that's a help. If your partner works hard to contribute to the finances, that counts.

After appreciating the basics of everyday acts, you could begin to notice the subtler, invisible acts of thoughtfulness. These might include noticing when your spouse asks how your day was and really wants to hear about it; or appreciating that she remembered to ask how a worrisome event turned out; it might mean recognizing that he went out of his way to pick you up because it was raining. Simple acts of acknowledgment register that consideration is happening.

Beyond your willingness to show appreciation, acknowledgment calls on you to recognize good intentions, even behind poor outcomes. One morning in a rush, a husband tossed the clothes in the dryer, not realizing that one of his wife's favorite sweaters had to be line dried. Predictably, it shrank. He apologized. She balanced her anger about the ruined sweater with an acknowledgment of his good intent, and accepted his apology. To further make amends, he surprised her with a beautiful handmade sweater on her birthday with the note "I got the right size this time."

At other times, acknowledgment extends reassurance about a hardship or struggle.

Brian was laid off from his job. Instead of freaking out and making him feel even worse, Michelle was calm and reassuring. She told Brian how much she appreciated his strong sense of responsibility, and reassured him that she could work more hours until he found a new job.

Here, Michelle gave Brian credit for his sense of responsibility. She reassured him that (in reciprocal fashion) it was her turn to help him now. Acknowledgment in a time of hardship allows a partner to feel understood and valued, independent of accomplishment or achievement. Even when life isn't going your way, acknowledgment can take the sting out of a difficult time.

The third way that acknowledgment bolsters fairness is by validating a partner's point of view. Remember—fairness is three-sided: how you see things, how I see things, and then a more complicated view that captures and meshes the multiple truths into how *we* see things. Acknowledgment soothes the experience of a grievance. That's the powerful scientific finding on the salutary effects of the validation of your reality. Scientists have confirmed what therapists try to teach couples: it's good for your relationship to acknowledge your partner's perspective. With validation, blood pressure goes down and the feeling of agitation diminishes. The underlying message of acknowledgment is, "I care about your experience enough to take responsibility for my actions." It means: "I understand a bit more what it's really like to be in your shoes—to be you." Beyond saying the words "I'm sorry," you're taking responsibility for your part. The goal is for each partner to give credit; recognize effort, intent, or struggle; validate a grievance; and remember there's your way *and* my way of seeing things.

The following vignette demonstrates the potential balm of acknowledgment after tensions arise. One morning a couple arrived to a session about five minutes late. The husband, James, grumpily complained that his wife, Myra, ran on Sternberg time (her family of origin). They were always late. I asked him if he ran on Smyth time (his family of origin). He nodded agreement, and recounted that "all hell would break loose" if he were late in his family. You just didn't do it. I then turned to Myra and asked if she had let James know that she was aware of the time stress for him. I wondered aloud if she tried, despite her own struggles with punctuality, to acknowledge his frustration. Myra replied, "Oh, I was very aware of the time this morning, but I didn't say anything about it. I'm always thinking about whether I'm running on time for his sake, knowing that the later I am the more irritated he'll be. But I guess I've gotten so tired of disappointing him that I don't even let him know that I recognize it." James turned to her and said, "If you had just said that you knew I was worried about being late, I would have been like a pussycat in a chair, waiting for you." Myra replied, "I'll try to do that more often." James took a deep breath, smiled, and looked noticeably calmer.

If we'd had a blood pressure cuff on James, it would have shown his reduced blood pressure following Myra's acknowledgment. As this vignette reveals, acknowledgment soothes distress, creates goodwill, and repairs the sense of fairness. But this vignette also exposes the complexity of fair consideration.

Acknowledgment works by validating reality. But remember, in a couple's relationship there are multiple truths. In the situation above, Myra was willing to validate why James was frustrated with her and take responsibility for what she could do differently, yet James didn't take any personal responsibility (that he was as much guided by his family's clock as Myra was hers). He stuck to his story that it was all Myra's problem with time. James had difficulty seeing that his chronic impatience contributed to Myra's silent response to his upset. He acted as if only his view counted. The failure to acknowledge the other's perspective creates a negative spiral, a downward emotional thrust. Instead of the soothing benefit of mutual acknowledgment, a standoff results when acknowledgment is withheld.

> *Exercise:* Think of a recent disagreement with your partner. Now think of your different points of view as stories. There's your story, your partner's story, and the story that an outside observer might tell. Write down each of these stories. See if this exercise helps you acknowledge the multiple truths in your relationship.

Withholding Acknowledgment: A Lost Opportunity

When you offer acknowledgment and give credit where it's due, your reward is a generous sense of partnership that motivates fair behavior. On the other hand, when you withhold acknowledgment the result is a stingy, deprivation model for relating. There's a lost opportunity for returning care, and insult is added to injury. Two couples illustrate the effects of withholding acknowledgment.

Frannie is very upset because Howie is too hard on the kids. She approaches him carefully, asking him to acknowledge the impact his screaming is having on her and their children. Howie calls Frannie a nag and dismisses her concerns outright. Howie's defensiveness further deepens the wound between them. Now there's the fact of his bad temper, and the additional relationship injustice to Frannie of being blamed instead of having her worries validated in any way.

Doug spends all day attending an event for his in-laws, but leaves before the party's over to complete a work assignment. Sheila is offended that Doug left early. Doug made a considerable effort even if Sheila was disappointed. Sheila fails to credit what Doug did (attend most of the event) and only expresses her frustration at what he didn't do (make more of a sacrifice by staying). If Sheila had first acknowledged the effort Doug made, this would have cushioned her complaint and left Doug more open to hearing her disappointment. Instead, they argue and never come to an understanding.

Withholding acknowledgment is a one-two punch of no credit but blame, which drains goodwill. It takes a gesture of consideration to restart the positive momentum. In the next scenes, the partner who has stopped the motion of reciprocity acknowledges his mistake and tries to make up for it.

Sid apologizes to Rob for being so critical of Rob's parents. Sid recognizes that he's driving a wedge between himself and Rob, and also between Rob and his parents. Sid offers to make dinner for Rob's parents.

Jonah regrets that he has always overridden Sylvia's wishes about remodeling their home. On the next home project, Jonah steps out of the way to give Sylvia the opportunity to take charge.

However, even if your partner doesn't offer the acknowledgment you deserve, you can *make a claim for fairness*—the third component of our new model.

A Claim: An Earned Request

A claim for fairness is a clear statement of your needs. You deserve the right to make a claim based on your past giving. A claim may be an action: "I'd like us to celebrate Christmas even though it isn't your religious tradition." Or a claim can be an appeal for a day-to-day change in relating: "I'd like us to greet each other when you come home." A claim can also be corrective feedback in the form of a stop action request to end unfair relating: "Stop drinking, stop calling me names, give me time to calm down." As the next couples illustrate, claims can be simple to meet:

Alejandro makes a claim for his wife to give him a few minutes when he first gets home before telling him the problems of the day. This helps him feel less overwhelmed and more interested in her day.

Leticia makes a claim for her partner to let her know before he commits to plans with his children from his former marriage. Leticia helps with their care and deserves this consideration.

Claims may also require a significant amount of change:

Drew makes a claim for his wife to enter a treatment program for alcohol addiction. He has endured many episodes of her drunken behavior, and needs her to get treatment for his sake, though it will also benefit her and hopefully save the marriage.

Sofia makes a claim for her long-term partner, Jade, to change jobs, after learning of Jade's affair with a coworker.

In the examples above, one partner identifies the meaningful consideration they need, and then makes a claim. As you read the vignettes, you might wonder if I'm just substituting the word "claim" for "asking"? How is making a claim different from asking? A claim is an earned form of asking. While everyone has needs, a claim is earned. You can ask for the earth, the moon, and the stars above, but that doesn't mean that you've earned the right to have your needs met by your partner. In order for a claim to be fair, it must be earned between the two people involved. You can't transfer the right to another person. You can't transfer what was due you from a past relationship. And you can't ask for more than you've given in a relationship (unless you've stockpiled enough trust). Claims are based on reciprocity.

Fair Claims or Unfair Needs?

At first, like learning anything new, making claims takes conscious work. First, you must identify your needs. The negotiation of fairness depends on partners' ability to state their needs; yet that doesn't necessarily guarantee that a need is intrinsically fair. If you haven't earned the consideration, it isn't a fair claim. It may be a need or a wish, but that's different than a claim for fairness. Since marriage is often a repository for unmet needs from the past, how do you know if your need is fair? How do you tell what needs are fair to claim? In order for a need to be a "fair claim" it must meet a few criteria:

- It must be a realistic expectation.
- It must not take advantage of your partner's trust in any way.
- It must be earned between the two relating partners.

Some requests are blatantly unfair: *"I want you to stop bringing your children to our house. I didn't marry you to have to share you."* Some responses are blatantly unfair: *"It's none of your business how much I drink. I'm a grown-up. Leave me alone."* But more often, the line between what's fair and what's unfair is blurred. A request for consideration may seem reasonable to one person but unreasonable and unfair to the other. In the next vignettes, the partners are operating according to different models for determining fairness. Try to decide whose claims are fair and reasonable as you read ahead.

Phoebe repeatedly asks Leo to stop leaving his toiletries on her side of the bathroom. He tries, but occasionally forgets. Phoebe is frustrated and thinks that if Leo really cared, he'd remember.

In the first scene, Phoebe has overly personalized the meaning of her husband's forgetfulness. She hasn't imagined, much less acknowledged, benign intent. While she has a reasonable need and has made a reasonable claim (don't leave your things on my side), she has an unreasonable expectation for perfection. It's clear that Leo is trying, but he's human. That doesn't take Leo off the hook for making a true effort, but it does require Phoebe to reset her expectations.

Andy wants to put a monthly limit on Rebecca's use of their credit card. She's been on a monthlong spending spree and Andy's had to dip into their savings to pay for it—and this isn't the first time. Andy worries that she could do some serious damage to their finances. Rebecca rejects his claim as she angrily defends herself: "I can't believe you think I'm so immature that I'd get us into real trouble. Stop treating me like a kid!"

Despite the insult Rebecca feels to her independence, Andy has earned the right to make his claim because he's literally paid the bill for Rebecca's spending. But Rebecca doesn't think so. Not *always* getting what you want when you make a claim is part of the push-pull of relationships. It rarely becomes a problem unless trust is low, or the collisions are frequent. When couples can't negotiate what's fair in such impasses, they begin to feel frustrated, then unloved, and a downward spiral ensues. The emotional rift widens when mistrust replaces fairness.

As these two microslices of relationships reveal, partners can have different feelings about what's fair. But feelings aren't the most reliable guide to fairness. I encourage people to think of feelings as offering important clues, while recognizing that feelings change—they're notoriously fickle. Remember that feelings are made up of assumptions and extra charges from past experiences and injuries, so things can *feel* entirely like your partner's fault without *being* entirely his fault. Painful feelings of hurt or anger are most constructively channeled into claims rather than through complaints, criticisms, resentment, or shows of contempt.

Criticisms versus Claims

Claims take work, because it's easier to identify what you don't like with a complaint or criticism than figure out exactly what you need instead. Whenever you make your needs known there's the risk that your partner cannot (or will not) comply. That's why it feels easier to complain, blame, or criticize— you don't feel vulnerable. Criticism allows your powerful feelings of irritation and anger to emerge. But the trifecta of complaint, blame, and criticism typically results in a partner's defensive response and a deteriorating situation. Claims differ from criticisms in the following ways:

Criticisms:
- point out what the other has done wrong;
- carry an emotionally hostile charge (from little digs to blaming);
- put people on the defensive.

Claims:
- encourage cooperative problem-solving (as opposed to fault-finding);
- are a request for consideration on your terms;
- assume benign intent (give the benefit of the doubt);
- give credit while asking for change;
- are earned.

Think about it. Even the most benign form of criticism, the complaint, feels like finger-pointing. In contrast, claims give credit while at the same time specifically identifying what needs to change. Let's review the next couple's situation to illustrate the differences between criticisms and claims.

Alice feels hurt by John's habit of responding to e-mails on his BlackBerry—he checks it constantly, even when they're out to dinner. She criticizes him: "John, you're so rude, can't you just cut off your Crackberry while we're out?"

[You can imagine John's response—huffy compliance, or irritable defensiveness: "I have to leave it on—my clients expect to be able to reach me. How do you think we can afford this dinner out?"]

And now the same scene, with a claim substituted for the criticism:

Alice: *"John, I know you feel obliged to be available to your clients [credits his reality], but I'd like you to turn your BlackBerry off while we're at dinner. I need some time when I can catch up with you without the distraction."*

John: *"You're right, Alice. These messages can wait. Sorry" [acknowledges the reasonableness of her claim].*

You may detect an intuitive vulnerability in making a claim. You are making yourself and your needs known. Since it's a possibility that your needs won't be met, why take the risk? Though it's counterintuitive, the very process of making a claim leads to an enhanced sense of self-worth. While you can't control the outcome (how your partner responds), you can ask for what you deserve. And you're much more likely to get fairness by making a claim than by finding fault. Some partners let silence speak for them. But your silence may create an invisible tyranny of either self-sacrifice or a punishing and childish expectation that your partner will mind-read. Self-silencing is a form of self-betrayal. It's unlikely that you'll get what you want very often if your modus operandi is silence. Instead, if you make a fair claim, even if your partner doesn't meet you halfway, you empower yourself by making clear your terms for fair and meaningful consideration. Let's play the last scene back one more time, but with the possibility of a rebuff in mind.

Alice: *"John, I know you feel obliged to be available to your clients, but I'd like you to cut the BlackBerry off while we're at dinner. I need some time when I can catch up with you without that distraction."*

John, sighing: *"Honey, don't you understand that this is part of my job? I'm on call 24/7."*

Alice: *"John, no one expects an emergency response to business on a Saturday night. I think it could wait at least an hour."*

John: *"You just don't understand."*

Now Alice and John are in the stuck position on their seesaw. If John doesn't budge, Alice may feel angry or she may accept that John has a problem. His need to feel important dictates his constant availability to his clients. That's his issue and she can't solve it for him. She'll have to decide what she needs to do with John's refusal to respond to her request. She may decline dinner out with him, or perhaps she'll invite friends along so she has backup company. But instead of saying nothing and stewing in anger and frustration, she has explicitly stated her needs. She has made a claim for fairness. You're only responsible for keeping your own balance on the seesaw. Now it's John's turn to right it.

Exercise: Think of a time when you recently complained to or criticized your partner. Now convert the criticism to a claim. First imagine his side. Give him credit for what you think is going on for him. Give him credit for his efforts or his struggles. Now ask for what you want to go differently. Use "I" statements rather than "you" statements, because "you" statements can feel like finger-pointing. Besides, a claim is about what you want. Let your partner know that you are making a genuine attempt at being fair to him.

Now let's take a look at how reciprocity, acknowledgment, and claims work together to restore fairness for a couple dealing with an everyday quarrel.

Putting Reciprocity, Acknowledgment, and Claims Together

A client in her forties drooped in her chair in my office and described this incident: "I went on a three-day business trip. Before I left, I took great pains to put the house in order and leave meals in the refrigerator for Jeffrey. When I came back, he'd made dinner for me. And he'd also made a big mess in the kitchen. At first I bit my tongue, but after I cleaned it all up, I lost it, and told him how upset I was with how he'd left the kitchen. Jeffrey refused to apologize. He said, 'But, Patty, I went to all this trouble to make your favorite meal. You know chicken Florentine takes several pans to make, so that's why there's so much to clean up. You're so ungrateful. All you do is criticize me and complain.' All I really wanted was an apology from him. Instead I got blamed for picking on him."

What's wrong with this picture? Neither partner gets what they deserve, despite the well-intentioned and reciprocal efforts. Patty takes care of Jeffrey by making meals before she leaves on her business trip. Jeffrey makes a lovely dinner to welcome Patty home, and expects some appreciation. But Patty wants an apology for the big mess he leaves for her. Then Jeffrey falls back on the old dodge: "How dare you say that after all I've done for you?" Jeffrey fails to acknowledge her point of view, while Patty fails to credit Jeffrey's effort. Instead, she complains rather than making a claim for him to clean up the kitchen because she's too tired. Both feel ill-considered. Love is not served.

My first directive to Patty and Jeffrey would be: "Stay glued together, get to a calmer place before you continue your argument." Going ballistic, or withdrawing into stony silence are punishing to your partner and destroy trust as well. Those reactions make it that much harder to recover. If you remember that your goal is a fairer and more trusting relationship, then you need to incorporate that goal when you disagree. Think about the other person's perspective before you try to have a more constructive discussion. Remember that love and fairness are served by acknowledging whatever truth there is in your partner's experience. The ability to get outside of your own vantage point and take a bird's-eye view is necessary for acknowledgment and fair claims.

The new order of fairness would go something like this: Patty acknowledges Jeffrey's good intent (to make a lovely meal to welcome her home). Instead of fuming about the mess she assumes he expects her to clean up, she makes a claim for Jeffrey to clean up the kitchen. She replaces blame with claims. Because Patty gives him credit for what he has done (rather than what he hasn't) Jeffrey doesn't defend himself. He understands why she's asking him to go the extra mile (and clean up). His acknowledgment is soothing. Then what? Either he cleans up, or they figure out that the dishes can wait, because both of them are tired. The dishes, after all, aren't as important as preserving the goodwill and fairness in the relationship. Yet people fight over little things like dirty dishes when they feel unacknowledged for their efforts, or when they're more accustomed to blaming each other rather than more consciously and thoughtfully making claims.

At this point you may be thinking that reciprocity, acknowledgment, and making claims sound pretty simple. Yet if they're so simple and so crucial to fairness and to relationship repair, why is this trio so hard to pull off? Most often, partners get stuck on stating their cases, which results in point-counterpoint, as if they're in a debate. People are so strongly motivated to *get* justice that they forget to *give* it. Winning becomes the goal—the only goal. Even taking a break from the heat of an argument may only result in the hardening of an adversarial stance between partners—time often spent honing the case against each other. Instead of recognizing the healing power of acknowledgment, many times partners want to prove their points (without acknowledging the merit of a partner's experience). Others get derailed from admitting personal responsibility because apologies can tend to make us feel down. Partners often exert a fair amount of energy resisting and wriggling their way out of apologies with defensive maneuvers. People begin to explain *why* they did what they did, rather than simply acknowledging *that* they did it. In our couple above, instead of acknowledging what he could have done differently, Jeffrey parried with *why* he'd made such a mess (the chicken Florentine defense) and then added how ungrateful Patty was in addition to being unappreciative of his efforts. The underlying message of Jeffrey's defensive response is "get over it, stop being an ingrate." Worse still, there's the "an apology wouldn't be necessary if you weren't so sensitive" under-tone—in other words, it's your problem, not mine. Acknowledgment always involves personal accountability.

What might the repair between Jeffrey and Patty sound like? Either could extend the olive branch first. Jeffrey could offer an *acknowledgment* of the mess. "I know cleaning up is a hassle. I'm sorry I didn't imagine that the way I left the kitchen would make you feel dumped on. Next time, I'll try to be more thoughtful." Then he *makes a claim:* "But I'm not a mind reader. I hope you'll let me know what you need, in case I don't get it." Jeffrey points to the fact that Patty has a responsibility here, too. Her responsibility lies in making a claim for what is fair to her, rather than resentfully complaining after the fact. Patty could now reciprocally *acknowledge*: "Jeffrey, I really appreciate the dinner you made. It was delicious. I could've done a better job letting you know that I was too tired to clean up. You were operating under our usual deal—one cooks, one cleans up. I feel good that we could work this out, and learn from it." The relationship recipe here is: offer an acknowledgment of the other person's reality, then claim the consideration you'd like. As this brief vignette illustrates, couples always stand to benefit from acknowledgment as it acts to restore fairness. Acknowledgment builds *trust*, the fourth component of our new working model of fairness.

TRUST

Trust is a vital part of a loving relationship that grows through reciprocal acts of care, mutual acknowledgment, and fair claims. Trust is always a two-way street. Trust isn't a static commodity, earned only once, but instead it's fluid and subject to fluctuations, breakdowns, and repairs. Trust grows when you have your needs considered (even when unmet) and shrinks when you get less than you deserve. As trust fluctuates, so does closeness. You have to have trust to feel close to your partner. In a healthy relationship, you're able to give freely and trust that you'll receive care in return.

Figure 3 shows trust as a well between people. When people fall in love, they're not relating from that well of trust, but rather from the early glow of

RELATING FROM THE WELL OF TRUST

THE NEED FOR TRUST IS CLOUDED BY
THE BLUSH OF FIRST ROMANCE

TRUST RISES WHEN BOTH PARTNERS FILL
THE WELL OF TRUST.

IT TAKES BOTH PARTNERS TO REPLENISH
TRUST.

IT TAKES BOTH PARTNERS TO REPLENISH
TRUST.

FIGURE 3

passionate love, with its surge in brain chemicals that produces the "falling in love" experience. Romantic love seduces us with the promise of unconditional love—unearned and wildly given. But as the old saying goes: "Marriage is between four people. The man you think you are marrying and the husband you actually marry, and the woman you think you are marrying and the wife you actually marry." At some point the fantasy wears off. When it does, you'll need a more mature reciprocity where love is embedded in trust.

Trust is continuously filled or depleted by the minutiae of daily life, as well as by momentous events. Trust rises when there is reciprocity and recedes when one or both partners act unjustly. Because this reservoir of trust exists between two partners, one person can't fill it alone. If only one person attempts to fill the well of trust, it's not only unfair, but also unsustainable. Acts that drain the well (and the relationship) of trust can be onetime events (an affair, an injurious secret, a critical remark), or chronic and repeated acts of unfairness (lack of appreciation, put-downs, disregard, not making a partner a priority, emotional or physical abuse, alcohol or substance abuse).

The health of a relationship depends on your reservoir of trust. Then when a partner is unfair, there's a trust reserve to be tapped into. Marriage merges the trust level that partners bring from their parent-child relationships, with the couple's experience with each other. If your trust level is high going into marriage, there's more room for your partner to make mistakes. On the other hand, if you start with a low level of trust, slight offenses can register as if they were major problems.

One couple I saw was living proof of how past and present balances of trust blended to reduce trust. Martin's chief complaint was Renée's jealousy. Their relationship of three years began when Martin was still married. Now their fights often devolved into Renée's wrongful accusations that he was cheating on her. Renée's insecurity was twofold. She anxiously concluded that since Martin had cheated on his wife, he could be unfaithful to her, too (this conveniently sidestepped the fact that she had also cheated—as his affair partner). But beyond the couple's complicated beginning, Renée brought a lower level of trust to their relationship from feeling unloved by an abusive father. Martin had a very narrow margin for error in this relationship, because Renée's level of trust was so low to begin with.

You can't trust if you don't expect to be fairly treated. You lose trust if unfair experiences aren't repaired. When partners have their trust broken, they may withhold care, love, affection, and finally, themselves. The loss of trust might be temporary, for a few hours or days, or it might be more lasting and result in the breakdown of the relationship.

However, if couples have a trust reserve, their relationship will be more likely to weather rough times. Later in the book, you'll meet Kate and Tim. Married with two young children, their relationship started off with a great deal of trust, which was drained by several years of Tim's alcoholism. In an early session, Kate reported the following: "It got to the point during the worst of Tim's drinking that I couldn't really remember the good times—but I knew that they'd existed. The drinking years were really pretty ugly, but I knew that I'd married a loving person. I just held on to that memory." At the crisis point when they called me, their trust was meager to be sure, but ultimately it was what held them together—that and their willingness to learn to become fairer to each other. Trust, then, can be all but drained, but still be a vital resource in intimate relationships.

While trust has a global and even abstract quality, fairness provides a factual map of daily life. Reciprocity, acknowledgment, and earned claims are the action components of the new fairness that you negotiate with your partner.

With your new model of fairness, you'll use these key components in a thoughtful negotiation. Now you're able to assess and evaluate your old assumptions, and review and revise what has counted as fair in the past. Since the feeling of what's fair sometimes defies logic, in the next chapters I'll talk about what leads partners to be unfair to each other. I'll start with the imbalances of give-and-take, and end with when to get off the seesaw for good and decide your relationship cannot be salvaged.

EXERCISE: RECIPROCITY: THE SEESAW WITH MY SPOUSE

Picture yourself and your partner on the seesaw that represents the give-and-take in your marriage.

Are you giving more often than taking, or vice versa? Now, choose an item that best reflects your relationship, from A, B, or C, and then complete sentence D.

A. In my seesaw picture I am on the receiving end (while my partner is grounding me) because:

B. In my seesaw picture I am on the giving end (while my partner is way up in the air) because:

C. In my seesaw picture my spouse and I are balanced. We take turns giving:

D. This suggests that my relationship is: _____.

Remember, good people are both overgivers and overtakers. Your position on your seesaw doesn't tell good from bad, only your ride in the balancing of your relationship. You're reading this book because you want a healthier relationship. You'll learn more about the problems with reciprocity in chapter 4 and then in chapter 5, you'll learn how you might have ended up in the position you did. But more important, you'll learn more about finding balance.

BALANCING
GIVE-AND-TAKE

In the last chapter we saw how important reciprocity is to a healthy and loving relationship. In order to implement the new fairness, you and your spouse need to identify your current patterns of give-and-take and understand the mistakes you both may be making. But what if one of you has an inherently inaccurate model for what reciprocity really means? What if your relationship is too often in the tilt position? What if you think you're doing most of the heavy lifting, while your partner is content to watch; or worse, wants to help by critiquing you; or worse still, wants an outside consensus on the definition of "heavy"? When do you know it's time to get off the seesaw because it will never be balanced? That's the trick with reciprocity—figuring out whether your balance is just right, temporarily off, or permanently tilted in favor of either partner. Across all of your relationships there's generally a pattern, whether you're in balance, or whether you're the giver or the taker. One woman who came to see me complaining of exhaustion and depression summed it up this way: *"It just never ends. First my parents expected me to take care of them—and I did. Then my husband wants me to cater to him—and I do.*

Now my kids treat me like I run Mom's Diner and Mom's Chauffeur Service. But the pay is lousy. There must be something wrong with me that it's always give, give, give."

Like the woman above, most of us have a degree of awareness that our balance is off, even if we can't quite figure out how it happened or how to change it. Sometimes we hold our spouse responsible for the imbalance:

He said: *"If she would just cut me a break when I walk in the door—instead of handing me the baby—like, I've done my job, now it's your turn."*

She said: *"If he could only see what has to be done—just pick up the laundry or wash one dish! But no, he thinks I'm supposed to be on call 24/7."*

It's always easier to see what someone did to us than it is to see what we did to someone else. In reality, both partners benefit from taking a closer look at the imbalances in reciprocity, which can signal two basic mistakes: giving too much (and expecting too little for yourself) and taking too much (and feeling little or no need to give in return). The Fairness Questionnaire in chapter 2 suggests whether any of your important relationships are skewed. Yet there are times that having an imbalance between you actually indicates a healthy reservoir of trust. You only get in trouble when the imbalance is significant, chronic, and substantially drains trust. But before we delve into the problems with reciprocity, let's look at the healthy imbalances in fairness that promote trust and love.

Healthy Imbalances

As you recall from the last chapter, healthy imbalances in give-and-take occur when one needs to meet the legitimate needs of another. The most universal examples are found in the asymmetrical parent-child relationship. Parent-child relationships begin with a slavish devotion to ensure an infant's survival and growth. This altruistic giving serves an evolutionary purpose— it keeps our gene pool going. But we aren't thinking of our gene pool during midnight feedings or during years of material, emotional, and physical dependency. We're mostly thinking, "I give because I love my child." And a dependent child is entitled to have his basic needs met by his parents. This is a healthy form of one-sided giving.

Healthy and temporary overgiving may also occur in symmetrical relationships, such as marriage. Situations that call for overgiving may include: the father-to-be who takes over most of the chores for his pregnant wife; the wife who agrees to work full-time so her husband can pursue a lifelong dream of painting; the husband who supports his wife's return to school by taking over child-care responsibilities in the evenings so she can study; the spouse who provides extended caregiving to a partner during a major illness; the wife who sponsors her husband for the fifteen hours a week he needs to train for his upcoming triathlon. These healthy circumstances of overgiving reflect trust that if I give now, I'll get a turn to receive when I need one. That's how healthy giving works. Let's list some reasons for healthy giving.

Healthy Reasons for Giving

- It feels generous.
- It's an ethic: Christian/Talmudic, Buddhist, Quaker, Muslim, "It is better to give than to receive."
- It's a matter of obligation.
- It makes me feel needed.
- It makes me feel like a good person.
- Others depend on me to be this responsible.
- Even when it feels burdensome, it feels like the loving thing to do.
- It's a way of showing that I'm a good partner.
- It shows that I'm doing the same as my mother/father did for me.
- I like myself more when I give.
- It demonstrates my love.

In balanced measure, all of the above reasons can be healthy. Healthy relationships can absorb temporary imbalances of reciprocity when each partner is attuned to both giving and receiving. But reciprocity goes awry when one partner overgives while the other too often takes. Then you've got a problem. What causes partners to make these seemingly obvious mistakes in fair relating? What happens when the giver doesn't know what they need? Or even that they *should* expect *something* back? On the other hand, what if one partner's expectations are unreasonable or even impossible for the other to meet? Conversely, what if the partner on the receiving end doesn't know what or how to pay back? Or what if they're unmotivated to pay back? What happens to the relationship then? Let's begin to find answers to these perplexing questions.

Unhealthy Imbalances

THE FIRST PROBLEM: GIVING TOO MUCH

Let's begin with the first problem of giving too much. You might ask, "Why concern ourselves with giving too much? Why not say, 'Three cheers for giving!'" After all, giving can be beneficial, even healthy for you. It can help you get beyond yourself, reduce depression, and create a "generous economy" in relationships. Giving more than is asked or even required can make you feel good. When you sensitively discern what someone else needs or wants, you feel needed and valued. So what's so bad about giving? Nothing, if you don't overdo it. On the whole, giving is a resource to others, and a wonderful quality. Again, the goal is balance—because overgiving can boomerang on individuals as well as relationships. When does giving become a problem? And how can you tell if you're giving too much? The first signs of overgiving often show up in feelings of individual distress, which then percolate down to your relationship. As you read ahead, check the signs of overgiving that you may experience.

Individual signs of overgiving include:
- emotional depletion and depression;
- resentment/simmering anger;
- disappointed expectations;
- not getting a turn.

Relationship signs of overgiving include:
- lack of reciprocity over time;
- failure to acknowledge contributions;
- lack of mutual consideration;
- feeling taken for granted.

See if you can identify any of the indicators of overgiving in the next scene.

A young woman, married only a few years, called asking for treatment for depression. Chief among the reasons she recounted for her depression was feeling poorly treated by her husband. He was easy to anger, preferred hanging out with his friends to spending free time with her, and took her for granted. When she cried about this, he told her to get over being so needy.

If you identified her emotional depletion and depression, her resentment and disappointed expectations, as indicators of overgiving, you're correct. Additionally, because her husband didn't acknowledge her contributions, she felt taken for granted. For all she gave, she wanted and deserved better treatment. She was the giver; he was the taker in their marriage. Her depression was a wake-up call that their relationship needed to change. Looking at their relationship from the outside, people often wonder, "Why did she settle for so little for herself," as often as they condemn, "How could he have treated her that way?" Let's take a look at both sides of that coin.

Low Entitlement

Why make the mistake of settling for too little and giving too much? People are motivated by different reasons. Some individuals who give too much feel undeserving of receiving in turn. They suffer from *low entitlement.* As you remember from the last chapter, when you give, you earn the entitlement (the "right") to receive. Individuals deserve to receive care and consideration (based on their giving), but if you have a low sense of entitlement, you won't *feel* entitled to an appropriate return of care. Your register for fairness will favor other people at your own expense. Your family fairness model left you with a lopsided notion of what is fair to you. You may confuse "self-interest," which is healthy, with "selfishness," which isn't. You may shortchange yourself by not asking for a fair return. Think back to Celeste in chapter 1. It was impossible for Celeste to ask for what she wanted because she believed that love meant being selfless. She oriented herself toward what everyone else needed, wanted, and (she thought) expected. Her family's spin on love resulted in protecting others, not burdening anyone, and so meant cheating herself out of asking for fair consideration.

The depletion of depression, or physical exhaustion, is often the first clue that you've overgiven. Depletion is your psyche's and your body's way of saying "I can't keep going like this." When you repeatedly shortchange yourself, a snowball effect occurs: if you don't know, and you don't advocate for what you deserve, you may be so accustomed to overgiving that you don't even know what you need or want. Yet the pain of depression can mobilize people to seek help, and to change their overgiving patterns.

We'll deepen our understanding of entitlement as we explore other facets of fairness throughout the book. For now it's enough to keep in mind that low expectations for the return of care and consideration spell trouble for reciprocity. Yet, there's an important distinction between people with low entitlement who don't expect to be treated well enough (but would welcome it), and people who aren't comfortable receiving. We look at the stingy receiver next.

The Stingy Receiver

Have you ever known anyone who had trouble receiving, who was more comfortable on the giving end of things? That's what I call the stingy receiver. Their resistance to receive reflects a lack of trust in being "too close." Have you ever realized that being on the giving end of a relationship ensures a degree of control? The baffling benefit of this kind of control is this: if you don't owe anybody, you can feel less vulnerable in relationships. You might not trust being on the receiving end because you're afraid of dependency and the risk of emotional closeness. If you've been burned before by someone who expected too much back, you may not want to chance owing someone. Some individuals trace their reluctance to receive to a childhood spent with a loving but overly needy parent who relied too heavily on them. Others may be reluctant to receive if they learned from a demanding parent that they could never do enough. In other words, stingy receivers aren't born but made. In intimate relationships, independence and the appearance of supreme self-reliance can provide a good cover for the fear of owing a partner too much—or anything at all.

The Stingy Giver

Stingy givers insist on an exact accounting of "who owes what" and "whose turn it is." The stingy giver doesn't trust that fairness will happen over time, and so keeps score. It's a tit-for-tat way of relating, which is technically equitable, but doesn't feel loving. *"I'll cook for you (only if) you buy the groceries. I'll let you drive my car (only if) you put gas in it. It's not my turn to watch the kids, but I will (only if) you put them to bed every night this week. I'll give in and go to your family's for July Fourth (only if) you take me to the beach the next weekend."* The terms for reciprocation might be okay in and of themselves, but the spirit's all wrong because it's conditional and imposed rather than trust-based and negotiated. A variation on conditional giving that diminishes a couple's trust reserves even further is *giving with strings attached*.

Giving with Strings Attached

Giving with strings attached turns giving into manipulation. It's a "Well, I did this for you, so now you owe me" bind. One man confided to me, "I'm scared to let my girlfriend throw me a big birthday bash because then I'll owe her for life. She'll point out all she's done for me, whenever she wants me to go to dinner with her mom or spend the holidays with her family. I'd rather not celebrate the stupid birthday." Giving with strings attached isn't true giving. With true giving you may either give with no expectation of a particular return, or you may give but negotiate what you need. Giving with strings attached has a hidden agenda that makes partners wary of receiving, because they know *that* you'll expect back, but don't know *what*. The models of the stingy receiver, the stingy giver, and the giver with strings attached reflect a lack of trust. What other beliefs reflect an unhealthy stance toward giving?

- I can't trust that if I don't take care of things, anyone else will.
- I can call in the chits because you owe me.
- I won't have to ask for my needs to be met, because since I'm so giving, you should meet them automatically.
- I'm doing what's expected, but eventually I'll get mine.
- I feel superior to others when I do more for them than they do for me.
- I need to be "strong" and absorb more than the other person.

Being in the credit column in relationships means you're owed. In healthy relationships, that's no problem. People take turns being on one side or the other of give-and-take. Where partners get into trouble is when one destructively uses the power of being owed to call in a debt. What would that look like?

For starters, you could leverage what you're owed by insisting on an unreasonable or even impossible return that your partner can't provide, and didn't even know they were obliging themselves to do. Or you could ask your partner to offer you continuous reassurance; to calm your irrational jealousy; or make up for past losses or insecurities. Partners commonly freight marriage with unfair needs and expectations in order to be rescued from their own inner struggles, to somehow magically be made happy. As James Hollis sums it up: "The truth about intimate relationships is that they can never be any better than our relationships with ourselves." Let's meet one couple whose reciprocity went haywire after the husband overgave for years, and then wanted a particular return.

In our first session, Carlos, a thirty-four-year-old man, recited a long list of ways he had tried to please his wife of eleven years. He was successful in his job, allowing her to stay home with the kids; he did all the home repairs;

he visited with her family more often than he preferred; he took her and the kids on two vacations a year. Carlos came up with three reasons for his overgiving:

> It made him feel like a good person.
> It proved that he loved his wife.
> It made him feel needed.

But his overgiving eventually left him angry and backfired on the couple. Carlos wasn't aware of the potential problems of his overgiving until he couldn't get what he wanted in return. In fact, up until this crisis in his marriage, he didn't really think about all he did in terms of what he wanted or needed back. He simply thought of himself as a good husband, as he'd been a good son, a good person—an all around good guy. It was clear to me that there was absolutely no manipulation intended in his giving. But Carlos's giving wasn't as free as he'd thought. His unspoken "deal" with his wife was that if he were so obviously generous, then she would "give" him a fourth child.

His wife, Sally, had been the willing recipient of all his generosity. But Sally hadn't known that her payback would be another child, something she felt she couldn't do. She was already overwhelmed with their three girls, one of whom had a developmental delay. Carlos couldn't understand her reasons; he couldn't understand what else he could do to change her mind. He logically offered solutions to all of her objections. But logic didn't sway her. Her refusal just didn't seem fair to him. The atmosphere between them grew tense and embittered, with Sally feeling terribly pressured, and Carlos, angry and resentful. Carlos hadn't initially known what he expected back. Later, like many spouses, Carlos misused his giving by haranguing Sally to give back on his terms.

I encouraged Carlos to uncover the reasons for his unyielding insistence on another child. Carlos discovered that he wanted this particular return because he was haunted by the childhood death of his youngest brother, and fourth sibling. Yet he hadn't realized the connection between his deceased brother and his need for another child (with his particular emphasis on needing a son). Carlos learned that he was asking Sally to assuage his unresolved grief. Rather than continuing to blame Sally, Carlos took on the hard work of consciously understanding the meaning of his grief. Sally in turn reassessed whether all she expected of Carlos was reasonable—perhaps she had taken him too much for granted.

Was there a happy ending for Sally and Carlos? It depends on how you define happy. They didn't have a fourth child. But Carlos made peace with his grief, and took more responsibility for knowing what he wanted (when he needed something back). Sally became more mindful of her guiding assumptions that she was entitled to have Carlos fulfill her many expectations just because he was her husband. As a result, they were each able to take more responsibility for becoming fairer, and reconcile with each other, instead of killing their marriage through disappointment and blame.

Of the two problems—giving too much or taking too much—it's simpler to solve the former. Reworking your beliefs, your expectations of yourself, even others' expectations of you, may feel scary and uncomfortable at first, but the immediate and obvious benefit is ending your depletion. It's easier to rethink your motives for giving too much, lose any remnants of martyrdom or victimization, and still feel good about yourself. If you give too much, you are, after all, in control of giving less. But if either you or your partner has the problem of taking too much, you'll have to work even harder to change that imbalance before one of you wants to get off the seesaw.

THE SECOND PROBLEM: TAKING TOO MUCH

Taking too much is the "How could you treat me this way?" mystery of relationships. Partners wonder: "What did I do to deserve this?" Often nothing. Unfortunately, if you're frequently asking these questions, you may be in a relationship with someone who is a chronic taker, who hasn't given you enough in return. You learned in chapter 3 that this kind of taking is called *destructive entitlement*. This "taker" operates from a highly distorted sense of fairness. He feels owed—but he isn't aware that he's trying to collect from the wrong person—you. A destructively entitled individual has had his trust used up earlier in life, and so feels entitled to get, without giving back fairly. Let's see how this dynamic looks in the life of our next couple.

The therapy began with only one spouse willing to attend. That's not uncommon, though what was atypical was that it was the husband, Simon, who initiated the therapy, and the wife, Allie, who was resistant. I gave Simon some tips on how to introduce the idea of therapy to Allie in a nonthreatening way. If you're ever in this situation, I've included those tips at the end of this chapter. In Simon's situation, I guessed that Allie was scared to come in, though Simon thought she was more angry than scared. Simon told me that Allie was very resentful at the demands his children placed on his time. I anticipated that Allie might worry that I would judge her for her stance against his children. I told Simon that stepparents, especially those without children from a former marriage, often feel like they're playing second fiddle. I asked him to reassure Allie that I wanted to help her, too; I wanted to strike a balance that would work for both of them. I also suggested that I'd be glad to talk to Allie, or see her by herself for a session, so that she wouldn't feel that I was biased against her from this one, first session with Simon. Allie attended the next session.

Simon and Allie were married for six years when I first met them. They described themselves as loving parents to their two young children. They said they loved each other, despite their recent intense arguments. But, as Simon reported, Allie bitterly complained about the time Simon spent with his teenage children from his first marriage. Allie was angry that she had to share her family time with her stepchildren. More recently, Allie refused to have them in "her" home. Out of earshot, she called them names, despite Simon's repeated pleas to stop her verbally abusive behavior. She counted every hour Simon spent with his teens, and demanded that he give their children "equal quality time." When he couldn't, there was hell to pay. In retaliation, Allie didn't speak to Simon for days at a time and sometimes made him sleep on the couch. Allie said she wouldn't be satisfied until Simon gave up his visits with his kids. Why was Allie so demanding? Her abusive behavior went beyond the normal strains of the blended family experience. Allie, like many people

who have a destructive sense of entitlement, felt entirely justified. Her ratio-
nales included:

- The children hadn't taken up so much time during their courtship,
  why should they now?
- Time with Simon's children robbed her of their time as a couple and
  nuclear family.
- Simon should choose her over them.

Allie's unfair expectations had their roots in her childhood, where she felt
treated like an unwanted and unlovable child. Allie's parents married because
her mother was pregnant with her. Her mother had just begun college and
was deeply ambivalent about going through with the marriage or pregnancy.
Later, her mother told Allie in a fit of anger that she had tried to abort the
pregnancy. This punishing information was deeply wounding to Allie. Not
surprisingly, Allie had a stormy relationship with her mother. Her father typically stayed out of it and in the process never developed a satisfying or
nurturing relationship with Allie. Allie's two younger siblings were the "fa-
vorites." On all counts, Allie was on the losing end in her family. The impact
on her marriage was her damaging determination that no one would make
her or her children feel like the castoff she'd been. Allie was so determined to
have her point of view prevail that she wasn't interested in being fair to Simon, much less his children. Hers was a childish stance of destructive entitlement resulting from childhood experiences that Allie only begrudgingly
acknowledged were related to the couple's problems.

In the couples therapy, I held Allie responsible for the harm she was causing. I also recommended that she seek individual therapy for the empathic
support, insight, and corrective feedback she needed. It probably takes a
therapist to be sympathetic toward someone like Allie, because as likable as
she was in many ways, she was outright destructive to her husband and his
children, and was burning up the trust and goodwill in their marriage. Yet a
therapist wouldn't do her any good by simply being sympathetic. Allie's pain
had to be validated—it was very real and very raw. But then she also had to

be held accountable to correct the distortions in her fairness model, and stop her attempts to force Simon to choose between her and his children. If the couple were to make progress, Allie would have to own up to the fact that neither Simon nor her stepchildren deserved her mistreatment.

For a partner on the receiving end of such damaging behavior, as Simon was, it helps to understand that the issue of taking too much belongs to the other person. Then it's easier to take it less personally. Yet beyond understanding, you must set limits to protect yourself and make a claim for your partner to solve the fairness imbalance where it started, rather than foist the problem off on you. For Allie and Simon, it was Allie's problem that had become Simon's (and Simon's children's) problem, and until they settled it, Simon had to hold the line on what was fair to him. If Allie didn't change her unfair behavior, Simon would likely need to get off the seesaw and end the marriage. After all, no one is obliged to stay in a relationship that is chronically unfair. While this book doesn't specifically or singularly focus on any particular abusive pattern of relating, and holds out hope that many problems of relationship can be solved, still I strongly encourage you to get professional help if your relationship falls into this abusive category. This is true even if your partner won't join you.

For Simon, holding a line meant not caving in to Allie's unfair demands. It meant calling her on her verbal abuse every time she did it. It meant not letting her snide remarks about his children slide. After all, the loyalty Simon owed was also to his children, and he owed more to them than he did to Allie. Simon needed to be prepared to leave the marriage if Allie wasn't willing or able to make significant changes.

And the ending? Unfortunately, Simon's children grew up before Allie did. The marriage limped along for several years. Allie never followed up with individual therapy and only came to couples therapy sporadically. Simon continued to see his older children and didn't let Allie interfere with the time he spent with them. As Simon's teenagers entered young adulthood, they refused to see their father when Allie was present. They wanted no relationship with her, as she had wanted none with them. Eventually, Simon got off the seesaw. He separated and divorced Allie. He stayed as long as he did in an effort to protect his youngest children from having the same fate as Allie—feeling like castoffs. Allie's destructive entitlement did the marriage in. And Simon? He's now remarried and content. He does mourn the years he spent (or, as he says, "lost") with Allie.

It's often baffling to the person on the receiving end of a destructively entitled partner, that she (in this case) doesn't see how unfair she's being. When destructive entitlement is operating, many of the causes are outside that individual's conscious awareness. Instead, they justify their behaviors without meaningfully connecting the dots between their low trust level coming into marriage and their current attitudes and behavior. Let's break these causes into two groups:

Destructive motivations outside of conscious awareness
- I never felt like I was No. 1 for anyone.
- This is how things were in my family.
- My parents did too little for me (I'm owed).
- You had it better than I did—you can take care of me now.

Conscious justifications for taking too much
- If someone offers, why not accept?
- If my partner feels angry at what I've done, then that's their problem.
- I never asked my wife/husband to do too much—that was their choice.
- My parents just demand, demand, demand. No way I'll be pushed around in my marriage, too.
- I'm entitled to get more; it's your job to look after yourself.

It's not easy to overcome the legacy of entering marriage with too little trust. That was Allie's situation. Yet if you work on developing insights into the origins of your unfair behavior, you're on the way to healing. You must have insight in order to take corrective steps for yourself, and then with the people in your life that either drained your trust by unfair treatment or whose trust you drained through your own destructive taking. The next chapter explores this idea more fully. But before closing this chapter, let's take a look at a slightly more benign version of taking too much, the problem of infantilization.

Infantilization

Parents, like the rest of us, are subject to the two mistakes in reciprocity. Parental overgiving begins naturally because each one of us starts life on the receiving end. Children from a young age, sometimes laughably and poignantly, grapple with their obligation to return care for all the parenting they receive—first for survival, and then in order to grow, physically, intellectually, and emotionally. Parents have to provide a massive amount of nurturing, yet at the same time avoid creating a bit of a monster by "babying." If a child is babied throughout childhood (or beyond) with little age-appropriate expectation of return, it distorts a child's fairness model and gets in the way of a child's task of truly growing up.

That's the catch with taking too much and remaining overly indebted to your parents—you never grow up. Indebtedness handicaps your chances for feeling good about yourself. You're likely to feel like a spoiled brat. It can also hinder your ability to invest in future relationships at a deep level. You aren't free to fully commit or be emotionally responsible. You likely have unrealistic expectations of what caretaking you "should" get from a partner. You feel entitled to receive more than is coming to you, because you're relating to your partner as you do to your parents—expecting to be on the receiving end of things. After all, you've spent your whole life there—so it feels normal.

This lopsided way of relating is more popularly known as the Peter Pan complex—the boy who never grew up, often taken care of by a Wendy, the girl who grew up to be an overgiver. Despite its name, the Peter Pan complex, or infantilization, is a gender-neutral offender. Both men and women can expect and take too much. A partner typically experiences this kind of adult as likable, but irresponsible, or increasingly unlikable if the bent is more toward selfishness and self-centeredness. In the upcoming chapters, you'll see how adults who were babied bring an inaccurate fairness model to their relationships, while justifying their behavior at the same time. You'll also see that the way out of indebtedness is to start giving back, in all relationships.

As you conclude this chapter, I ask you to recognize that it's challenging enough to keep your own balance with reciprocity, and disorienting when confronted with your partner's different stance. There will be many more examples throughout the book of the problems on both ends of the reciprocity seesaw, and the possibilities for a new and fairer balance. But what about getting off the seesaw altogether? How do you know if it's the right decision and when it's the right time? It's almost certainly the right decision if you're concerned for your safety or the safety of your children. But how about a marriage like Simon's, where there's no physical violence or threat but a chronically and significantly unjust climate? Each individual's context is different, so there's no one size, no certain answer, that fits all. Simon remained with Allie because he felt his youngest children would benefit from that decision. And perhaps they did. However, his older children suffered because of Allie. Did he do the right thing? The wrong thing? I would say he did what he believed at the time was the best thing to do. Only Simon can say if he made the right decision. Do you think you might have made a different choice and yet not judge him for his? Each individual and each marriage comes with its own unique balance of reciprocity, the couple's particular "deals," their histories and models of fairness that impinge on the question "Should you leave or stay?" Therapy can be especially helpful in discerning your particular context as it weighs whether to stay on or get off the seesaw. But whatever you decide, explore your own history and identify the unfinished business you're likely to bring to a future relationship. Exiting one relationship and taking the same habits, beliefs, and expectations with you may take you right back to where you are—on a chronically unbalanced seesaw but with a different partner at the other end.

In the next chapter we'll explore in depth how basic childhood needs for fairness have later implications for couples. Your earliest learned pattern of relating (and being related to) can be quite impervious to change unless you recognize and understand it. As the author Anaïs Nin observed: "We don't see things as they are; we see them as we are." Becoming conscious of the key childhood experiences that shape your ability to be fair is the next goal.

 ## SOME TIPS TO GET YOUR PARTNER TO JOIN YOU FOR COUPLES THERAPY

In a first session when one partner has initially refused to attend, I coach the other spouse about how to enlist the absent partner to join.

Demonstrate your sincerity to your partner by indicating that *you* want to learn what you can do to make your relationship better. Reassure your spouse that you don't want to do couples therapy to "get your ticket punched"—to say you've tried and now you can get a guilt-free divorce. People sometimes come to couples therapy so angry and frustrated that they want a "psychological dispensation" to end the marriage. They hope that I'll agree that it was never a real marriage, and there's nothing more they can do. Sometimes that's true, but more often people are simply worn out and just need new ideas for making their relationship better. My goal is to help partners develop the skills they need to preserve their relationship or, if that's not possible, take a new set of skills with them to improve their future chances. Lesson: approach your partner with reassurance.

Don't threaten therapy as if it were a punishment—*I'll divorce you unless you go to therapy with me!* Lesson: ask more nicely. But what if you've asked nicely, even pleaded, and your partner still won't attend? Try to figure out what your spouse is afraid of. Many partners anticipate that they'll be blamed for all the problems. Let them know that you want to understand their side of things. Alternately, they may say that you're the one who needs therapy, because the problems are all your fault. We've all heard these justifications for not getting help. But the fact is, these rationalizations are fundamentally about the fear of the unknown. What to do? Go back to your new working model of fairness. Offer your partner some credit for the legitimate reasons for distress. I genuinely and empathically try to imagine what it's like for the absent spouse. This helps partners who are present reframe their understanding and develop a broader perspective. It also shows I'm balancing my concern for the person in front of me, with my concern for their relationship. It won't do their relationship any good if I merely side with one person's grievances, however legitimate they might be. After all, the individuals who are present have to go home to the problems with their respective spouses, and need to understand what is within their control to change, even if their partners never attend.

Other ideas? Suggest that you both meet for a first session with more than one therapist, and let the reluctant partner choose the therapist for the couples therapy. Suggest that you commit to a set number of sessions—say twelve—to see if you make progress on your problems. If you don't have any word-of-mouth referrals—please turn to the resources appendix at the end of the book for a list of professional organizations with specialty training in marriage and family therapy.

EXERCISE: THE PROBLEM WITH RECIPROCITY: PRESENT BALANCES

Once again, put yourself on the seesaw of give-and-take. Now ask yourself about whether you currently consider yourself a giver, a taker, or in a balanced relationship with each of these important people in your life: your mother, your father, your spouse, your children. If the balance is tilted, does it represent a healthy indicator of trust? If not, what would it take from each of those individuals, including you, to bring it back into balance? What would need to change?

(continued)

EXERCISE: THE PROBLEM WITH RECIPROCITY:
PAST BALANCES

Think of your own family, growing up. First think about the balance of
give-and-take between your parents. How did they balance the responsibilities of family life? Did one do more, one less? Was one more a
caregiver? How did you feel about that? If one made too many sacrifices, what did that teach you? If one didn't do enough, how did you
come to understand it? Do you model your own gauge to fairness on
their relationship?

Next think of yourself and your siblings . . . was one too much in
charge, too burdened; was another babied? How did that shape them,
or you?

Finally, think back to the balance of give-and-take between you and
your mother and then you and your father. Can you identify how they
gave to you? Do you appreciate what they gave, or have pain about
what they didn't give, or both? Do you know what you contributed to
them? Was what you could return valued? Did it feel like you'd done
enough? Too much? How does this model for fairness play out in your
relationship with them today? How does it shape how you relate to
your partner? To your children?

THE BAGGAGE YOU BRING
TO RELATIONSHIPS

"Everybody's got baggage, but my ex-husband was *not* a neat packer."

(Ellie, married sixteen years, divorced five years)

"It's just endless. I repeated my crazy relationship with my father with my husband, and now my daughter is doing the same thing in her life."

(Jane, married twenty-seven years)

"You keep bringing up the past, and my family, but the past is the past. In the past I wore diapers, too, but what's it got to do with today?"

(John, eight years, second marriage)

How many times does something have to happen to you before it occurs to you?

—ROBERT FROST

Everybody brings baggage to a relationship. The trouble is sorting it into piles of yours, mine, and ours, and then figuring out what to do with it. It's often easier to pin the blame for relationship problems on a partner, rather than claiming your own baggage. Your baggage consists of experiences from past relationships that have shaped your expectations, affected your level of trust, and recharged hot buttons from childhood. While we often think of baggage as the mess left over from old romances, have you ever noticed that people have an uncanny way of picking partners that match their unfinished business from childhood? In order to avoid changing partners, but dancing the same dance, you need to unpack your baggage, stop repeating unhealthy patterns, and strengthen your marriage.

You might challenge, as John did—what's the past got to do with today? Remember Allie and Simon from the last chapter? Allie brought many unreasonable expectations to her marriage, transferred from her unhealed parent-child relationship. Her baggage had hidden explosives, detonated by the demands of sharing family life with her stepchildren. While your baggage never technically leaves your possession, your parents did help you pack it. Now you need to claim your baggage that propels the cycle of unfairness forward.

Reworking your unfinished business helps you avoid repeating mistakes. Most of us make promises to ourselves about what we'll do differently from our parents—whether that's with a partner or as a parent—*I won't be a screamer, like my mom; I won't be a workaholic, like my dad*—*I'll go to all the kids' games*. People also loyally value and carry on traditions and behaviors from their families—because baggage doesn't imply there was no good, just that everyone has a mix of experiences, some wonderful, some painful, that we have to fully digest in order to grow up.

Another reason to care about baggage are the rather scary divorce statistics in the last generation. Your odds for divorce rise if your own parents were divorced (anywhere from a 50–100 percent rise). But this correlation isn't fate. The good news is, it isn't your parents' marital state (blissful or vitriolic, married or divorced) that most impacts your chances in your own intimate relationship—it's how your parents related to *you*. That's where sorting your baggage comes into play. What counts most in creating a successful relationship is learning how to take responsibility for your baggage and developing the skills to negotiate a new fairness.

This chapter asks: What was it in your own upbringing that leads you to act fairly or unfairly now? How did your childhood experiences shape your model of what you owe and deserve and your beliefs about love and fairness? Were your parents fair in how they related to you? Were you expected to reproduce your parents' values? Was that good for you? Were their expectations reasonable? What if there was a mismatch between your parents' expectations and what you could or did do? Does love in your family permit you to question what's fair? Does love in your family mean "Everyone did their best, so let's understand and move on"?

It would be a mistake to confuse taking a harder look at fairness between you and your parents with whether they loved you or whether you loved them. Love, fairness, and injustice coexist in relationships. Yet, how do you make sense of this paradox? Since all parents relate unfairly to their children at times, there are bound to be some unhealed grievances. Children are capable of hurting their parents, too, of course. It's just that there are different consequences when the passenger in a plane misbehaves than when the pilot does. Childhood injustices that aren't righted (or at least addressed) teach unhealthy ways of relating that burden marriage. We'll discover the six basic rights that children are entitled to have parents meet. When parents can't or don't provide a child with these fundamental needs, there's fallout long into the future. Let's begin our exploration of the baggage you bring to marriage by tracing unfairness from childhood to adulthood.

The Trajectory of Unfairness: From Childhood to Adulthood

We live our lives forward, but understand them backwards.

—KIERKEGAARD

As a parent, daughter, and psychologist, I have a keen understanding of the weighty responsibilities of parenthood, and the human limitations parents bump into, balanced by a major respect for the damaging consequences of unfair parenting to a child. I extend understanding with one hand and accountability with the other as I ask both parents and children in my practice, growing and grown, to reflect on the fairness record between them and its effects. Many people have parents who both loved them and couldn't adequately meet their needs for nurturing and advocacy. Despite that, parents often try to give more to their children than they got (both materially and emotionally) from their own parents. Since unhealthy patterns of relating often travel from generation to generation within a family, I encourage you to think about your own family history as you read ahead.

Your History

When I ask people to talk to me about their experiences of unfairness in their families, they often begin with particular memories, usually of onetime painful events. *There was the time Dad punished me for breaking a window and I hadn't done it. Once, Mom slapped me in the face in front of my friends. When I was seventeen, Dad got so drunk that he got into a fistfight with me. Mom told me that I dressed like a slut. I got grounded a few times when I was covering for my brother.* Onetime events get burned into our memories, stuck in the playback loop even when we wish we could erase them. But curiously, it usually isn't the onetime event of injustice (unless it's an event of very high emotional intensity or violence) that has the most far-reaching consequences—it's an unfair pattern of relating, repeated over a long time. Those patterns might include emotional or physical abandonment, abuse or neglect, poor boundaries, or ongoing criticism. For example, Allie will never forget the day her mother angrily told her that she had tried to abort her pregnancy. But it was the ongoing injustice of knowing her siblings were loved while her mother was mean to her, and her father emotionally disengaged, that most shaped Allie's destructive behavior with Simon and his children. Let's explore the mechanism for the transfer of these unfair patterns of relating from childhood to adulthood.

But, you may still be protesting: *The past is the past. You can't change the past. They did the best they could.* Or: *My brother got the worst of it. I wasn't affected.* Or: *I had Ozzie and Harriet for parents; it's the in-laws who are the lunatics.* Or: *It feels wrong to be poking holes in my childhood.* Or: *They're too old to change. They might have a heart attack if I upset them.* Or the whitewash: *My mother was too young to know what she was doing. Yes, my father hit me too much, but I was a handful.* And the ultimate defense: *Can't we just respect the dead?* But you can't just rationalize unjust experiences away, even if it feels bad to take a hard look.

Why does it feel bad? Because it feels disloyal. But is it truly disloyal? No. It may be counter to what your mother or father would want. It might offend them. It might hurt their feelings if you question what they did. But it isn't disloyal. In fact, it's an act of obligation to explore your childhood experiences, because examining them is your best chance for healing them.

The ability to step back and gain perspective about your family's context is a more complicated but compassionate and empowering way of relating to your parents, as well as to yourself. You're shouldering this task rather than bringing unfinished business to your marriage, or forwarding it to the next generation. That's an act of courage and responsibility. So even if it feels disloyal at first, I'm asking you to return to childhood memories and recall emotional experiences that may limit your ability to be fair to yourself and to your partner today. Ultimately, it's good for you and for all of your relationships.

Connecting the Dots: Past to Present

Now let's connect the dots between your parent-child baggage and your intimate relationship today. Emotionally fraught childhood experiences are the hot buttons your partner reactivates. When you get your buttons pushed, it won't look the same as in childhood, but it will feel the same. It's your psyche's way of saying "I've been here before." Take Julio for example, who hurls insults at his wife because she forgot to pick up orange juice at the grocery store. Julio's screaming fit makes no sense, until a glimpse into his childhood reveals a mother who was verbally abusive when he made the slightest mistake. His wife's absentmindedness triggers a torrent of anger disproportionate to the offense, which is similar to what his mother unleashed on him. And like many partners who haven't claimed their own baggage, Julio has taken his revenge on the wrong person. His excessive and punitive expectations forged by painful childhood mistreatment, have transformed him into a justice-seeking bully in marriage.

Every partner, no matter how good and loving, is unfair at some point, since even good people can find themselves behaving in a grossly unfair manner. Conversely, partners put up with unfair or even abusive behavior for reasons often unknown even to themselves. We'll explore the reasons for enduring injustices later in the book. When you've been treated unfairly it's all too easy to pathologize your spouse (and often your in-laws, too). But it's both too simple as well as too unproductive to simply be someone's victim. If you've been treated unfairly, whether by your parents or spouse or both, at the very least you can learn from it. You can learn how your own familial script has shaped what you expect and how you relate. Insight helps make sense of suffering. On the flip side, when you've acted unfairly, it's crucial to take your share of responsibility. But it's also too simple, as well as too debilitating, to just be the bad guy. Being in the doghouse forever, unable to earn and receive forgiveness, results in the loss of hope. As one husband said to his wife after many months of repair efforts, "I'm tired of trying to make good. I might as well have done nothing." She replied, with vengeance getting the better of her, "Good. Maybe now you'll know how I felt all those years." They were in a standoff, risking their marriage by maintaining their old roles of victim and victimizer.

In order to grow from unfairness, you'll need to move beyond being either a victim or victimizer. You can set this process in motion by searching for the roots of unfairness—the familial script of expectations, of skewed give-and-take, of wounds—and set out to heal them. Rather than tally blame, I encourage you to make a searching inventory of the legacy of unfairness. In order to understand the roots of unfairness, you have to look for clues, beginning with your relationships with your parents. Of course, some unfairness is obvious: *My father beat me black and blue.* But more often unfairness is less apparent: *My mother never wanted to spend time with me. My father never made a fuss over anything I did—I felt invisible.* Whether obvious or not, damage gets done. No matter whether your parent-child relationship was mostly fair, flagrantly unfair, or unfair in subtler ways, it's essential to understand how it shaped you.

In searching for clues it's important to consider:

- how you may be repeating old patterns;
- how your unfinished business plays out in your expectations of yourself and of your partner;

- how it may feel easier to hold your spouse responsible for pushing your buttons than hold your parents accountable for installing them;
- how your marital experiences may have deepened old wounds; and
- how healing unfair childhood treatment can be a tremendous resource for your marriage.

Parental influences are often a mixed bag of both positive and protective factors along with dysfunctional interactions. When parents relate in a warm and nurturing way, show interest in a child's activities, and set good limits, they are relating fairly, and providing what a child deserves. Fair parenting also means modeling healthy skills for resolving conflict at home, where it first takes place. And because no one is fair all the time, good parenting can require one parent to advocate for you when the other is being unreasonable (or worse). These ways of relating show love, teach fairness, and build a child's trust. Fair parenting teaches a child a balanced model for give-and-take that promotes emotional growth and healthy relationship skills. These positive factors are predictive of a long and loving marriage.

There are also negative modes of parent-child interactions that contribute to later marital distress. These dysfunctional patterns include: 1) inappropriate parent-child boundaries—such as the kind of poor limits that put kids in the middle of parental problems; 2) topsy-turvy roles where the child has adultlike responsibilities or worries; 3) uninvolved or emotionally disengaged parents; 4) critical parent-child interactions; 5) harsh, inconsistent parental discipline; and 6) poor conflict-resolution skills.

But life is a bit more complicated than a list of positive or negative parenting factors. The consequences you sustain from these patterns of interacting are partially determined by who you are as an individual. For example, for one child, very strict parenting instills a sense of order and self-discipline. The meaning that child makes of his exacting upbringing is positive. That child grows into an adult who praises and repeats his parents' approach to child rearing. But in the same family, another sibling may experience the stern expectations as stifling and punitive. That sibling grows to adulthood full of resentment and anger, feeling overcontrolled and unfairly treated. No doubt the marriages of these two siblings look different. So, your outcome, for better or worse, depends not only on how your parents related to you, but also on how good a match you were for their expectations (reasonable or not) and their parenting style (ranging from fair to dictatorial).

To help you tease out the positive or negative tilt in your parent-child relationships, it's helpful to look at the six childhood entitlements, or "rights," that promote fairness and define the trajectory of fairness from childhood to adulthood. Think about your own childhood as you review these rights.

Six Childhood Entitlements that Promote Fairness

1. Protection and preservation of the primary relationships with your mother, father, siblings, and extended family
2. Safe, reliable, and nurturing parenting
3. Appropriate give-and-take between parent and child
4. Being valued
5. Negotiation of fairness issues
6. Repair and restoration of fairness and trust

Unlike marriage where give-and-take is expected to be reciprocal, parent-child relationships begin with parental responsibilities to provide care. Parents owe it to children to meet basic needs that promote the development of trust. Children are entitled, by virtue of their utter dependence and vulnerability, to have these birthright needs met. The world of childhood starts with these rights. Together, these six entitlements make up a relationship ethic for what parents owe and what children deserve.

If you were chronically deprived of one or more of these basic entitlements, your take on fairness is likely to be skewed. Just how much depends on the nature of what you experienced and whether you had protective factors, such as one "safe" parent who shielded you and advocated for you, your own inborn resilience, or a nurturing adult outside your family. Let's review the six basic entitlements and then see how growing up without them can encumber your ability to be fair, whether to yourself, your spouse, or to both. As you reflect on these basic rights, think of their meaning to you and any resulting unfinished business.

Entitlement #1:
Protection and preservation of the primary relationships with your mother and father, siblings, and extended family

WHEN DEPRIVED OF #1, THE CONSEQUENCE IS: YOU DON'T TRUST

The preservation and protection of your parent-child relationship is an irreplaceable legacy. Ideally, this relationship is based on love, but whatever the circumstances—which may affect how you feel about the relationship—you are connected by birth. The long history of parenting further connects you, whether biological parents, grandparents, adoptive parents, foster parents, or some combination of parenting figures raised you.

When primary relationships aren't protected, a child's trust is damaged. The headline story of a mother who abandons her infant is an example of treating a child as if he or she was disposable and the relationship meaningless. It makes the news because we share a moral repulsion for the broken bond of parental protection. But more commonly, the parent-child bond is cut off or devalued in a less dramatic but trust-diminishing way. Parent-child cutoffs may be temporary estrangements or permanent disconnections. There are four general ways that the ecology of primary family relationships may not be protected or preserved:

1. **You were abandoned.** You knew who your parent was, but he or she dropped out of your life. Perhaps one parent disappeared soon after your birth. Or you had such infrequent contact with a parent that you felt rejected or even abandoned.

2. **You were a pawn.** You were put in an impossible bind, in which your emotional security depended on choosing one parent over the other (a split loyalty). Rather than a parent rejecting a child, the child (with the support of the other parent) rejects a parent. A split loyalty often creates a physical or emotional estrangement between a parent and child. Perhaps you were asked to explicitly take sides in the drama of a custody battle, or implicitly expected to side with your mother or father (one against the other) in their day-to-day tensions and arguments. You felt the need to rescue or at least support the more vulnerable-seeming parent. Split loyalties also occur when one parent repeatedly "bad-mouths" the other, and encourages a child to feel the same way by devaluing, having contempt for, or even cutting the other parent off.

3. **Your family cut off extended family relationships.** Family conflict led to cutoffs with grandparents, aunts, or uncles, who were lost from your life. The underlying message: relationships are conditional, and your loyalty belongs to one side, not the other. It isn't safe to invest in any relationship—you could be cut off, too.

4. **You were adopted, or put in foster care.** Adoption, foster care, or alternative, temporary arrangements offer invaluable parenting resources, but this instability may create significant emotional disruptions for some children. An age-appropriate sharing of information, which may include "open" adoption, can minimize the impact of these losses on a child's experience of mistrust and split loyalties.

The failure to protect a child's entitlement to primary relationships is a major and consequential loss that often translates in adulthood into baseline mistrust, the use of emotional distancing, and cutoffs as a way of managing hurt and protecting yourself from further experiences of rejection and loss. This kind of loss also colors your choice in a partner and may lead to over-simplified and distorted views of love and fairness. Let's meet Roberto and Angie to see how the loss of this entitlement impacts marriage.

Roberto: Cut Off from a Parent: Consequences for a Marriage

Roberto is a successful fifty-three-year-old husband and father of two. He'd always scoffed at the idea that his lifelong estrangement from his father had caused any problem for him. His parents never married, and separated when he was a year old. Roberto hadn't seen or spoken to his father or his paternal grandparents since he was five years old. His mother discouraged the visits and disparaged his father for being an "irresponsible bum," blaming him for the breakup of their relationship. Roberto spent most of his life trying to be the antithesis of who he thought his father was. He was devoted to his mother and her family. He was a high achiever in school and went on to excel in college. He married Angie, his high school sweetheart. He owned a car dealership. With each accomplishment, Roberto secretly felt proud that he put more and more distance between himself and his father. Roberto wasn't the kind of guy who would seek therapy for his parental loss, or for any other reason. He prided himself on not needing anyone's help.

That was before his affair. Angie, his wife, issued an ultimatum after learning about his infidelity: go to therapy or move out. Shortly thereafter, his youngest daughter was hospitalized for depression—she had swallowed a handful of aspirin. Roberto couldn't understand how this could be happening to him, or to his family. After all, he puzzled, he was a much better husband and father than his father had been—because he was *there*. How could things have gone so wrong? Over the next year, Roberto faced the consequences of his estrangement from his father. He learned that his difficulties with emotional intimacy, both in his marriage and with his children, were a direct result of how he coped with the cutoff from his father. In adulthood, as in childhood, he rejected his father out of a sense of loyalty to his mother. He felt indebted for all his mother had done, and so (unconsciously) repaid her by rejecting his father. This took a toll on his ability to be vulnerable or to trust. Roberto's affair temporarily gave him the illusion of great closeness and intimacy with his affair partner. But while Roberto's issues seem more clear-cut and obviously destructive to the couple's trust and fairness, Angie also contributed to their fairness impasse in a different way.

Angie: Not Being Safe and Secure: Consequences for a Marriage

Angie's father also abandoned Angie in her childhood—but emotionally, not physically. Her father was a quiet drunk, who worked the second shift. When he came home, he sat in front of the TV and drank his six-pack. Angie accepted the emotional distance that came with her father's drinking as normal. His unavailability taught her to have low expectations for what she could get from a man. Angie didn't consciously articulate this conclusion—she just unwittingly lived it.

When Angie met Roberto, he actually seemed the opposite of her father. He enjoyed doing things, didn't sit at home drinking beer, and had ambition. Angie didn't recognize that her marriage was emotionally remote. After the early rush of romance, they settled into a pattern of hard work, raising kids, and what seemed like a good life, though neither of them leaned on the other very much. Angie was always trying to please Roberto, who had a critical streak. When she'd gone through a couple of hard times—a stillbirth, her brush with cancer—she turned to her mother and sister for support. She didn't really expect Roberto to be there for her, because she expected very little from a husband. Due to the emotional void with her father, Angie accepted the low level of emotional intimacy with Roberto as normal. She took solace in the fact that Roberto didn't drink and was a good provider. Because Angie had never faced up to the childhood origins of her low sense of entitlement, she couldn't identify the repeating dynamic in her marriage because Roberto seemed so different from her father. She felt satisfied in her marriage for many years. But when she discovered Roberto's affair, Angie found herself floundering and angry. She knew she wanted more than someone who cheated on her; now she realized that she wanted more than a distant, but functional relationship. She wanted a more emotionally intimate partner.

Roberto and Angie had each grown up with a negative slant on paternal love. Their shared experiences of absent fathers (physically or emotionally) had bonded them initially. But once the romantic stage of their relationship ended, their unfinished business handicapped their ability for emotional connection with each other. The crisis in their marriage forced the couple to evaluate and work to change these patterns.

Entitlement #2:
Safe, reliable, and nurturing parenting

WHEN DEPRIVED OF #2, THE CONSEQUENCE IS:
YOU DON'T FEEL SAFE AND SECURE

A good trust base requires consistent, available parenting and a physically and emotionally safe family environment. When these are missing from a child's life, the child enters adulthood with significant deficits in the ability to trust. There are two parenting patterns that deprive a child of a safe family environment and a secure parent-child relationship:

1. **You experienced neglect or abuse.** This could have been due to physical neglect, harsh parental discipline, or physical or sexual abuse. Children in these circumstances lose trust.

2. **Your parent was emotionally unsafe.** By emotionally unsafe, I include parents who were overly critical, called you names, blamed or made you a scapegoat, dismissed your concerns, or threatened you with the loss of love. Sometimes that same parent runs hot or cold. Emotionally abusive parenting creates an insecure attachment that damages a child's trust.

Let's talk about the ways that having unsafe parenting can later affect who you choose for a partner, and how you relate to your partner. If your trust was drained early on, your expectations for reciprocity in your marriage will be off-kilter. You may expect either too little or too much from your partner. It's hard to predict out of context which outcome will occur, but let me offer a sketch of these variations.

If you expect too little, you won't stick up for yourself enough. You'll invest too much, and overgive to create more security for yourself. Paradoxically, one way to be in control and to feel safe is to expect less, like Angie. If you don't expect much, you won't be terribly disappointed (at least for a while). You'll settle for an emotionally remote relationship because it "feels" normal. Secondarily, and out of your awareness, you'll choose a partner to repeat this pattern with, not because you're inherently masochistic, but to understand and gain mastery and control over your childhood experience in hopes of having it turn out better this time.

In other individuals, never feeling secure or important enough controls the relationship. Instead of expecting too little as a result of an unsafe childhood, you may find your neediness burdens your partner with the expectation that marriage will cure your childhood insecurity. In effect, you expect your spouse to be a better, more caring, less limited parent to you than your own parents were. Early romantic love tends to fool you into thinking that you'll always be taken care of, and initially reinforces your unrealistic and unreasonable expectations. After the dazzle of passion fades, you find that you haven't been rescued from your childhood needs. Your search for an idealized form of love and validation may continue through an affair, overworking, or emotionally leaning on your children to meet your needs. Let's look at how this plays out in Donna's marriage.

Donna: Unsafe Childhood: Consequences to a Marriage
Donna's childhood was characterized by a combination of strict parental discipline, emotional distance, and abuse by a sibling. Donna's mother was overwhelmed by the demands of nine children. Her father worked two jobs to support the family. Donna was third in line, with an older brother and sister and six younger siblings. Her older brother was put in charge of the children whenever the parents were out of the house. Donna remembers being terrified of him, and rightly so. When he was in charge, it was every man for himself. He hit Donna and taunted her with sexually inappropriate suggestions. One day when she was about fourteen, she remembers locking herself in her second-story bedroom, planning to jump out the window if he broke the lock. Donna didn't feel close enough to either parent to confide in them. Because of her unsafe childhood, Donna came to her marriage very needy, though she had the veneer of professional accomplishment and the outward appearance of a very caring and charming woman. Donna expected her hus-

band, Rafael, to provide frequent reassurance about her looks, pep talks about how her job was going, and comforting words about how much everyone loved her. Beyond that, she often chided her husband for what he could do better—be more attentive, make more money, make her feel desired. Her needs were always couched in terms of what her husband *should* do.

Donna expected Rafael to meet her needs without having needs of his own (mimicking the feel of an early parent-child relationship). When Rafael voiced his needs, she felt angry—this wasn't "the deal." Donna could only be her good, charming self if Rafael took care of her. After a few years of this, Rafael was worn out. The less he gave, the more she drank. Rafael wanted her to get help, but Donna refused because "he couldn't tell her what to do." However, she was actually protesting the conditionality of love. Wasn't she ever going to be loved absolutely? Her unsafe childhood led Donna to self-defeating behavior. I saw her drinking as an angry revenge exacted on herself for not being loved unconditionally, either by her parents or Rafael. Donna didn't get help or face the earlier trauma of her unsafe family life until treatment was court ordered, after she was arrested for drunk driving.

Entitlement #3:
Appropriate give-and-take between
parent and child

WHEN DEPRIVED OF #3, THE CONSEQUENCE IS:
YOU DON'T KNOW WHAT'S FAIR TO GIVE OR TAKE

In chapter 4 you learned about two basic mistakes with reciprocity: you can give too much or take too much. Parents, being human, sometimes stray onto one side or the other of this divide. If short-lived, the experience of either imbalance of give-and-take can be appropriate and growth promoting. For example, parents may baby you temporarily (and appropriately) when you're sick. You get a break from the usual expectations and chores of family life. Conversely, a child may have to pitch in and take on more responsibilities than usual—for instance, when a parent is ill or is caring for an elderly family member. Receiving care when you need it, and helping out when it's reasonable, builds trust in the fairness of give-and-take between parent and child.

But when parents chronically err by either giving too much or taking too much from a child, it can be emotionally damaging and cast a long shadow over that child's development. In some families, one sibling, often older, has too much expected, while a younger child is babied. Each imbalance handicaps an individual and their relationships with an unrealistic model of fairness. Let's look at what these imbalances look like in childhood, and how they manifest themselves in intimate relationships.

Parents Gave Too Much

As you recall from the last chapter, *infantilization* occurs when parents don't hold children accountable for age-appropriate behavior or responsibilities. Children might get a pass on tantrums or disobedience at a younger age; or excused for never getting anyone a Christmas present, though they expect theirs; the rules for them might be more relaxed than the rules for their siblings; they may take for granted that they can live at home forever and have their laundry done and meals cooked. This tilt of the seesaw creates an unrealistic expectation of remaining on the receiving end in relationships. It cripples a child's maturity and warps his notion of fairness. In adulthood these individuals experience difficulty taking appropriate responsibility. While you might find it hard to feel sorry for these adults, they have paid a high price for receiving too much—they've never grown up emotionally. In fact, some of these adults literally never leave home. They may become a parent's companion and eventually their caregiver. If they do leave home, the infantilized adult likely takes his fairness skew with him. Let's follow this dynamic in the lives of Andy and Jan.

Andy: Infantilization: Consequences for a Marriage

Andy agreed to enter couples therapy because Jan, his wife of twenty years, was often mad at him. Jan loved Andy's joie de vivre, his charm, and his larger-than-life personality. But she was enraged by his irresponsibility. Andy begrudgingly acknowledged Jan's more notable grievances. Jan was the primary wage earner since early in their marriage. While Jan became a partner in a large public accounting firm, Andy set up a solo accounting practice. Andy attributed (and hurtfully dismissed) Jan's advancement to a gender-driven bias in the corporation. He joked that her success was "panty hose promotion." Andy was unsuccessful in his own practice. In fact, he had neglected to file or pay estimated taxes for a two-year period, and hid this problem from Jan. When this resulted in an IRS legal action, Andy reluctantly told Jan because he needed her to apply for a thirty-thousand-dollar loan to cover his debt. He had already burned through his credit line. Perhaps most personally painful to Jan was the fact that Andy never bought her a gift, despite all that she did financially to support him and their three children. She told me sadly one day: "My seventeen-year-old daughter came in while I was wrapping a birthday present. She said, 'Who's that for, Mom?' I said, 'It's Dad's gift to me. Who do you think buys them?' She looked at me stunned. I guess I've hidden the sorry reality pretty well until now."

While Andy recognized himself in Jan's description, he lacked a realistic take on the severity of the consequences to his marriage. He tried to make Jan laugh things off, or worse still from her perspective, convince her that he knew best. He assumed a superior, dismissive position regarding her frustrations with him. What caused Andy to hold these unrealistic expectations for a marriage and for life? Because Andy's parents had never held him accountable, Andy continued his unspoken "deal" with them in adulthood—being the pampered son who never grew up.

Andy's father was emotionally remote from both the children and his wife, Natalie, who was fifteen years his junior. Andy was the firstborn and the child his mother turned to for both practical chores that her husband didn't do and also for emotional connection. His mother absolutely adored Andy and never really wanted him to leave home. She did his laundry, she served him his meals before she served anyone else theirs, she bought him cars which his father told him were to be repaid (but never were), and she later loaned Andy money without his father's knowledge (or Jan's, either). The legacy of his mother's overgiving left Andy feeling entitled to be on the receiving end. Andy wrongly applied this model for give-and-take to his marriage (a wife, like his mother, would give and he would take).

This story didn't have a happy ending, but a fair one. Jan loved Andy, but divorced him due to his unwillingness to take his fair share of responsibility. She concluded that despite love, she wasn't obliged to remain in a marriage that grossly disregarded fairness. Years later she ran into Andy. He volunteered, "It's a good thing you divorced me; I'm in another relationship, but I haven't changed."

Parents Expected Too Much

On the other side of the fairness fence is the situation of *parentification*. Parentification, as the word suggests, is a topsy-turvy role assignment in which the parent leans on the child in an age-inappropriate, adultlike way. For example, a child may be put in charge of younger siblings—from getting them dressed, to getting them to school, to disciplining them. Or a child may take over other parental functions such as meal preparation, or negotiating for the family with the outside world—for example, when there is a language barrier with immigration or when a parent feels incompetent. Potentially even more burdensome than overt role reversals is emotional parentification. That child may be under pressure to "be perfect," or make up for a parent's lost dream, or function as a best friend or a confidante, sometimes being turned against the other parent in the process.

Parentification creates a belief system for a child that equates meeting expectations (however unfair) with being loved. Because caretaking is reinforced, a self-fulfilling prophecy occurs: the more you do it, the more valued you feel, which in turn diminishes your ability to ask for a fair return. While you've earned the entitlement to receive, by virtue of all you've given, paradoxically, your capacity to ask, or even know what's fair, is handicapped by your parentification. Since children typically don't know what's fair to give, they just give what's expected. The outcome in adulthood can go a few ways.

The first outcome is a reduced sense of deserving for yourself (also called *low entitlement*) and usually results in overgiving. The second outcome in adulthood occurs with the combination of excessive parental expectations and a low level of parental nurturance. This contributes to *destructive entitlement*, (where you *feel* more deserving than you are) and shows up in expecting too much from a partner. Let's first see what low entitlement looks like in the marriage of Mark and Shelly.

Mark: Parentification: Consequences for a Marriage

Mark was depressed. He had a low energy level, problems concentrating, and was irritable. His sleep wasn't good, and he'd gotten in the habit of having a couple of glasses of wine every night just to "take the edge off." But even with antidepressant medication and a reduction in his alcohol consumption, Mark remained depressed.

Mark's wife, Shelly, had a chronic illness. While some days were better than others, it made it hard to enjoy their lives as they had before her diagnosis. Weekend after weekend, the couple's plans were lost to a bout of Shelly's illness. Hearing this, I wondered: Was Mark's depression biological, primarily situational, or was there unfinished business that worked against him even now?

As Mark described his growing up, he said that whenever he complained, his father scolded him for being selfish. Mark learned that love meant sacrificial giving. But how could he realistically change any of this now, since he needed to be in a caregiving role to Shelly, and even to their kids? Typically, Mark tried to keep these stresses to himself, but as a result he was often grumpy and withdrawn from Shelly. He thought, "What good will it do to say how I feel? Complaining won't change the facts—I'd just be dumping on Shelly." How could *he* feel frustrated about losing another weekend? After all, his wife was sick—he wasn't. He felt selfish for even having those feelings. He reproached himself, just as his father had. Rather than accepting his feelings as legitimate and talking with Shelly about their mutual frustration, he withdrew, and his depression deepened. His old belief about love and fairness contributed to his depression because he felt he must give, without ever asking for a turn. His parental mandate, "It's stronger to absorb your suffering and weaker to burden others," hadn't served him or his marriage well, either.

I challenged Mark to consider the possibility that his withdrawal, which was intended to protect Shelly from the "burden" of his feelings, actually created further distance for both of them. I suggested that he would feel more connected to Shelly if he could share his sadness about their lost weekend plans. This was different than complaining about her illness. After all, she was frustrated and disappointed, too. His attempts to be unselfish, unintentionally made Shelly feel apologetic, and made their stressful situation even worse. With my encouragement, Mark decided to share his distress with Shelly, which was a conscious contradiction of his family's mandate: "Don't complain; don't ask for yourself."

To his surprise, Shelly was relieved when Mark opened up. She felt less alone and less guilty about her own helplessness. Finally she could offer him some care in return by simply acknowledging that he was struggling, too. She encouraged him to make alternate plans when she wasn't feeling up to joining him. Mark began to think about what hobbies and activities he would enjoy. His depression lifted as he learned that balancing care for Shelly alongside his needs wasn't selfish—and it was better for the relationship, too.

Like Mark, many parentified children are often highly functioning and very responsible adults—sometimes too responsible for their own good. As children they've learned that giving earns love, but love is conditional upon overgiving. When you overgive your way to being loved and valued, this eventually leads to depletion and depression. But parentification isn't always even this benign. The second and more destructive face of parentification results when a child is both burdened and not valued (the one-two punch of all burden/insufficient care). Then you're more likely to find a partner with exacting standards and punitive, even destructive, behaviors.

Once again, think back to Allie in her marriage to Simon. Allie was demanding, punished Simon, and mistreated her stepchildren. She was the Cinderella of her childhood, the unwanted child, blamed for ruining her mother's life. Her mother was critical, her father was hands-off, and her extended family lived out of state. There were few protective factors for Allie. Allie's adult relationship with her family of origin remained distant and conflictual. In marriage, she felt greedy for her husband's time and attention, and was determined that her children wouldn't feel second best as she had. Her stance was unjust, but followed a clear trajectory of how unfairness can get transmitted from childhood to adulthood, and from generation to generation.

These examples show that give-and-take is lopsided in both situations of infantilization and parentification. Each imbalance handicaps both individuals and their marriages. Of course, partners don't wear a sign announcing, "Hi, I was an infantilized or parentified child." Children don't have the perspective to know whether their family's model is fair or not. As one adult commented about understanding fairness in her own childhood: "Children are good observers, but bad interpreters." An accurate interpretation of the baggage you bring takes thoughtful evaluation. As an adult, you owe that to yourself. Keep this ongoing balancing act of give-and-take between parent and child in mind, as you explore the fourth entitlement of being valued.

Entitlement #4:
Being valued

WHEN DEPRIVED OF #4, THE CONSEQUENCE IS:
YOU DON'T FEEL VALUED IN YOUR ADULT RELATIONSHIPS
Most children try their best to figure out and then meet parental expectations and values. That is a child's loyalty return. Children typically keep trying, long into adulthood, to continue to meet these expectations in some way in order to feel valued. But feeling valued is different than knowing you were loved. People can know their parents loved them, without feeling valued. When I work with patients, I often ask: "What did your parents appreciate about you?" Sometimes people are stumped. Sometimes they point to their achievements—but then I frustrate them further by asking, "Not only what

you did, but who you are?" Frequently adults don't know what they contributed to their parents or family growing up. More often they can identify whether their parents were disappointed in them. If you don't know how you were valued, then what effects might this have today? As you read ahead, identify any of your own experiences listed below:

- You achieved love through your accomplishments. You felt valued only if you were "perfect" or met exceedingly high expectations. Now you feel more like a human *doing* than a human *being*.
- You were a disappointment to a parent, despite your best efforts. Now, you're especially hard on yourself.
- Your unique contributions and efforts weren't acknowledged. Now you feel insecure, and need frequent reassurance because you don't feel "good enough."
- You were primarily valued for "being good." Now you're worn out trying to live up to other people's expectations.

Any of these inward struggles takes its toll on an individual and marriage, as Tonia learned.

Tonia: Not Feeling Valued: Consequences for a Marriage

Tonia felt deeply hurt that her parents had paid for her brothers' college educations, but refused to pay for hers, despite her better grades and stronger academic interests. Her parents thought college would be a waste of money because Tonia would get married and never use her degree. Neither her mother, who never had career goals, nor her father, who had a very traditional view of women's roles, valued Tonia's love of learning. Despite Tonia's protests at the unfairness of their position, they were unyielding. Soon after completing high school, Tonia started a job to save her own money for college. She also began dating a college student. Within months of dating, she became pregnant. She was devastated. She didn't want to go through with a pregnancy or a marriage, and for Tonia, abortion was out of the question.

In contrast to her feeling of despair about her pregnancy and impending marriage, her parents were delighted with the prospect that her boyfriend came from a good family and was headed for medical school. Many years later in my office, Tonia tearfully reported that at the time, she had asked her parents to support her wish to call off the wedding and help her place the baby for adoption. But through a combination of guilt and shaming, they talked Tonia into getting married. Tonia concluded that neither her mother nor her father really cared about how she felt. No one cared about her lost dreams for her future. Tonia tried to cope by pushing her feelings away. She married. Not long after their son was born, Tonia began an affair. When her husband found out, he left her, and even questioned if their child was his. She moved back in with her parents, who helped her raise her son.

Not being meaningfully valued in childhood contributed to Tonia's self-defeating behaviors. While her acting out may be seen as immature, I often find that similar behaviors are fueled by a deep sense of injustice. Individuals like Tonia often hold themselves hostage to show others the damage they've done. Tonia's affair was an indirect way of holding her parents accountable for pushing her into a marriage she didn't want, and for not valuing her life aspirations. Tonia's experience combines not being valued with the loss of the fifth entitlement—fairness isn't negotiated, but decided unilaterally.

Entitlement #5:
Negotiation of fairness issues

WHEN DEPRIVED OF #5, THE CONSEQUENCE IS:
YOU CAPITULATE OR CLING TO CONTROL

The sense of fair treatment is forged by the way parent-child conflicts and disappointments are managed. Ideally, both parent and child (in an age-appropriate way) get a vote about what's fair. In healthier families, differences and disappointments are openly discussed—even welcomed. But when parents don't value or incorporate a child's perspective and feedback, the result is misunderstandings and hurt feelings. Because no one person, not even a parent, can be the sole judge of what's fair in a family.

Yet a young child doesn't have the information, judgment, or comprehension to determine what's in his best interests. But all children need and deserve parenting that is sensitive to their input. Parents have the dual responsibility of being realistic about their own circumstances, and then reasonably offering their child choices. For a child this has the positive effect of knowing that your input counted. Even when you don't get what you want, it helps to know that what you wanted, mattered. In this model, fairness is negotiated in a way that takes into account the best interests of each individual.

But what happens to a child's development when a parent was a fairness dictator? When a parent's "I don't care what you want, do it because I say so," style of relating drains trust over time? What if choices were made for you, even when they felt wrong to you? What if, like Tonia, you objected and were told to stop being foolish or ungrateful? When a parent decides fairness unilaterally, a power-based relationship operates that fails to teach conflict resolution skills. Instead, the style of a fairness dictator breaks trust and teaches a child to either capitulate, rebel, or manipulate. The capitulator doesn't stick up for herself because she has learned helplessness. The activist becomes a powerful advocate for others, in personal life or in career choice. That individual partially heals her own childhood injustice through a quest to get justice for others. Finally, more simply and destructively, if a child doesn't trust that she'll get a say, that child may cope by sneaking, lying, or manipulating—strategies that often find their way into marriage, as Charlise discovered.

Charlise: Life with a Fairness Dictator: Consequences for a Marriage

Charlise and Paul arrived for couples therapy. Paul stated, "I'm always picking up the pieces for her bad decisions." He turned to his wife and said in an exhausted tone, "I feel so disrespected by you. The word 'negotiate' doesn't exist in your family. Any difference becomes an all-out fight." Paul then went on to describe what he meant.

Charlise hid things from Paul. They might be small matters—a shopping purchase she anticipated would get Paul's veto—or large—quitting her job. Eventually, when Paul found out, he'd feel betrayed and burdened by the un-planned financial impact. Sometimes Charlise angrily defended herself: "It's my life and these are my decisions." Sometimes she was remorseful. Either way, Charlise maintained a pseudoadult, "in control" stance, while she con-tinued to put Paul in a parental position. Like a naughty child, Charlise side-stepped Paul's anticipated objections by leaving him out of the loop, only later to need his help to fix the problems. How had Charlise, an otherwise very likable young woman, learned to relate in such a grossly unfair way?

In Charlise's childhood, her father ran the show. He made the decisions, both large and small, for everyone. They might involve where the family lived, what time dinner should be, or on any given day, whether the children could have dessert. Or his decisions might even intrude into very personal areas—such as his insistence that the children (through their teen years) be naturists (nudists) on their family vacation, like he was. Any minor attempt to assert her own opinion was met with consternation, disapproval, or an all-out fight. Charlise's mother, though distressed by her husband's rigid man-ner, deferred to him. Charlise learned to sneak behind her father's back. Charlise turned to manipulation when there was no possibility for fair ne-gotiation with her father, just as her father relied on power instead of trust to get his way. Therapeutically, it was important for me to acknowledge that Charlise had experienced grossly unfair treatment by her authoritarian father—coupled with the lack of advocacy by her mother. Then, I asked Charlise to recognize that she was doing to Paul (making decisions without regard to him) as her father had done to her. With this insight, she was moti-vated to change her behavior and treat Paul more fairly. It was a win-win scenario for Charlise to learn a new model of fairness and risk trusting that Paul would consider her needs. As Charlise related more fairly, she earned Paul's trust that she would no longer go behind his back. Charlise learned to truly negotiate decisions, big and small.

Entitlement #6:
Repair and restoration of fairness and trust

WHEN DEPRIVED OF #6, THE CONSEQUENCE IS:
YOU CARRY AND PERPETUATE UNFAIRNESS

After childhood, it becomes your responsibility to recognize and right the effects of unfairness—because the past awaits you when unfair experiences are unhealed. No matter what relationship you're in, you bring your baggage with you. The trajectory of unfairness brings us to our sixth experience: What happens to you when unfair experiences have never been acknowledged? Can you get over them simply by putting the past behind you? Or is there something to gain by returning to the source of the injustice? Is it possible that "the hand that hurts can be the hand that heals"? The extent of the damage from breaches to the first five entitlements turns on the crucial sixth: the repair and restoration of fairness and trust. Injuries from the past can be mitigated by your attempts to heal them.

When parents and grown children attempt to right a wrong, and restore fairness, they can create more trust in their relationship. But the first barrier to true repair is the denial that damage was done. Parents and children may each deny the extent of harm done. It's a bit more intuitive that a parent would deny harming their child (after all, no parent wants to think that). But why would the child, who experienced unfair treatment, remain in denial even into adulthood?

With this denial we come full circle, to the beginning of the book, where we began our first exploration of the family fairness model. This deeply ingrained model may have a skewed take on fairness, full of unreasonable expectations and beliefs that aren't particularly rational. Denial about this painful reality is a loyal defense that serves a vital purpose during childhood—it's an accommodation to the family culture. Many people protect themselves from the distressing recognition of parental injustice by clinging to myths such as: *I had a happy childhood* (which may be partially true); or the best offense is a good defense, like Roberto's cover: *I rejected my father; he didn't reject me*; or the overly simplistic myth: *My mother was a saint and my father was a jerk* (or vice versa). Myths help explain things, but unconsciously they function as a defense against loss, and protection from feeling disloyal to your parents. But life and relationships are usually more complicated than the myth that denial allows.

In addition to denial, the defenses of avoidance and blame may be used to shield against future reinjury. Psychologist Leslie Greenberg reminds us that people overlearn emotional pain in order to avoid repeating it. Because unfair treatment is painful, people sometimes fool themselves into thinking that the past is the past and won't be repeated. So you might resent, blame, or even silently forgive your parents for some hurtful experience, but still repeat patterns from those relationships in your romantic life. And many people avoid thinking about their relationship with their parents altogether. They muscle their way through the pain of the past, rather than heal it.

For it's not only the fact of injustice but also how you deal with the past that makes all the difference in the world. I encourage you to think about your unfinished business as you ask yourself these next questions:

- Did your parents assist you in expressing your feelings about unfair or hurtful situations, or was this discouraged?
- What happened when you protested unfairness? Did you feel considered or dismissed?
- Was showing your feelings considered a weak thing to do? Were you expected to just "get over it"?
- Did you worry that you were hurting your parents if you questioned how they related to you?
- If there wasn't a good way of resolving unfairness, did you protest, or did you "give up" and withdraw emotionally or physically?

Your responses reflect whether you developed a repertoire of behaviors to protect yourself from further injustice and hurt. Old coping behaviors—the defenses developed from past injuries—are designed to make you feel less vulnerable. Now, instead of showing you feel hurt, you show anger; now, instead of speaking up, you opt for a wounded silence; now, when you're disappointed, you pull a third person into the mix to side with you; now, when you feel bullied, you lie; now, when you feel mistreated, you seek revenge; now, when you don't get what you need, you blame; now, when things are grossly unfair, you resolve never to speak again. The problem isn't that you developed these defenses—we all did to some degree—it's that you still use them—despite the fact that they're outdated and no longer constructive. Once upon a time, they felt protective. But now in your intimate relationship, these childhood defenses can be downright detrimental. The truth is, the events from your past are affecting your intimate relationship today. And while it may be difficult, working to repair holdover issues with your parents can enhance your relationship with your spouse. You can finally let go of the baggage for good. You're probably wondering, "But how?"

Revisiting Unfinished Business with Your Parents

Again, remember that you aren't exploring childhood injustices for the purpose of an interesting archaeological dig into the past, but because of their current impact. Most of us experience a mixture of fair and unfair treatment. Hopefully, the fair experiences can give you courage to address those that were unfair.

What Good Would It Do?

While the paradigm for repair is similar for parent-child relationships and intimate relationships, the reasons you might resist repair differ. Let's look at the most common rationalizations that adults give to avoid addressing their unfinished business with their parents.

- They're too old (old can mean anything from age fifty on).
- They did the best they could. I don't want to be a parent basher.

- What good would it do? The past is the past.
- "Sure, when I was nineteen, I screamed at my father/mother about what happened, but they never apologized." (Screaming accusations isn't generally conducive to an apologetic response.)
- It's better to forgive and forget.
- They're still the same—they'll never change.
- Back then, parents just didn't talk openly with their children.
- I shrug it off.
- I become cool and distant, and assume that if they care, they'll notice something is wrong.
- I forgave them a long time ago. Why should we talk about things now?
- What unfairness? I had a happy childhood.
- My childhood has nothing to do with my marriage.
- How can you resolve something with someone who's dead?

I understand that for many of the reasons above, you may not want to run the risk of reentering the maze of your parent-childhood experiences. Anticipating a dialogue with a parent about experiences in the past evokes a familiar pain. But you forget—perhaps both you and your parents have grown up some. Perhaps both of you would welcome a chance to clear up unfinished business before it's too late. Perhaps you need to remind yourself that the primary reason to risk healing wounds of unfairness is the empowerment to you and the benefits to all of your relationships. Repairing unfinished business can liberate you from sad or bitter feelings from your past, and free you for your future.

The Benefits of Repairing Unfinished Business

Since imagining gains is sometimes harder than predicting problems, it's important to understand the benefits of repairing unfinished business. You need to understand not only the risks of engagement, but also the potential benefits as well. Here's what you stand to gain:

- an increased ability to take personal responsibility;
- an increased empowerment and self-advocacy;
- an interruption of a cycle of unfairness; and
- the skills for relating in a new way.

In order to illustrate the trajectory of unfairness and then how repair works, the next vignette describes a significant issue of unfairness in my own family many years ago.

Healing for the Future

I was a classic case of the emotionally overfunctioning, parentified child. Fortunately, I was also loved and valued. But I was burdened by my special role of confidante to my mother about her unhappiness with my father. My favored status with my mother turned me against my father. In this way, I lost the entitlement to have my primary relationship with my father protected. For as much as my mother gave me, I was obliged to return care more on her terms. She leaned on me. That was the deal. I didn't recognize any of these concerns as fairness issues, nor even how burdened I was—emotionally, I was much older than my years. I certainly didn't recognize my family's questionable assumptions about fairness and love that had been in place for generations. I simply accepted the myth of a happy childhood with a mother who loved me, and—oh, well—a distant and ill-tempered father.

My first clue that something was wrong occurred in my young adulthood, after the very unhappy ending of a serious relationship. I became symptomatic—despondent, depressed, lost trust in men, and yet was drawn to emotionally remote partners. To get away from all this pain, I took the geographical cure and I moved across the country.

My situation was this: I had recently completed my first graduate degree in psychology. I found my new psychological insights both enlightening and depressing. At last I knew why I was a mess—because my family was. My mother and father had a tense marriage. My father was irritable and unpleasant to be around; my mother was depressed. I was still quite close to my mother, who continued to confide in me about her disappointments with my dad. Her complaints certainly seemed reasonable to me. I was also having similarly disappointing experiences with men. Like my mother, I gave too much in relationships, I expected too little, and then felt hurt and disappointed in return. In my experience, life and relationships were definitely unfair.

My ideas about life, love, and fairness were about to be shaken up. My second graduate degree was in marriage and family therapy. I trained with pioneers in the field of relationship ethics—what people owe to and deserve from parents, partners, and family. My indebtedness to these great thinkers and generous colleagues—Drs. Iván Böszörményi-Nagy, Barbara Krasner, and Margaret Cotroneo—is lifelong. From them, I learned how to understand fairness within the context of the family sweep of generations and in the present. I learned how to offer and claim fairness in primary relationships, on behalf of my relationships and myself.

But before I could do this, I had to examine my own unanalyzed set of assumptions about what I owed and what I deserved in relationships. I had to acknowledge that the fairness model I had learned from my parents wasn't always a good guide. I had to recognize the misconceptions I held about my parents, my family, and myself, and learn what to do about them. I had blind spots in my model of fairness, which were causing significant problems in my life. I had just about every distorted belief about love and fairness there was. I thought that being "strong" and putting the other person's needs first was paramount; I thought that I instinctively knew what was fair because I was such a caring person; I thought that my take on the issues with my mother and father was accurate; I thought that my mother had never treated me unfairly because her love for me was so evident. After all, she chose me to confide in—I was special in her eyes. I had no clue that these issues were governing my choice in a partner and in my own tendency to be sacrificial and then disappointed in return.

Until I challenged my assumptions, I didn't realize that I needed to change. I didn't know that what seemed normal (if depressingly so) was in fact a way of relating, guided by a fairness model that I had learned, and so, could change. Before I could become a competent couples and family therapist and help others, I had to take a new look at my own family. I had to make a claim for my own entitlement to a relationship with my father, unimpeded by my loyalties to my mother (Entitlement #1). I had to right the balance of give-and-take between us, so that I wasn't the child emotionally taking care of the parent (Entitlement #3); I had to stop perpetuating a cycle of injustice that had a play-it-forward component (Entitlement #6). Here's what I did:

With the first insight that my mother had been unfair by using me as her confidante, I felt more depressed. Had my mother set out to treat me unfairly? Of course not. Most parents do the best they can. But my mother—due to her depression and the neediness of her own mother—had blind spots in her expectations of me. Without realizing it, she leaned on me in ways that were unfair to me. Then there was my father. I thought I was fair to my father—I wasn't. I had never even imagined his side of things. Now I was disappointed in my mother, my father, and in myself. What good was this doing?

Slowly I understood that I needed to move beyond my insights and address these unfair experiences with my parents directly. I decided to do this for the sake of my relationships with them, but also for my own future relationships and in order to have integrity with my clients. I couldn't very well give advice that I hadn't followed myself. I had to risk changes in all of my relationships in order to gain a better balance of give-and-take.

How did I deconstruct the old beliefs that made up my dysfunctional fairness model? First I had to reevaluate my assumption that because I was a good person, I could know with conviction what was fair. In my own case, I felt that I had tried my best to be a good and thoughtful daughter. But when I looked at my relationship with my father, I saw that I had held him, and perhaps all men, at a distance. My mother's disappointments with my father had shaped my negative expectations both of my father, and of men in general. These insights would shift the ways I related to each of my parents and the ways I related in other close relationships. Beyond insight, I knew I needed to confront this unfairness directly.

Some readers might wonder if I simply lacked the skill of being assertive with my mother, or perhaps I was having this difficulty because I just wasn't autonomous. Those are reasonable questions, but in other relationships in my life I seemed to have no trouble standing up for myself. I thought leaving home some years before reflected my self-sufficiency—living on my own across the country, managing my own finances, and generally being very self-reliant. So why hadn't these skills helped me with the years-long injustice of being my mother's confidante?

First, I was lost within the fairness model that I had learned in particular from my mother. I didn't even see the injustices. I was in denial. My family's fairness model was so much a part of who I was, I couldn't see it for what it was. And second, perhaps as important, I was powerfully motivated to be my mother's loyal daughter. Since loyalty is both a way of being connected and paying back a parent, I was returning care to my mother (totally outside my awareness at the time) by taking her side. I had been loyal to my mother at the expense of my relationship with my father. If I insisted on creating new terms, I now understood that I would be breaking all the invisible, powerful, unspoken rules about how mothers and daughters relate, and had related for generations in my family. Mothers and daughters had been closer to each other than husbands and wives were. I would break the unquestioned fairness deal that had been in place since before I was born.

How did I change this unfair pattern in which I was implicitly asked to take sides against my father and accept the premise that men were just disappointing? The change was part revolution and then years of evolution in my relationship with both parents. The revolution began with a talk with my mother. I was visiting my parents during my midwinter break in my second year of family therapy training. On this particular day, which I will always remember, I broke the biggest rule in the unspoken assumptions about love between mother and daughter in my family—I made a claim for fairness on my terms. I summoned up the courage to tell my mother that she hadn't been fair to me. She had leaned on me too much in my role as her confidante, at too early an age, and had hurt me by repeatedly enlisting my sympathies against my father. For my mother, such an encounter with me was a radical departure from my typically comforting role. I pressed on, asking her to care about me by leaving me out of her disappointments with my father. I told her that I wouldn't continue to be drawn into discussions about my father's temper, and other enumerated shortcomings. I cared deeply about her, but as much as I loved her, I didn't owe her this, because I owed something to myself, and to my father, too. The old model wasn't fair to me, and it wasn't fair to my relationship with my father.

I let my mother know that I had to separate her marital problems from my relationship with my father as a parent. I needed to relate to my father through my own experiences of him, not her experiences of him. I couldn't give my father a "fair shake" and still take sides with her against him. Until then, I hadn't even cared to know my father with any degree of complexity. I wasn't entirely sure how my negative view of him had influenced my own ability to choose a loving partner, but I knew it couldn't be helping that I held such a pessimistic view of men. I had begun to realize that the past was not the past; it was bleeding into the present.

As I spoke, my mother was stunned with hurt and anger. Tears welled up in her eyes, and she replied indignantly, "I would have never said that to my mother!" The clear implication was that I had done the unthinkable by telling my mother that she had been unfair to me. By taking this risk, I had revealed the difference between love and fairness. The change I needed in my relationship with my mother had nothing to do with not being "loved enough," but it had everything to do with fairness.

Now, my mother rightly prided herself on what a fair-minded, good, and generous woman she was. Yet she had a large blind spot about fairness. This blind spot developed particularly in her relationship with her own mother. While her mother languished in bed, depressed for months at a time (sadly, there was no psychopharmacy available in that era), her father was more available, but periodically debilitated by a heart ailment. My mother learned to be a competent, highly independent child, who couldn't show her own needs. That was how she gave back, and how she had overgiven to her mother since early childhood. She had never risked talking with her mother and father about this lopsided balance, and was unable to set her own limits for giving. Instead, she passed the debt forward—to me. My mother expected (without knowing it) that in repayment for all that she had done to "be strong" by taking care of her mother, while never asking for fairness for herself, that her children would give her the same. I had done so until that moment.

Had I continued to accept this payback system of being "strong" and giving sacrificially, I would, no doubt, have passed it down to my future spouse and children as unknowingly as my mother had done. This imbalanced way of relating was already negatively impacting how typically "used" I felt, how little I expected for myself, and how generally angry and depressed I was. I also realized how little I had really gotten to know my father, and how unloved and unlovable that made me feel.

Now, in that moment, I was asking my mother to give me something that she had never asked for and certainly never gotten—an acknowledgment that what I had given had cost me too much. I stood still before my mother's intergenerational call to retreat, her claim of "I would have never said that to my mother!" Somewhere, from the depths of both my pain and hope, I had the courage to respond, "Well, then I'm glad I have you for a mother, because I wouldn't want that kind of relationship." I hugged her and hoped that neither of us would shrink from the challenges of fair relating.

With that first dialogue, nothing apparently dramatic changed overnight, except for my mother's wounded and wary regard for me and my new studies. But I was freed almost immediately from that old way of relating in which I was depleted and let down. While this exchange may sound simple, it struck terror into my heart. I knew at a deep level that not only was there far more to gain, but also far more to lose, in claiming fairness. I had risked disappointing my mother in the deepest emotional way. But these were the necessary losses that accompanied the gains in pursuing fairness. I didn't know if my mother would remain distant from me, or if we would grow into a healthier and closer way of relating. I hoped, but didn't know, that this beginning dialogue would become a paradigm for fair relating in all of my relationships. I hoped, but didn't yet know that I would again feel close to my mother, because I could risk saying what was fair to me, and she could embrace this new way of relating where love doesn't trump fairness. Now love was based on a new model that encompassed truth with compassion and mutual respect as well as love.

The new fairness that emerged transformed my relationship with my mother over time, from one in which I had felt very loved but also exploited as a confidante, to one of freedom and great mutual respect as well as love.

My gains from this dialogue quickly changed my ability to reconnect with my father. He and I developed a closer and more understanding relationship. I no longer simply saw him as an angry man, but a hurt and rejected one, deeply scarred by the early deaths of both his parents. As I expressed this understanding, and cared about getting to know him, my father was able to show remorse for how his anger had affected me. To my father, I was the lost sheep, returned after many years of emotional distance. I was again his loving daughter. He was again my loving father—something I hadn't felt for years and years. I also was able to ask for a fairer balance of give-and-take in many of the other relationships in my life. Whenever my courage wavered, I would remind myself that if I could hold my parents accountable for fairness, I could ask for fairness from anyone—the rest of the world was a piece of cake. Some time later, the new way of relating that I'd developed helped me when I met my future husband. All of these crucial shifts, all of the love that has followed, were made possible because I was becoming more fair-minded.

Shortly after reworking these lost entitlements with my parents, my father had a massive stroke. He never regained much of his speech, but our renewed bond remained powerfully present until his death some years later. My mother and I have had the gift of over twenty-five years of working through fairness issues. To her enormous credit, and my relief and gratitude, after some years of struggle, we came to terms with the past. Readers may wonder how my relationship with my mother, now in her eighties, fared after she read my account of this time. With some trepidation, and sensitivity to her feelings, I asked her to respond to this excerpt before it was published—that was only fair. I asked whether I had offended her by any of my reflections. She immediately responded, "Why should I feel hurt? It's all true." I can think of no higher compliment anyone could pay this book than her declaration upon reading it: "I wish I'd had a book like this when your dad and I got married."

As my story shows, and you'll see in later chapters, working on unfinished business from the past benefits both you and your relationships. My experience of reworking unfairness, rather than merely understanding it, transformed my beliefs about love and gave me the conviction that healing injuries, even severe ones between family members, is possible.

As you move on to Part Two of the book, you'll be applying your new insights to four kinds of dilemmas in couples' relationships. Some will make you laugh at your reflection, mirrored in the couples arguing over the smallest details of day-to-day life. Others will remind you of challenges you've already encountered (or prepare you for those you may face). And others will move you as you feel a couple's heartache, and rejoice as you watch them heal. We begin chapter 6 by entering the drama of one of the earliest and most crucial balancing acts requiring fairness between partners.

 EXERCISES FOR CHAPTER 5

EXERCISE: SIX ENTITLEMENTS: CONNECTING THE DOTS . . . CONSEQUENCES FOR A MARRIAGE

For each of the six entitlements below, write a statement that relates the entitlement from your parents (whether or not you received it) to how you suspect that outcome plays out in your relationship with your partner today:

1. Protection and preservation of relationships:
   What I got:
   What I didn't get:
   Consequence for my marriage:

2. Safe, reliable, and nurturing parenting:
   What I got:
   What I didn't get:
   Consequence for my marriage:

(continued)

3. Appropriate give-and-take:
   What I got:
   What I didn't get:
   Consequence for my marriage:

4. Being valued:
   What I got:
   What I didn't get:
   Consequence for my marriage:

5. Negotiation of fairness issues:
   What I got:
   What I didn't get:
   Consequence for my marriage:

6. Repair and restoration of fairness and trust:
   What I got:
   What I didn't get:
   Consequence for my marriage:

EXERCISE: ADDRESSING CHILDHOOD ENTITLEMENTS

I encourage you to reflect on the entitlements of this chapter and relate them to your own experiences growing up. If you choose to address any area of your relationship with your family members, as I did, do so with preparation.

Before you address any issue of unfairness, it's helpful to imagine a more benign explanation for the occurrence. What did a parent struggle with? How did their own parenting shape them? At the very least, this may help you depersonalize an injustice—and recognize it as more their problem than yours. This may free you of the confusion surrounding love and unfairness.

Next, ask for their care. Let them know that you wish to talk about an area that is still impacting you today. Sometimes it's safer to start by asking about their family history before speaking about your history with them. Be prepared for the possibility that you may meet with resistance, such as denial, hurt, or defensiveness. Resist the urge to point fingers. Be specific about what you're hoping for, and what claim for change you're making.

Preparation may include consultation with a family-trained therapist, or in a session designed for that purpose. Don't feel any pressure to tackle these challenges without help, or if it doesn't feel safe.

Part Two

REPAIRING EVERYDAY INJUSTICES AND BREACHES IN FAIRNESS

All virtue is summed up in dealing justly.

—Aristotle, Nicomachean Ethics

FAMILY LOYALTY CONFLICTS:
THE TIES THAT BOND AND BIND

"First, at the top of the pyramid, there's my wife. Then there's her relationship with our son. Then there's her closeness to her family. Then come her friends, then her coworkers and her career, then the dog. Then me. I'm never chosen. With my wife, I'm at the bottom of the heap." *(Greg, second marriage)*

This husband of thirteen years is describing a marriage with misaligned loyalties. The drama of loyalty conflicts is like none other for couples. Loyalty tensions between partners have the potential energy of the immovable object (what your mother/father wants) meeting the irresistible force (what your partner wants). The tensions might include: *Whose family do we spend the holidays with? Do we open gifts on Christmas Eve or on Christmas Day? Do we give gifts at all, since that's considered childish and materialistic in your family? Do we follow the Orthodox tradition of your parents or the Reform tradition of mine? Do we spend our vacations mostly visiting family, or pursuing our own interests as a couple? Do we spend more time with your family or mine? Do we take time away from the kids like your parents did, or spend more of our time supporting the kids' interests like my family did?* Loyalty dilemmas involve making choices between your spouse and your parents; between your children from a former marriage and your present partner; and even at times, between your spouse and your children.

Loyalty can be a healthy bond that provides security and connection, or a tight obligatory bind that holds you hostage. Resolving loyalty dilemmas is a prerequisite for feeling fairly treated in general, and is an early and critical task of relationship formation and stability. Yet loyalty is often overlooked in favor of the higher-profile problems that couples report, such as money, parenting, division of labor, sex, and career conflicts. At most, loyalty makes it into the Ann Landers column under advice about the in-laws. Indeed, loyalty seldom appears in popular books on relationships. Then why give loyalty top billing in this chapter? Because unsolved loyalty dilemmas are the over-arching contributors to common fairness conflicts. The other problems in relationships are topics; loyalty is a dynamic. Loyalty is the secret code to decipher the moral imperative of "what you owe me (and I owe you)" for parents and partners alike. As such, it powerfully shapes both significant and seemingly insignificant interactions between partners. I think of loyalty as the umbrella under which all the "spokes" of money, parenting, division of labor, sex, career conflicts, and in-law squabbles radiate. So before we tackle the other problems most couples experience, let's return to loyalty, to understand its impact on you and your marriage.

Two Tribes

Freud once said, "When you marry there are six people in the bed." The other four occupants are parents and in-laws. The merger of two families supplies the makings for a couple's loyalty conflicts. Each individual in a couple brings familial expectations and traditions to the mix. It's as if two tribes were negotiating the unspoken assumptions of who is "right," what traditions are "better" (and will be passed on), and what is fair. As with most tribal behavior, there's a strong propensity to defend your family's customs and traditions, even if the customs are wacky and the traditions questionable. For example, in the tabloids recently, a celebrity husband took his celebrity wife to task for driving with their baby in her lap. Not only was this illegal, it was dangerous. She defended herself (and her traditions): "Well, my daddy always did it with us, and nothing bad ever happened."

Why justify a behavior that could have disastrous consequences? Loyalty.

Loyalty to your parents and family of origin can trump reason, and even make your own interior critiques of them feel wrong and ungrateful. Families transmit not only their customs and traditions, but also their expectations and assumptions, from parent to child, marriage to marriage, and generation to generation. These may promote an individual's growth or be unhealthy and hamper it, like the celebrity mom who remains loyal to her father's ways—as unsafe as they are. Family loyalty is one of the kinks that can stop partners from relating fairly. That's because marriage makes a third tribe—a third loyalty system.

And Marriage Makes Three—Loyalty Systems

There are three loyalty systems for a couple—your family's, your partner's family, and then the loyalty system you and your partner create as a couple. In the early stage of relationship formation, your in-laws and their loyalty system become apparent. Now you come face-to-face with the unfamiliar tribe of your partner's family, and their customs and expectations. While challenges to family traditions and expectations that come from within the tribe are regarded as disloyal, challenges that come from outside the tribe are treated as mortal threats. Thus, the trouble with in-laws: you, as a new partner are a threat to the established pecking order—the "who comes first?" question. And until you've been together quite a while, forget addressing any perceived slight with your in-laws—you're just not enough of an insider to pull it off. Until then, it takes a team effort. The adjustments of each spouse separately and together to form their own team, their own tribe, are an ongoing process. The problem with forming a new tribe is that you often have to make choices between your partner and your parents. Even if you want to please both, sometimes you can't. Besides, even if you could, pleasing everyone else often leaves out what's fair to you. A couple's task is to integrate the loyalty expectations each brings from their families and then create a third system together. But first, you have to sort out your own family loyalties.

Your Parent-Child Loyalty

When you married, you weren't thinking, "Oh, each of us is bringing our in-herited family legacies and traditions from both our mother's and father's sides. These legacies have been shaped for generations through experiences of illness, death, immigration, rituals of celebration and loss, financial con-straints or material success, emotional resilience or emotional illness, sup-portive extended family or estranged family relationships, open expressions of feelings or silence, loyalty expectations of utter devotion and sacrifice, or limited expectations." No, I bet you weren't thinking that. After all, what you've lived feels pretty normal, so you weren't sizing up your loyalty issues at the altar. You simply absorbed these powerfully experienced loyalties as a matter of belonging to your family.

Being obliged to return care—trying to figure out what's fair to return—is a universal parent-child dilemma and a direct result of the loyalty bond. Now multiply this problem by a factor of two, as each spouse brings many variations on the theme of loyalties to their marriage. When you haven't thoughtfully evaluated your fairness model, you're more likely to ping-pong between guilt-ridden obligation and sacrificial compliance, where your par-ents' and partner's expectations will be pitted against one another. Each person must find a way to return care by meeting reasonable parental ex-pectations and challenging those that aren't. Then you're truly free to grow up and prioritize the new and competing loyalty commitments to a spouse.

By my definition, to truly grow up you must stop bouncing between what your parents want on one side and what your partner wants on the other. You must thoughtfully act from a place of deep maturity with neither wholesale acceptance of parental beliefs and expectations, nor with a knee-jerk reaction or oppositional stance to your parents, to your partner, or to the world. Grow-ing up emotionally doesn't follow a chronology—there is no charted course. But growing up always involves coming to peace with loyalty expectations.

In addition to negotiating the parental expectations in your head, those sometimes loud voices of pride, concern, or disapproval, you must also deal with the real people (your parents) weighing in on the "right" answers. Even if your parents are no longer alive, you still know what they'd want. But it's not that you have to do what your parents think best; rather you owe it to yourself and your partner to get beyond either blindly conforming, or simply reacting to parental expectations and obligations. To do so, you'll need to settle whether you share the same or different expectations and values, and the same or different models for give-and-take. You'll need to risk what it may cost you to diverge from who you were expected to be and what you were expected to give. Your partner also has his or her own loyalty obligations to settle. Once you're married, your competing loyalties to parents and spouse will be tested, reshaped, and retested. Successfully integrating the triad of loyalty systems is an important task of early relationship formation. Yet for some, these loyalty dilemmas take a lifetime to resolve. Most couples can't wait a lifetime.

Marital Loyalty: Choosing Between

Where do loyalty commitments run into trouble for a couple? Did your wedding vows include the phrase "and forsake all others"? Well, sometimes your spouse is going to expect you to forsake your parents, too, or at least put them on a lower rung of the ladder. Loyalty often presents itself as a "choose between" dilemma. In early marriage it often takes the form of choosing sides between your spouse and your parents, or choosing between differing traditions. After a divorce, and in subsequent relationships, it may mean choosing between your new partner and your children from your former marriage. In these situations the couple must decide what's fair, what they owe to each other, and what they owe to their other loyalty-based relationships, particularly when the two are on a collision course. Loyalty is a deep bond, but it can also be a deep bind when you have to choose between two sets of people you love and are obligated to.

Because marriage forms new loyalties, you have to balance what you owe your partner, with what you owe yourself, your parents, and extended families.

Loyalty Juggling Acts

Loyalty conflicts that appear early on in relationships:

- What if my boyfriend can't stand my family? Should I marry him anyway?
- How important is it to marry someone with similar values as my mom and dad?
- Your parents are Catholic, mine are Jewish. Do we have a priest and a rabbi, two services, a civil ceremony, or just throw up our hands and elope?
- Should we raise children in our two different religions, in one tradition, or in none?
- Whose family should we spend the holidays with?

Once couples are in a long-term relationship, familial expectations underlie many issues:

- *Love in my family means helping out in every way you can. Love in yours means an annual visit.*
- *Love in my family means pleasantries and avoidance of conflict. Love in yours means hashing things out, and then feeling closer.*
- *Will we have children to make our parents happy?*
- *In your family, men take care of finances and women take care of kids— what if that isn't what I bargained for?*
- *Do parents argue in front of the children, or is that only done in private?*
- *Will we celebrate birthdays like in my family, or only do that for the children, like in yours?*
- *Will we save money for the future like your family did or live paycheck to paycheck like mine?*
- *If I make the money, do I get to control how you spend it?*
- *Whose family's values do we follow regarding the children's education?*

- *Who makes the decisions in the family?*
- *Can I still have my own personal time like my parents did, or will you feel rejected because your parents were never apart?*

Couples are left to negotiate the tribal customs and the particular family loyalty expectations. A new couple may have a difficult time functioning as a team if either feels they're letting their parents down. Let's first take a look at a few early loyalty conflicts before we explore those of later and second marriages.

Parents and Engaged Couples: Loyalty Conflicts Emerge Before the Wedding

Joe and Nicole had discussed eloping, despite the fact that they were both warmly accepted by the other's family. The problem was Nicole's parents. They were driving the couple crazy over the wedding plans. Nicole's parents wanted a society wedding, despite the couple's preference for a more modest celebration. Joe came from a working-class family and felt very uncomfortable with the extravagance. At first he tried to go along to get along with Nicole's parents, but soon the couple was arguing over everything from silver patterns to table linens, to engraved invitations, to the size of the invitation list. Eventually, Joe became so frustrated that he pressed Nicole to take his side. Although Nicole was also stressed out by her parents, she felt the need to defend them. She begged Joe to be more understanding. After all, she was their only daughter—and they were paying for the wedding. And besides, they had just given them money for a new car. Nicole felt she owed it to them to indulge their wishes for her wedding.

Soon, Joe was beginning to rethink getting married at all, while Nicole just wanted to run away and elope. Wasn't this supposed to be the happiest time of their lives? Nicole had never seen this side of Joe—impatient, irritable, and disapproving. And Joe hadn't known how much he would come to judge Nicole for her inability to stand up to her parents, not to mention his growing dislike of them. Each began to secretly worry if they'd made a huge mistake in their choice of a partner. Each wondered: was this a preview of what marriage would be like? Should they get out now? I'll return to Joe and Nicole shortly, while you think about what you would do if you were in their shoes. Now, let's meet our next couple.

For the first time, June could envision a future, a lifetime with a partner. She and Alex felt very loved and cherished by each other. But June's parents refused to attend her wedding to Alex. Previously, June's parents had objected to the boyfriends she'd brought home. They'd been of a different religion, or were divorced, or didn't have good enough jobs. Alex, on the other hand, met all of June's parents' criteria except one—Alex was a woman, Alexandra. June kept the nature of their intimate relationship a secret for months. The boyfriends she brought to meet her parents in the past were just that—friends. She had never felt comfortable telling her parents about her lesbian relationships. Despite knowing this, Alexandra felt deeply hurt that June wouldn't come out to her parents—they were serious, after all. This became the couple's ongoing fight theme. Alexandra argued that she had risked a lot to be with June. She had moved from another state and left a secure job. Finding another good position had been hard. Alexandra insisted, "Can't June take a risk for our relationship, too? Wouldn't that be fair?" June pleaded, "Couldn't you just give my parents more time? You just don't get what it's like. I love my parents. You've never even forgiven yours for their miserable divorce, and getting moved across the country after that. I just need more time."

Finally, Alexandra threatened to leave unless June told her parents. June felt pressured and misunderstood. June knew that Alexandra couldn't anticipate how disapproving June's parents would be. They had really liked Alexandra when they thought she was just a good friend and roommate, but now June knew they'd feel differently. Alexandra persisted. Despite her reservations, June finally disclosed the intimate nature of her relationship with Alexandra. Neither June nor Alexandra was fully prepared for the aftermath. June's parents stopped speaking to her. They didn't invite them to holiday dinners. They excluded them from family celebrations. Later that same year,

June sent her parents an invitation to the civil union ceremony that she and Alexandra were planning. June's parents didn't respond.

June kept the door open, hoping her parents would be back in touch. They finally were—after her father's near-fatal heart attack. June felt tremendously guilty. Had she caused her father's heart attack? How much had she hurt them? Would things ever be the same? June blamed Alexandra for pushing her so hard. June had chosen Alexandra over her parents, but now she wasn't sure that her loving feelings for Alexandra would ever return. Could this couple's relationship recover from the aftermath of a loyalty conflict that had nearly cost June her relationship with her parents, and to June's way of thinking, almost cost her father his life?

For both couples, Joe and Nicole, and June and Alexandra, fairness dilemmas arose from the choose-between tensions of split loyalties. Was it fair for Joe to lose his patience and insist that Nicole take her parents on? Was it fair for Nicole to be such a wimp, unable to tell her parents to butt out? Nicole had never settled what she needed to reciprocate for what her parents so extravagantly gave (and she accepted). Until their crisis over the wedding plans, Nicole repaid her parents with compliance. Was Joe's model of return to his parents any better? At best, he maintained a polite but coolly distant relationship with his mother and father, which was also characterized by occasional blasts of Joe's annoyance at them. At least Nicole's relationship was close, even if it was too close for comfort. As for the second couple, was it fair for Alexandra to threaten to leave June? Was it fair for June to blame Alexandra for the aftermath of coming out to her parents? In both relationships, the unsolved loyalty dynamics had nearly drastic consequences for the couples. But what's easy to overlook is what these dilemmas also tell us about each partner's ability to balance competing needs and loyalty obligations.

Nicole, with encouragement and support, was finally able to let her parents know that as much as she appreciated their wish to give her a wedding on a grand scale, she needed them to back off. Instead of taking the easy way out—and pinning the blame on Joe—Nicole was a grown-up. She came to terms with the fact that for all her parents had given and she had received, she didn't owe it to them to have her wedding strictly on their terms. Nicole told her parents what all the pressure was doing to her, and asked them to let her make the remaining decisions without their input. She made a claim for them to put a more honest and balanced relationship with each other above their desire for a socially proper wedding. Nicole's parents benefited from hearing their daughter's side of things. Initially, they were taken aback, but they came to understand that a wedding their daughter didn't want was not a gift, but an albatross-like expectation, and one that was creating a rift between them.

Beyond being assertive, Nicole had cut through a much larger dynamic— the justice aspect of loyalty, which requires rebalancing what consideration an adult owes to parents with what the parents owe their child. For Nicole, this was a defining moment in her relationship with her parents, and also in her own personal growth. She had made a claim for a new level of give-and-take with her parents, no longer trading their indulgence for her compliance. And Joe was back to his old cheerful, lovable self. Once again, they looked forward to their life together, and now to their wedding, too.

June was not so grown-up. She continued to blame Alexandra for the year-long estrangement from her parents, and for her own guilt feelings about her father's health. It was true that Alexandra had pressed June. She hadn't been as understanding or patient as she might have been. She hadn't been entirely fair. Out of hurt and frustration she had threatened to leave the relationship. Yet Alexandra was owed something, too. She'd made significant sacrifices to be with June. She hadn't counted on having to maintain a secret existence.

Before this loyalty collision between her parents and Alexandra, June had looked like a grown-up, but emotionally she was still her parents' little girl. June's challenge now was to balance more fairly being a loyal daughter who honored all her parents had done for her, with her own entitlement to set terms for their relationship. June needed to recognize that she couldn't be responsible for her parents' disappointment about her sexual orientation. That wasn't fair to her. She couldn't protect them from who she was. When she had tried to, it had been at a high price to her individual growth, and wreaked havoc on her relationship with Alexandra as well. June would have to give up a childlike dependency in exchange for her own freedom to relate more maturely. Was there another choice? June's only remaining option was to revert to her former way of meeting her parents' needs while hiding her own. She could be so loyal to them that she betrayed herself. June could stay stuck and sacrifice herself, Alexandra, and their relationship.

While June's parents had been generous in many ways, they hadn't given her permission to grow up emotionally—to have competing loyalties. They had disapproved of every relationship that June had had, relationships that vied for her time and devotion to them. Over the course of a few months in therapy, June struggled with changing the focus from her resentment of Alexandra to a crucial recognition of how her parents had burdened her by their emotional demands and neediness. It's often the case that it's easier to blame a partner than hold parents accountable for the unfair tug on loyalties. After all, partners can be replaced. But the problem with changing partners is not only all of the accompanying losses, but the failure to resolve the underlying loyalty conflicts, which will only be repeated with a new partner.

June had understandably been terrified to recognize the lopsided nature of her relationship with her parents. They had already demonstrated the conditionality of their love. She didn't want to lose them to another cut-off. She knew at a gut level that they had made her the center of their world as an only child, after years of infertility. It was easier to be mad at Alexandra, than her parents, for whom she had so much love and compassion. Until this time, June had spent her life trying to be the daughter her parents wanted. She did this with her unquestioning loyalty and protectiveness. June was stuck. She bounced between their expectations of her and Alexandra's. She couldn't settle what she owed herself and them—at least not at this time in her life. June's loyalty bond remained a bind. When I last saw them, June and Alex had decided to stay together, but their thematic tension over "who comes first" continued, and would doubtlessly create future conflicts.

These early loyalty conflicts are easy to see because they pose such stark choices. They test fairness in a way that either strengthens or strains the bond between partners. Colliding loyalties often come at a high price for a couple in an early stage of their commitment to each other. If a couple is unable to resolve their loyalty conflicts, their relationship carries an unending feeling of unfairness. What other loyalty clashes lie down the road? Let's meet

Sandra and Charlie for a look at the ongoing penalty a couple pays for unsettled loyalty dilemmas.

Who Do You Love Best?

Sandra first came to see me when she and Charlie had been married only three years. They hadn't solved the early and almost universal task of how to prioritize and choose between competing loyalty commitments. Their dilemma was: Who comes first, the couple or the parents and their established traditions? Couples don't explain it this way of course. More often, like Sandra, they can't quite figure out why they're so upset. Sandra began her story this way:

"This is really silly, because I don't even really like my aunt and uncle, but I want to spend Thanksgiving with them. The last Thanksgiving dinner we spent with them was four years ago, just before my mom died. My relatives didn't cook, but took us to a cafeteria. When we left, Charlie said to me, 'I'm never going back there again.' I know that Charlie will insist we spend Thanksgiving with his family. It's a lovely meal. But it's not my family. And it'll be a big deal if we don't go. Charlie's mother keeps him on a short leash. One year, just before we got married, Charlie's mother sent a Christmas card to Charlie addressed to my mother's house. Charlie was living with his parents at the time, but that was his mother's way of letting Charlie know that he wasn't spending enough time with his own family. Now that both my parents are dead—my dad died when I was a kid—we've spent every holiday with Charlie's family. My uncle is the only relative left on my mom's side. I know if I don't go to Charlie's family for the holiday, he'll think I'm being mean to him, and his family won't understand, either. He never picks me over his family." She began to cry softly, and said, "Wow, I had no idea I felt so upset about this."

Sandra initially struggled to define the problem, thinking at first she was being petty: it wasn't so much the holidays, but how Charlie always seemed to put his parents and his family first. In the past, he just brushed aside her mention of spending holiday time with her mother's extended family. Even though he swore he loved her, he chose them. It's been four years now since it was her family's "turn." Why should this year be any different? Sandra discovered that her loyalties to her mother's family were deeply meaningful, especially since her mother's death. Despite her ambivalent feelings about her aunt and uncle, they're the last link to her mom.

At first, Sandra kept her distress to herself—it felt so irrational since she didn't really even enjoy spending time with her relatives. But her resentment grew that Charlie put her second. Her upset became compounded and commingled with the couple's other disagreements. She believed that Charlie just "didn't get it," didn't get her, and didn't care to. She began to feel unloved. As the holidays approached, Sandra prepared to go to her aunt and uncle's by herself. This preemptive strike wouldn't give Charlie a shot at being fair. Nor would it give the couple a chance to work out their loyalty conflicts and become a team. I encouraged Sandra to make a claim for fair consideration. She had earned the right to ask for a turn because she had spent so many holidays and other occasions with Charlie's family rather than her own. The fact that Charlie complained about her uncle's politics and the cafeteria food had nothing to do with what was fair to her and between them.

The premature deaths of Sandra's parents had made her fearful of taking any risk that might threaten the harmony of her marriage. She couldn't take any more loss. Her worst fear was that Charlie might leave her if she wasn't her usual very agreeable self. I helped her to identify how her worry about this improbable outcome arose from her anxiety about losing relationships. I suggested to her that it was easier for her to silence herself than ask for what was fair. With that insight, Sandra realized that she needed to make a claim for fairness. But she worried that it was weak or pathetic to have to ask. Would Charlie think she had changed or stop loving her? I encouraged her with the reminder that she stood a much better chance of getting fair treatment if she could make a claim for it. From where I sit, it takes much more courage to risk being known, and asking for what's fair to you, than setting yourself up for disappointment (and setting your partner up to let you down). Still braced for disappointment, Sandra took the chance and asked Charlie to spend the holidays with her family. She fully expected him to resist or reject the idea. His response surprised her: "I never knew your aunt and uncle were that important to you. I thought since my mom and dad really went out of their way to make you feel more like a daughter, that you were okay with being at my family's. But I see how upset you are. I understand, and I'll make sure that my parents do, too."

Charlie acknowledged that his assumption about continuing to spend the holidays with his family wasn't mutual or reciprocal. Charlie realized that they both needed to remain connected to their families. Sandra recognized that in the past, she had shortchanged herself and Charlie when she avoided the risk of making a claim for what was fair to her. Sandra promised Charlie that she would speak up from now on rather than silently build resentment and distance herself from him. Speaking up was both empowering and counteracted her fear of loss. The couple agreed to actively discuss how to spend future holidays rather than making assumptions. Their new fairness opened up a way of relating that felt better to both of them. Facing their loyalty dilemma head-on built trust and strengthened their commitment to each other because they were able to work through problems. Now they knew how.

These vignettes reflect loyalty tensions that surface early in the course of an intimate relationship. These "choose me" dilemmas can feel impossible to resolve, because loyalty means that you owe something to everyone, but whatever you choose, either parents or partner are likely to feel disappointed, even rejected. How can you possibly be fair under those circumstances? What people often overlook is what they owe themselves. Resolving loyalty conflicts is a basic and vital task for partners. However, if either spouse defers answering the hard questions of what they owe themselves, their partner, and also their parents and families, they're likely to encounter loyalty dilemmas throughout the duration of their marriage as our next couple did.

Loyalty Dilemmas Over Time

Dan and Eliza have been married just over fifteen years, and have two sons, ages thirteen and eleven. The loyalty dynamic in their marriage keeps pop-ping up in chameleon-like fashion—the more it changes, the more it remains the same. Dan often feels pulled between Eliza and his mother, Rose. Dan and Eliza's honeymoon foreshadowed their long-playing loyalty dilemma. Eliza recounted the time with disgust.

"It started out very romantic. We planned a cruise for our honeymoon. I had always envisioned a time we'd remember forever. The day after our wedding, we drove to our departure city, boarded the liner, and got settled. After unpacking, we left our cabin for our first evening of dancing and dinner by candlelight. We went into the dining room, and from across the room I saw another couple at our table. I thought, 'Hmm, that's strange.' As we got closer, I couldn't believe my eyes. It was Rose and Ed, his mother and father. They had booked our cruise. I felt stalked! I wanted to get off the ship at the next port. But Dan didn't even get upset with them. Then to add insult to injury he wanted me to be okay with their invasion. And what could I do? I was new to the family. I couldn't pitch a big fit, right then and there. I couldn't throw them overboard, although I felt like it. My in-laws made sure I remembered my honeymoon forever—they ruined it. But it gets even worse. The next summer we took a train to our vacation destination. At the arrival station, waiting for us, were his mother and father. Again, Dan greeted them with a big smile on his face. 'What a neat surprise,' he said. Again, I was supposed to understand. I have not felt chosen for, ever since. I don't trust that Dan will choose me when it's between his parents and me. In fact, I know it."

Dan has spent much of his life trying to live up to his parents' expectations, especially meeting his mother's emotional needs, because she easily feels neglected and hurt. The upside to his parents is their generosity and willingness to bend over backward to help them out. If the couple needs a babysitter, they're there. If Dan needs help in his office, his mom or dad pitch in. Dan wishes Eliza would handle his mother the way he does—humor her, keep her happy, and keep going. When the mother-in-law theme isn't in play, they're a warm and loving couple that takes great pleasure in their lives together. But when Rose is demanding the limelight, Dan gives in and Eliza gets mad. Eliza would trade all their babysitting, if only Dan would stand up to them. At times, Eliza feels so helpless and desperate that she threatens divorce.

How are we to understand the problem that Eliza has outlined? Dan and Eliza began their therapy with me by trying to understand why Dan didn't take a stand when his parents were intrusive. Dan responded by saying that he always felt he owed his parents. He never had the sense that he'd done enough, especially for his mother. Rose has reinforced his perception by taking center stage at Dan's graduation, his wedding, and events for his sons.

Rose was a devoted mother, but with the twist of wanting payback on her terms. Rose dedicated herself to the many activities and interests that Dan and his sister had as children, while she also promoted their success in school. Rose gave a lot, but she still needs to be center stage in her children's lives, even now. Rose is demanding a loyalty overpayment from Dan. When parents look for a lopsided return, there's often an underlying history of sacrifice or loss that inflates their loyalty expectations. For Rose, this loss occurred a few years after her marriage. Rose was a promising concert pianist who reluctantly gave up her career for motherhood. Neither her husband nor her own parents supported the continuation of Rose's career after she became pregnant with Dan. Consequently, Rose needed motherhood to make up for the career sacrifice she'd made. Rose never fully acknowledged to herself or anyone else how painful that choice had been, or how much she missed her music career. Instead, she converted the loss of her own identity and achievement into the role of motherhood and her need for her children to both be successful and devoted to her. Rose unconsciously feels entitled to her son's attention because it makes her sacrifice feel worthwhile. The result for Dan and Eliza has been a loss of joy around important family events and celebrations. Dan gives an example of one such scene:

"After my commencement from grad school, we were all invited to give brief tributes at the departmental party. I thanked my mom, dad, and Eliza for all of their support, as most grad students did. Well, later that night, Mom went AWOL. I found her in a back room, crying. She said I hadn't said enough about all the ways that she had helped me get into school, and that this was her alma mater, and that she felt that I wasn't spending enough time with her at the party, or making a special point of introducing her to my professors and friends. I was dumbfounded. But I tried to reassure her that I really did appreciate all she'd done, and how much I wanted her at the party. Eventually she stopped crying and I got her to rejoin us. I have no idea where Dad was during her meltdown, but that's usually the way it goes. And even when he's around, he's not any help to me. Dad just wants Mom to be happy."

Rose's disappointment with Dan wasn't fair, but a cheap shot aimed at getting Dan to pay attention to her. From Rose's vantage point, she deserved a little fuss. Before his marriage to Eliza, Dan had accepted this tilt in his mother's favor. His sense of obligation was distorted but felt normal because he had internalized her expectations in his childhood. And like all children, he tried to meet her expectations because loyalty and his sense of being loved and lovable were at stake. Since children into adulthood take their cues from their parents, often it's a spouse who insists on a reevaluation or shift in perspective that may be long overdue.

Now Dan needs to right this lopsided imbalance with his parents. If he doesn't, he'll continue to be more understanding of his parents' needs (particularly his mother's) than he is of either his own, Eliza's, or those of his kids. Up to this point, Dan has expected Eliza to be as understanding as he is. When she isn't, he experiences her as unsupportive of him. Dan is doing to Eliza what his mother did to him: expecting unquestioning sacrifice. Dan has to develop a better lens for seeing what's fair, and then use it to see and challenge unjust parental expectations. Otherwise, he'll jeopardize his marriage.

Some fifteen years after their honeymoon, Dan and Eliza are still struggling with the same theme of unresolved and competing loyalty conflicts. Eliza anticipates that Dan's upcoming birthday could be ruined by another of Rose's dramas. Dan doesn't want a fuss over his birthday and complains that Eliza keeps "bugging him" about dealing with his mother ahead of time. As usual, Dan has procrastinated in making plans with his mother, and now a marital crisis looms. As the session begins, Eliza is barely able to contain her fury, while Dan looks stricken.

ELIZA: "This is the last straw. It would seem to most people to be a minor incident involving his mother, but the fact that Dan couldn't say no to her . . . It affects my life and my marriage. I always bake a chocolate layer cake for Dan's birthday. It's their favorite cake—Dan's and the kids. This year, his mother called and told him that if we hadn't made plans (it was a month in advance, so we hadn't), she wanted to bake the cake and do the dinner—on a night I couldn't attend. Without talking to me, Dan said that was fine. To most people, this wouldn't sound like a big deal, but I just can't take it anymore. So now here are my lousy choices: if I'm 'understanding,' and go along, then Dan caves in to his mother, and I lose all respect for him. If I protest, I get to be 'the problem.'"

DAN: "But I said we'd have our own dinner, too. And you can both bake me a cake."

ELIZA: "You don't get it. I need you to choose me."

DAN: "But why does there have to be a choice?"

ELIZA: "Because you never stand up for yourself, much less for me or for us. We're not functioning as a team. You're not a partner to me."

DAN: "But they're sick now and old."

ELIZA: "What was your excuse fifteen years ago? I'm ready to divorce you."

DAN *(alarmed)*: "I just didn't understand. I'll call up and tell them we're going to have the dinner another time because you can't be there."

ELIZA: "Look—intellectually, I understand that you've had a hard time coping with your mom when she's intrusive and then acts hurt, which, by the way, she has done your whole life, but you need to do something about it. Now! And don't make me the scapegoat! In your family, it's peace at any price, and I'm sick of paying the price! How about telling her that *you* want me to bake the cake and *you* want me at the dinner? And don't try to hang it on me—like you usually do: 'Eliza has this problem or that problem.' That's a coward's way out—you need to finally own this one!"

Dan was stuck. He couldn't take care of his mother and Eliza at the same time. His old peacekeeping mode (modeled on his dad) was to yield to whichever woman was making his life more difficult at the moment. Sometimes that was his mother, sometimes Eliza. But capitulating wouldn't solve the loyalty conflict, or the issue of fairness to himself. It would be just another replay of what always happened. How did Dan get out of this Houdini-like bind that had taken them to the brink of a divorce?

Dan first had to figure out what was fair to him, rather than simply giving in to pressure. Through weeks of intensive work in therapy, Dan started to see that he owed himself something, too—namely a right to his own needs. Because Dan had spent his entire life trying to please others (especially women), this was a groundbreaking thought to him. He came to understand that his needs were a legitimate aspect of self-interest and were just as worthy of consideration as those of his mom, his dad, Eliza's, the kids'—anyone's. Next, Dan had to discern what he actually wanted. At first, Dan had a hard time focusing just on himself. He began by saying he wanted both his mother and Eliza to be okay with any plan for his birthday. Then he realized this answer simply avoided his responsibility to determine what was fair to him.

Dan decided that he truly wanted to celebrate his birthday when Eliza was available, rather than having two dinners—the one to please his parents and the other to please Eliza. Dan knew that it was right to have his relationship with Eliza take precedence over his parents. He found the courage from this crisis to reorder his loyalty commitments and appropriately prioritize his marriage.

Dan's claim for this new fairness began with a call to his parents, telling them that he needed to change the birthday plan for a time when Eliza was available to host the dinner. His mother and father initially protested. "But we've really counted on our evening with you." His father fell silent as his mother continued to press, "Couldn't you just do both? Why not? What's the big deal? What's Eliza's problem?" Dan held his ground and asked them to respect the fact that he wanted Eliza to be present and to bake the chocolate cake, as she usually did. But rather than leave it at that, tinkering with the details and avoiding the underlying loyalty conflict, Dan took the leap and told his parents that he often felt pressured to meet their wishes. He often felt caught in a no-win situation. This wasn't fair to him, and he intended to let them know when this happened.

His mother began to weep. "How can you be so mean? I only wanted to make your birthday special. Why are you being so difficult? Why can't you stand up to Eliza?" Then his father sternly rebuked him: "Look how you're upsetting your mother. Why are you doing this? I hope this makes Eliza happy." Dan again spoke courageously: "Eliza has really been very gracious for many years. This is my problem with you. I never spoke up about how you intruded on our honeymoon or vacations. I've rarely let you know when you've been out of line. I love you both, but I need you to know that I'm feeling run over by you. Just because I'm not crying like Mom doesn't mean that I haven't been hurt. This is a hard thing to tell you because I know it's not what you want to hear. But I'd rather be honest with you instead of keeping my distance and making phony excuses."

The phone went silent. Finally Dan broke the silence and said he hoped they'd attend the rescheduled birthday dinner. His parents muttered good-bye and hung up. A couple of days went by and Dan called them again. While the reception was decidedly cool, his parents said they would be there for the dinner. It was a politely subdued evening, but Eliza and Dan emerged as a team at last. Soon after the dinner, Dan said to Eliza, "I feel like I'm waking up from a forty-year coma. I just never thought about what was fair, only about how I could keep everyone happy."

After many years of marriage, Dan had set a new course for making his marriage the priority. He had resolved the loyalty impasse with his parents. Challenges with his parents would undoubtedly emerge in other ways, but he felt confident in his new ability to be fair to himself while considering the needs of everyone he loved. Eliza felt relieved that Dan had stopped being a ping-pong ball, giving in to either her or his parents. Eliza knew that in the future she might not "get her way," but she knew it was so much better for Dan to finally be free to say what was fair to him.

And what about Eliza? Was Dan the only one bringing baggage and left-over loyalty issues to their marriage? Of course not. Life and marriage are never that simple. In the course of asking Dan to make challenging changes, Eliza also reexamined her own beliefs about love. She learned to truly appreciate that despite the ways his parents had burdened Dan, they had loved him beyond doubt, if imperfectly. For Dan's sake and the sake of their children, Eliza became more welcoming to his parents, as Dan made her feel more secure in his commitment to prioritize their needs as a couple. In turn, Dan asked Eliza to stop threatening divorce when she was distraught. Her threats were a gratuitously harsh way of saying how unhappy she was. Eliza agreed to stop her threats and became determined to hold herself to a fairer standard.

And what about Dan and his parents? Dan got them to come into therapy for one session. Not that they "believed" in psychotherapy, but because he asked them, and because they were hurting, too. In that session, Rose, for the first time in Dan's memory, was able to talk at length about the big void in her life since the children left home. His dad, Ed, still enjoyed many hobbies and social outlets since his retirement, but Rose didn't golf or play bridge. Dan thanked his mother for acknowledging the reality that she had looked to him all these years to fill that empty space in her life. He asked her why she had given up playing the piano, even casually? Rose said it made her too sad to hear herself play so poorly now, compared to how she liked to remember herself. And besides, now her hands were arthritic. There was no easy answer to her losses, just as there had been no magic wand to relieve Dan of his conflict. But in that session you could see that each of them was finally free to speak unspoken truths. I hoped that they would continue to tap into this newfound way of relating. At least now, they had experienced it.

As you can see from Dan and Eliza's struggles, loyalty dilemmas that aren't resolved early on continue to play out years into the future. They can pop up in the "little" examples of who'll bake the birthday cake or they can loom large in repeated major conflicts. Our next couples face the geometric growth of loyalty collisions following divorce.

Loyalty Conflicts in Second Marriages: Choose Me, Not Your Children

The loyalty dilemmas of second marriages have a compounding effect, because there are so many deeply connected people with competing needs and desires. Most second marriages are not the "Brady Bunch," an idealized, parallel match of two partners, with children of approximately the same ages. More often there are complications of children at different life stages, the usual questions of degree of stepparent involvement and tensions over different parenting styles, as well as issues about how the former spouses play their parts. Arguably, the most challenging, from a loyalty perspective, are the remarriages where only one partner has children and the other is childless. The childless partner has to manage feelings of competition with the ongoing presence of the former spouse (and other parent), as well as his (or her) new role as a stepparent. The children in the mix have to face their feelings of loss (and later gain) at having to accept a stepparent. The spouse with children has to delicately balance his (or her) time and energy between the children and new spouse, and perhaps ongoing guilt feelings about how a child is faring in this new arrangement. What do these loyalty pulls sound like?

- You always put your children's plans ahead of ours.
- I don't want to set aside money for your children's tuition. The least your ex could do is pay for college.
- You broke our deal by taking a job that will take me away from my grown children.
- My kids were first to schedule that vacation week with us; your kids will have to wait.
- I want time alone with you.
- You're a pushover with your kids.
- Can't you just get along with each other for my sake?
- How long are you going to let your kids guilt-trip you for your divorce?

Let's see how these tensions play out in the lives of two couples.

Jacqui is a thirty-two-year-old graphic artist married to Matt, an advertising executive twenty years her senior. Loyalty issues have set the stage for ongoing tensions. Jacqui began a session by describing a defining moment in their marriage. Shortly after their first anniversary, Jacqui became pregnant. As luck would have it, on the weekend that she was due to deliver their first child, Matt's eighteen-year-old son was graduating from a high school across the country. Matt reassured Jacqui that if she went into labor, he wouldn't fly out, but otherwise he planned to attend his son's ceremony. His son already regarded him as an absentee dad. If Matt didn't attend the graduation, he feared that his son would write him off for the inattentive father who he had sometimes been. In the session, Matt defended his decision for what sounded like the umpteenth time, arguing that he needed to be there for his son. Matt hoped that Jacqui would be more understanding than his son would be if he didn't show up.

While the literal problem was that Matt couldn't be in two places at once, the underlying conflict was his need to balance the realistic needs of his pregnant wife, against the reasonable needs of his son, who was counting on Matt's attendance. Matt asked Jacqui to be supportive. She wasn't. Matt flew to the graduation.

Despite the fact that Jacqui didn't go into labor that weekend, she has never forgiven Matt for choosing his son over her at that time. Jacqui bitterly recounted that at her most vulnerable time, Matt left her. Theirs was a King Solomon–like predicament. Who was more deserving of being chosen? What was fair: To Jacqui, to the baby (due any minute), to Matt, to Matt's son? What if there was no "right" answer? Each couple has to sort out these crucial priorities using the context of their own lives. But for Jacqui and Matt, this situation became the symbol for every future choice Matt made that triggered Jacqui's feelings of abandonment.

For Thomas and Josie, married five years, their loyalty problems get played out most weekends. Despite years of trying, they have no children of their own. Thomas, however, has two young teenage children from a first marriage that lasted only a few years. His sons spend three out of four weekends with Thomas and Josie. When the weekend comes to an end, Thomas wants to spend some time alone with Josie. While Josie would like that, too, she winds up cleaning the house instead and getting ready for the busy work-week. Thomas does his share of housework, but there's still too much to do. Josie explains: "Cleaning up after having two messy teenagers in the house takes up most of Sunday evening, and then I'm wiped out. It's an issue that has plagued us for our entire marriage. I can't seem to meet everyone's needs, that's for sure."

Josie reflected that her efforts to be a good sport—to help out with the kids, and not complain about how little time she and Thomas had to them-selves on weekends—were in part a cover for feeling like a third wheel. She thought her choices were to be mad or accepting. She took out her frustration in a whirlwind of housecleaning. But she hadn't thought about what was fair to her. An obvious solution was for everyone to pitch in with the housework. Thomas could get his kids to clean up before they left, and free up more of Sunday evening for the couple. But at a deeper level, Josie needed to make a claim for an evening out with Thomas on a weekend, even when the kids were with them.

To her surprise, her request was a relief to Thomas. He wanted her to feel cared about, but hadn't imagined what she needed before. He went a step further, and made plans for them to have a weekend getaway in addition to more frequent evenings out.

And unexpectedly, as Josie claimed more time with Thomas, Thomas felt freer to occasionally spend time alone with the kids. Now, no one was so wor-ried about stepping on each other's toes. And the kids? As they helped out more around the house, they developed a better sense of belonging and felt closer to Josie. They felt less like guests and more like part of the new family.

The vignettes in this chapter reflect the loyalty dilemmas that arise early in a couple's relationship and have to be renegotiated as marriages mature, and in second marriages. With loyalty, you always owe something to each important relationship, including the relationship to yourself. In the next chapter, you'll see the added charge loyalty brings to the everyday abuses of fairness, as you learn the steps to restore fairness and rebuild trust.

"STUPID" FIGHTS: HOW THE RELATIONSHIP SURVIVAL KIT HELPS DAY-TO-DAY UNFAIRNESS

Evelyn couldn't believe it. Chuck had polished off the very last Dove Bar. She'd had a crummy day, and was looking forward to her special treat. She opened the freezer, and nothing—no Dove Bar. "Jeez, there were two, why'd he have to eat them both?" Next time she'd hide them. No more sharing Dove Bars with Chuck.

Studies show that when people are committed to a relationship, they usually content themselves "with a perfunctory quid pro quo for the day's small abuses: he's not helping with the party, let him find his own food. She's burning money on the cell phone, time to misplace it." While some marriages suffer major violations of trust (affairs, substance abuse, abandonment), all experience small, everyday abuses of fair relating. Think about your own marriage. Have you ever begun to describe a disagreement with the words, "Well I can't believe we were fighting over something this stupid, but . . ." The example might be:

- You left your used Kleenex on the bed when I've asked you not to, over and over again.
- I'm always stuck walking the dog.
- You left the gas tank on empty for me to fill up.
- I got up with the kids in the middle of the night, when it was your turn.
- You accepted a holiday invitation to your mother's house without asking me.

- I can never reach you on your cell phone.
- You left the dishes in the sink for me to wash.
- I can't believe you spent fifty dollars on THAT!

Though most couples manage these everyday abuses with little more than a mild complaint and without lashing out, for other couples they take on great significance. When left unaddressed, these "stupid" fights fray the fabric of a relationship and deplete a couple's well of good feelings. The couples in this chapter might very well illustrate scenes from your own relationship, where such examples seem meaningless without a prior context, but are actually highly symbolic. In this chapter you'll meet Leslie and Caleb, whose little disagreement over loading the dishwasher leaves each feeling unfairly treated. You'll learn why sometimes, no matter how hard you try, you can't seem to let go of an annoyance because of its underlying meaning. Since it's easier to experience unfairness than to right it, you'll need a relationship survival kit—the four key steps to repair fairness and rebuild trust. In the final chapters of *Try to See It My Way*, you'll see how these four steps can be applied not only to the everyday abuses of fairness, but also to the challenges that most relationships face and even to the most serious violations of trust. Let's turn now to the little things that shouldn't matter, but do.

"Stupid" Fights

Every couple has their own story of the ways their idiosyncrasies exasperate each other. At times these spats can lead to all-out war, and at other times, laughter. Everyday lapses can become a humorous, even endearing part of a relationship. Let's look at a few of those first.

Nina and Scott both laugh about their very first run-in while they were dating. Nina recalls, "It was about cutting cheese. I watched Scott cut this block of cheese from all sides and at all angles. I thought: 'That's amazing; he's doing it all wrong.' I explained that he needed to cut the cheese from one end only." Scott smiles and then tells his side: "My knee-jerk response was:

'Are you kidding me? You think I need to be told how to cut cheese? You're out of your mind.' But now I do it the way she likes because it's no big deal to me. It all tastes the same." For another couple, their "stupid" fight was over dinnertime. "Beth says dinner will be at a certain time but it's usually thirty or forty minutes later than that. We used to argue about it, but then I realized that I had to stop acting as if there were a plane to catch, and just cool my jets." Beth adds, "I'm not as organized as Ray. Before I used to say, 'It'll just be a few minutes till dinner,' so he'd stop bugging me. Now when I'm running late, I try to give him a more accurate time, so he knows what to count on." She smiles and adds, "The emphasis is on *try*."

Another couple, Rich and Willa, married for nearly ten years can now laugh about their first argument. "The first fight we ever had as newlyweds was about folding his socks and undershirts," recounts Willa. "I had never given a second thought to a 'right' way of folding underwear, and Rich was appalled. To him, there was only one way to do it. You have to fold—not roll—socks, and you have to fold the shirts in thirds. That's the right way according to Rich. I was offended being told that how I was doing it was wrong. Plus, I didn't feel very much appreciated, as you can imagine."

Rich smiles at Willa's recollection: "At the time, I thought I was just teaching Willa how to fold underwear. She'd fold them her way and then I'd have to undo them and refold them. I was so put out that I even griped to the guys at the shop about it. One guy, who'd been married a long time, told me, 'Dude, are you crazy? Your wife is trying to help you out, folding your clothes, putting them away. What's your problem?' I thought, 'Yeah, he's got a point.' What am I trying to prove here? I realized that I had to let go of 'being right.' You know, I still like my way of folding better, but you can spend your whole life fighting over who's right instead of seeing the effort someone's making. And I knew Willa's heart was in the right place." The surprising outcome for both of them was that once Willa felt appreciated, she let go of defending herself and decided that if she was going to make the effort, she might as well do it the way Rich preferred. Rich's experience bears out the adage "It's better to be happy than right."

Theresa and Jed are still frequently annoyed with each other over little things. Theresa is miffed that she's the only one who fills the ice-cube trays. "I mean, there are six of us and almost every day I find the trays on the counter or, even worse, back in the freezer—empty. It just gets to me. Apparently that suits everyone—but me!" Jed's pet peeve is the pile of papers Theresa leaves on the kitchen counters. "It drives me crazy that she throws everything in this pile—from appointment cards, bills, contractor estimates, paint samples, you name it. If I kept my desk or the workbench that way, she'd kill me." Theresa and Jed's spats don't amount to much. "We're like best friends, so we get over it." Both can shrug off the "stupid stuff."

These scenes from a marriage probably sound familiar to you. While your "stupid" disagreements may not involve slicing cheese, folding underwear, or filling ice-cube trays, all couples have their irritations with each other. When your relationship has the warmth that comes from appreciation and reciprocity, you can let go of the little things, and let the daily annoyances of domestic life slide. But when give-and-take with your partner otherwise feels unfair, then you're more likely to keep track of things such as: *Isn't it your turn to clean the toilets? Why should I ask about your day? You never ask about mine. I did this for you, why don't you do the same for me?* You can only be happy and stop "keeping score" when you expect to be fairly treated. Therein lies the problem with such conflicts. If you *don't* feel fairly treated, those dirty Kleenexes, dishes in the sink, or empty ice-cube trays take on powerful significance. They become the daily reminders that you're not getting what you need and want. Let's first explore the meaning behind these examples, then see how to repair the damage caused by them.

When Are "Stupid" Fights Not So Stupid?

The ability of a couple to resolve an everyday affront—or to simply brush it off—often depends on how fair-minded each partner is. A healthy model of fairness is a tremendous resource in the resolution of everyday abuses. Without it, situational irritants often mutate into meaningful and enduring conflicts that drain trust between two people, as you'll see in chapter 8.

Our next couple can't shake a "stupid" fight. In their first session, I asked Caleb and Leslie what had prompted them to seek therapy. Leslie nodded to Caleb to begin:

"Well, what I want to get out of this therapy is more wild sex with Leslie." Then he broke into a wide grin as she burst out laughing. I had my first clue that whatever their problems were, at least they could still make fun of themselves and laugh together. Caleb went on: "No, seriously, I love Leslie to death, she's a great person, but she drives me nuts. I only ask for a few simple things, but it's like I'm speaking a foreign language. That's why we're here. We're bickering all the time." He then recapped a recurring argument over loading the dishwasher.

CALEB: "I can't believe we're paying to tell you about this stupid fight, but here goes. I came downstairs before leaving for work and said to Leslie, 'Are you going to start the dishwasher before breakfast?' And she snapped back, 'Stop criticizing me for how I run the dishwasher!' I wasn't criticizing her. I just asked a simple question."

LESLIE: "Yeah, but I know what you meant: 'Don't you dare start the dishwasher before you load all the breakfast dishes.' If you've told me once, you've told me a thousand times how to run the dishwasher and how to keep the house. In fact, you think there's a right way to do almost everything, and it happens to be your way. But when I make a simple suggestion, you say, 'If you don't like how I do it, you can do it yourself!'"

CALEB (now aggravated): "I don't know why you don't listen to how I'm telling you to run the dishwasher. I mean, it's not rocket science. You wait until it's fully loaded before you start it. Otherwise it's a waste of money—hey—we could've gone on a cruise with all the money you've wasted on hot water."

Then the tone of Caleb's comments shifted as if he were talking to a five-year-old. "I've shown you that you can get more cups and bowls in the top compartment if you load it right. If I've told you once, I've told you fifty times not to turn it on while you still have space; but you don't pay attention. I work hard all day and all I'm asking you to do is use some common sense."

Caleb next turned to me and asked, as if this were a trial with irrefutable evidence: "So, Doc, can't she just understand that this saves hot water *and* money? It's more efficient—it's the right way to run it. I just want a yes or no answer."

I challenged: "Caleb, this can't be just about the dishwasher."

Caleb swatted away my response: "Sure it is."

Not buying it, I continued: "Well, I have a hunch that there's more to it than that. Caleb, you can make a case for waiting to run the dishwasher full, but you're going to get a Pyrrhic victory—a win at too high a price. You can browbeat Leslie into doing it your way, but that will cost you her trust."

Caleb seemed frustrated by my response. Caleb had wanted me to judge that he had the objective truth on his side. But their "stupid" fight had little to do with loading a dishwasher, and everything to do with the moral certainty of his fairness model that led him to believe he was absolutely right. Caleb was so intent on winning his point that he didn't seem to care that he was demeaning Leslie in the process.

What about Leslie? Leslie's fed up with Caleb's corrections, implied or otherwise. Caleb wants to deal with the content only—"Leslie, my way is more efficient"—but he ignores the real issue—the underlying message that he is the authority and she is not. Here a seemingly trivial issue has taken on significant proportions and deep meaning. As Deborah Tannen, the renowned linguist who studies communication between men and women, suggests: "It may seem natural to suggest that others do things the way you would do them, but given the underlying meaning of the message (*I'm competent and you're not*) . . . the expense in spirit and goodwill is more costly" than, for example, being efficient and saving hot water. Tannen validates Leslie's frustration: "Being corrected all the time is wearing. And it's even more frustrating when you try to talk about what you believe they implied and they cry literal meaning—denying having 'said' what you know they communicated."

Caleb and Leslie are now in a power struggle over who is "right," who will control what happens, who defines reality, and whose expectations are reasonable and fair. Why can't either one yield? Their argument has hit a nerve—for each of them. As the psychiatrist Dr. Irwin Rosen confirms, these are the "small events in everyday life that can look insignificant until they touch some old conflict, some long-standing betrayal, or shame the person." What do Caleb and Leslie need to understand about the influence of their fairness models on their fight?

Caleb's family model dictated that you *owed* respect if you loved someone. Caleb was the oldest son, and his father's favorite. His father was the dominant parent, a great guy, as Caleb described him, but one who demanded absolute respect. "There was no arguing when he was mad at you, it was just, 'Do as I say, don't talk back, don't look down, look me in the eye, and no sassing.' If you talked back you got backhanded." His mother had a much milder personality and deferred to her husband. Now Caleb insists on getting his version of respect. He dictates, rather than negotiates his needs with Leslie. There is no fairness in their household, either. Caleb is unfair without even recognizing it. Caleb, like his father, operates from a certainty that he's right. When Leslie opposes him, or simply doesn't see it his way, Caleb angrily blames her. He wants her (without being aware of it) to respond like his mother did to his dad. It's the worst combination for Leslie—no appreciation, just blame.

The couple's dynamic is complicated by the unfinished business Leslie brings from her own family. Leslie tried hard to please her parents, but her efforts went unnoticed. Her parents thought of themselves as the givers, and couldn't recognize how hard she tried to make them proud through her schoolwork, and by being a thoughtful daughter. She got the sense that her mother, in particular, was disappointed in her. Leslie's take-away lesson was, "try harder, because what you give back isn't enough." She grew up feeling inadequate because she couldn't meet her parents' expectations. In her marriage to Caleb, as in her family, she feels unappreciated. But she's getting tired of trying. Caleb's ongoing corrections worsen Leslie's low sense of deserving for herself.

Caleb and Leslie don't recognize how their childhood baggage operates in the present. Their unfinished business creates reactive loyalties (repeating the family models) in their marriage. Caleb still feels really close to his father, and rationalizes his father's harshness. Leslie thinks that her remedy of keeping a friendly but polite distance from her parents leaves her unaffected today. Caleb thinks of himself as the giver in the marriage (and Leslie, the taker), because he believes that as the wage earner he deserves more respect, more attention to what's important to him. Over time, Leslie begins to withdraw emotionally— much as she did as a child when she couldn't do enough to please her parents.

Eventually, their tension spills into every area of their lives. Caleb thinks Leslie is punishing him by her lack of interest in sex, to speak nothing of "wild sex." Leslie protests—how can she want to have sex with someone who doesn't see her efforts, only her screwups? Leslie feels taken for granted, and turns to the kids for love and support. Both think the other needs to change. Neither of them knows how to put things back together again. They're trapped in a cycle of unfair relating and don't see the way out.

As you begin to see from our couple, even seemingly superficial disagreements can transform into destructive patterns of emotional estrangement and general hostilities. Any one of these behaviors may appear obviously destructive and even self-destructive, yet viewed in context, they are also indirect protests about what's not fair. Unfortunately, these response patterns are the equivalent of throwing gasoline on a fire. Caleb and Leslie's marriage already shows these inflammatory signs.

Like many couples, they've discovered that their "stupid" fight is hard to forget, harder still to resolve, and spells trouble ahead. To restore fairness and goodwill, they'll need to trade in their defensiveness for curiosity about the underlying meaning of their repetitive argument, and develop the skills to relate fairly. Until now, *how* they've talked has made things worse. Let's review the common pitfalls on the road to repair.

Why "Stupid" Fights Can Be Hard to Forget

Fast-forward. The incident has blown over. Maybe you've said, "I'm sorry." Maybe your spouse has, too. Or maybe you haven't spoken for a day. Perhaps you've had makeup sex. Then, why can't you get over it? Did a grudge register despite your resolve to let it go? Little things that bother us in relationships are sticky; they build on themselves, because even the petty things in life deserve to be handled fairly. The greater insult to a relationship often occurs not from the disagreement itself, but from how a couple handles it, talks about it, and repairs it.

Research on marital arguments has shown that criticism, contempt, defensiveness, and stonewalling are the four most destructive factors in a fight. Yet, all couples are guilty of engaging in unfair fighting sometimes. But it's a serious problem when these dynamics are dominant. The single-most important factor in creating and maintaining a healthy and enduring marriage is the ability to restore fairness and repair the harm done. But before repair is possible, a couple first needs to learn to disagree without damaging their relationship even more.

Couples often make the mistake of "saying their peace," venting, or telling the other person what they did wrong in an attempt to clear the air. But the "let it all hang out" school of thought has been out of session for a long time. In its place, fair fighting includes no name-calling, no digs, and no contempt. Most therapists and relationship researchers consider fair fighting an important baseline skill. Beyond ending destructive responses, you can also make things worse by offering lame apologies.

Most often when you can't let go of an incident, it's because your partner hasn't made a genuine attempt to acknowledge your side of things. Instead you got a halfhearted apology, that's a politically correct maneuver of saying the right thing without taking true responsibility. I call these halfhearted efforts *sham apologies*. Sham apologies are characterized by "make it go away" responses, "yes, but" defensive responses, and competitive misery—"You've hurt me worse than I've hurt you." Unless you truly care about your partner's experience, then you aren't being fair, and you won't be able to fake an apology. Let's review these impostors to true repair efforts.

Sham Apologies

A sham apology is deceptive. It looks like an apology and sounds like an apology, but it doesn't feel like an apology. In fact, it usually makes a partner feel even worse, less loved. Let's listen for the underlying message sham apologies send, as we see the results of Caleb's sham apologies to Leslie.

Caleb: *"Well, I'm sorry, okay?"*
(Translation: *Would you please get over it?*)

or . . .

Caleb: *"I'm sorry your feelings got hurt."*
(Translation: *Too bad you made such a big deal out of nothing.*)

or . . .

Caleb: *"Well, I'm sorry you're so sensitive to criticism, and that your feelings got hurt. I wouldn't be so stressed out if you just took care of the few things I ask you to do. I knew your mom's house was a disaster zone, I don't know why I thought you'd be any different."*
(Translation: *It's your fault, and your mother's, too.*)

Anyone reading this may be familiar with that old knot in the stomach when things have gone from bad to worse. In the sham apology, partners want to see the issue go away or even win their point at the expense of true repair. This reinforces their sense of being "right." Predictably, nothing improves. Caleb's last sham apology destructively uses knowledge about Leslie's issues without taking any responsibility for his own contribution to their problem. Caleb doesn't offer genuine care or responsibility. He doesn't attempt to understand Leslie's perspective, which results in a deepened sense of injustice. It's a case of adding insult to injury. Caleb wrongly concludes that talking about a conflict is useless (without realizing that it's his blaming, right/wrong model of relating that's the culprit).

Sham apologies can include:
- **Building a better mousetrap.** You try to find flaws in your partner's logic in order to win the next go-round.
- **No acknowledgment.** You tell the other person what they did wrong without crediting their perspective.
- **Shirking responsibility.** You don't own up to your own responsibility. The "What else could *I* have done differently?" is missing.
- **Saying scripted "right, polite" words.** You say the right words, but with no heartfelt expression of understanding. This sham apology is the equivalent of telling your spouse, "I know your feelings got hurt this morning. I'm sorry you took it so hard." Sounds polite, but is dismissive and sends the underlying message "Sorry, sorry, now get over it." It also lays blame with its emphasis of "I'm sorry *you* took it so hard."

EXERCISE: EXORCISE THE SHAM APOLOGY: REPAIR THE RELATIONSHIP

Talk to your partner and tell him or her you would like to have a fairer relationship. Think of an example of the last "stupid" disagreement you had with each other. Practice replacing sham apologies with mutual acknowledgments.

First, get to a calmer physical state so you can recognize the interior script you have in your head about what your spouse did wrong. Fight your urge to continue down that road—it feels good in the short run, but it's not good for your marriage.

Next, stop yourself from building a better mousetrap, in which you find flaws in your partner's logic in order to win the next go-round.

Then, think about what it is you need to have things go better next time. Include your own acknowledgment of what you can do differently in the future.

Before you address your partner, imagine where they were coming from. Can you think of any benign explanation for their actions? Okay, now begin the dialogue, using their perspective as your starting point. Credit them first. Then take responsibility for your own contribution to the problem. Finally make a claim for what you would like to see go differently. (Use "I" statements rather than "you" statements.) Resist the impulse to become defensive. Identify concrete changes, even tiny ones that would help you feel more fairly treated.

"Yes, but": Competitive Suffering

In this situation a partner first acknowledges the harm he's done, but quickly trumps it with an even greater wrong you've done to him. This defensive maneuver sidetracks the couple into competing for the worse injury. Of course this totally undoes any progress and depletes trust even more. Let's use our warring couple to hear how competitive suffering sounds:

CALEB: "I'm sorry I picked a fight over how you loaded the dishwasher."

LESLIE: "Okay. Thanks."

CALEB: "But you know, you can be pretty hard on me, too. I barely get in the door before you're hittin' me with 'Weren't you going to call the plumber? You forgot to take the trash out this morning. The kids are driving me nuts—Johnnie scratched Billy—but don't scream at the kids.'"

LESLIE: "So it's my fault that I never do anything right?"

CALEB: "I didn't say that, you did."

As you can tell, exchanges of competitive suffering cause further damage to a relationship.

It's All in the Timing

Alternately, you can neutralize your apology with an immediate defense of your actions. You prematurely tell your partner why you committed a particular offense. In this case, you haven't allowed your spouse to truly feel understood and cared about before you explain why you trounced on them.

CALEB: "Sorry I made a federal case about how you load the dishwasher."

LESLIE: "Thank you for saying that."

CALEB: "You know I wouldn't lose my temper if you only showed me some respect and took what I said seriously."

LESLIE: "So it's still my fault?"

In this sound bite, Caleb isn't offering an apology, but a justification for his own behavior. Again, more damage is done. As you can see, self-defense isn't an apology. And you even have to be careful about offering well-meaning explanations of your actions before your apology has truly sunk in. If Caleb had let his apology stand, he could later have more reasonably asked Leslie to consider him—not because he was right, but because each position was understandable. Caleb's position: "Let's save money by only running the dishwasher when it's full"; and Leslie's: "It's full enough, and I need the extra plates in time for dinner."

In these examples of sham apologies, talk can feel pointless, and may even be destructive. That's when you need your relationship survival kit. If you don't know how to repair these "stupid" fights, the more likely you are to find yourself in a relationship nosedive. Let's see how to repair the "stupid" things before they veer out of control.

Repair: The Relationship Survival Kit

As important as better communication patterns are, fairness goes beyond these skills to the active repair of harm done—even when it's harm done by a so-called stupid fight. In the everyday abuses of fairness illustrated in this chapter, repair is key, since we all do harm sometimes, even unintentionally. A repertoire of repair skills is the equivalent of a relationship survival kit, and has four essential steps.

The relationship survival kit for restoring fairness builds on our new fairness model of reciprocity, acknowledgment (as positive affirmation), making a claim for fairness, and trust, with the emphasis placed on *restoring* fairness. The four steps are: 1) recognizing the injustice done; 2) acknowledging the (harmful) consequences; 3) making a claim to restore fairness; and 4) replenishing trust. Repair is most efficient, and in most instances most healing, when it occurs between the relating partners. While this seems obvious, couples often fall into the trap of complaining to a third party or trying to let things slide without addressing them. While it's tempting to gripe to a friend about your spouse, that isn't going to help the marriage. Your friend, after all, is more sympathetic to you. The end result is that now both you and your friend think badly about your spouse (making for even tenser get-togethers). Or, if you handle grievances by keeping them to yourself, then your partner has no chance to make amends. In fact, he may not even realize why you're upset. This is when you need the survival kit.

Your survival kit assumes that you and your partner together can heal the emotional and relational distress by restoring fairness. Effective repair involves action steps. Each person must make an honest inventory, and take personal responsibility for the trouble between them. This mutual accountability provides partners with common ground for restoring fairness. You'll use the same model for repair whether incidents of injustice are everyday or enduring, minor or major, because the four components for repair remain the same. It takes the same skills to right unfairness, regardless of the gravity of the event. This new model challenges you to stop fighting to "win" and start playing fair to rebuild trust. Let's review these steps, starting with the recognition of an injustice.

Survival Kit Step One:
Recognizing the Injustice Done

Sometimes the most challenging barrier to true repair is the painful awareness and acceptance of personal responsibility for wrongdoing. Your personal acceptance for unjust behavior may challenge deeply held beliefs you hold about yourself. The recognition of injustice must replace the tendency of partners to cross-blame. Blame may point to a partial truth, but not the whole truth. For repair to occur, you have to first stop counting "who hit whom first," because when it comes to feeling injured, you don't count accurately. You're more likely to remember what caused you to return fire than to recognize the damage you've done. You have to give up the justification for retribution: "I don't fight, I only fight back." The recognition of injustice requires you to stop pointing fingers and start accepting responsibility for hurting your partner, even if it was unintentional, even if you were hurt, too. Again, this isn't a whitewash of hurts—*Okay, we both did damage, we're even*—it's assuming your share of responsibility—that's what's fair to do, and what's within your control.

I think of the act of asking for and offering accountability as a gift. You care enough to close the distance that injustice creates. When you relate accountably, you owe an understanding of your partner's side, as much as you deserve to have your side validated. For all of the potential gains, why is it difficult to recognize and right unfair relating? Why isn't it an intuitively easy thing to understand, much less to do? There are inherent risks of recognizing injustice. You may question why it makes sense to make yourself vulnerable again if you've been hurt before. You may worry about the response you'll get. But the scariest risk is the potential for the loss of the relationship. What if things actually get worse? You may feel safer (if unhappier) not upsetting the applecart.

The Risks of Recognizing Injustice
- You don't want to confront your old beliefs about love and fairness.
- You understand why your partner behaves as he does, and you've just "accepted it."
- You may not get the answer you want . . . and then what?
- You may shake the foundations of the relationship and that's scary.
- You know your partner so well that you predict the outcome won't be pretty. Better to put up with it.
- Your partner may not see your side, and that will feel worse.
- You may break "the rules" of the relationship by claiming a new kind of fairness.

YOU DID HARM

If you accept the risks, the recognition of injustice reveals an apparent paradox. You are sometimes *both* the injurer and the injured party, and sometimes more the one than the other. Yet you may have trouble recognizing that you did harm if:

- You love your spouse.
- You wouldn't deliberately set out to hurt your partner.
- You think of yourself as good, kind, caring, and scrupulously loyal.
- You aren't accustomed to taking responsibility for your actions.
- You feel very hurt by your spouse.
- You have a strong sense of certainty that you're in the "right."

These obstacles to self-awareness and the recognition of injustice prove the saying "Hurt people *hurt* people." Let's return to Caleb and explore the barriers to fair relating that were initially out of his awareness.

REPEATING THE HARM DONE

Many people, like Caleb, overreact when their hot buttons are hit. Their partner who pushed the button (in this case, Leslie with her "lack of respect") is held more accountable than the person who installed it (Caleb's father). At first, Caleb didn't see that his loving but unyielding father laid the groundwork for Caleb's reactivity to Leslie. And because Caleb rationalized that his father's parenting had been good for him (it toughened him up), Caleb had an even harder time accepting that the pattern he was repeating was damaging his relationships with Leslie and their children. Because Caleb had a blind spot about his family's fairness model, he replicated it. Yet Caleb, like many people new to the idea, resisted this truth.

Initially the couple just felt hurt by each other and didn't see that Caleb was repeating his father's demand for absolute respect, while Leslie had chosen a partner who related to her in a similarly devaluing way as her parents had. In the couples therapy with me, Caleb initially made excuses for his father's harsh expectations. *He did the best he could. You're not going to get me to throw him under the bus. He had to be hard on me—I was a handful, and I got in a lot of trouble at school. Don't forget, he worked two jobs and didn't have time for any of my nonsense at the end of a day.*

But after we got through the sugarcoating of his childhood, Caleb started to accept that his father's uncompromising expectations were mirrored in his treatment of Leslie and the kids. Caleb had converted his childhood fairness model into a presumption that Leslie (and the kids) owed him absolute respect—which to Caleb meant doing what he thought was "right." Until his marital crisis, Caleb had viewed his father's demand for respect as a positive feature. Now Caleb understood that these experiences had made him rigid, not stronger.

In his marriage, Caleb's loyalty to his father let his father "off the hook," by displacing the injustice onto Leslie. Because he wasn't as harsh as his father had been, Caleb rationalized his own damaging behavior. This defense of "better by comparison" only served to diminish Caleb's sense of responsibility for the harm he did. Caleb learned that to improve his marriage, he had to learn a different and fairer way of relating.

Caleb was beginning to see that instead of being "right," he'd done more of the damage in the marriage. Leslie sometimes thought she'd made a mistake marrying Caleb. First, she'd had parents who were disappointed by her, and now she'd married someone like that. She hadn't yet recognized that if the two of them were to heal, she couldn't simply think of herself as Caleb's victim. Let's remember that people can be both victim and victimizer, as Caleb was both victim of his father's harsh demand for respect, and victimizer to Leslie (and his children). Leslie was both victim of her parents' and her husband's lack of appreciation, but paid Caleb back by turning the children against him. Caleb and Leslie needed to take the next step in restoring fairness—acknowledging the harmful consequences of their actions.

Survival Kit Step Two: Acknowledging the Harmful Consequences

Acknowledgment can be a show of appreciation, or, in its repair mode, can function as a validation of injustice. When you relate unfairly, you drain trust. To refill trust, you must take responsibility for harmful actions and their consequences. Acknowledging the harmful consequences means truly seeing the hurt, not just from your side (that's easy to do), but from your partner's side, too. It includes actively imagining and expressing, in words and in deeds, your concern for your partner's experience—even when you also feel hurt. Here are some components of this repair effort.

Acknowledging the Harmful Consequences

- **Validate your partner's experience.** "I can understand that my comment sounded critical."
- **Talk about the extra charge you're adding.** "Because my father always talked to me like I was stupid, when I just 'get a whiff' of that from you, I respond indignantly, the way I wish I could have to my father."
- **Offer care and accountability at the same time.** "Thanks for taking on more of the housework. I'm sorry I left too much on you."
- **Be curious about your partner's experience.** "I didn't see your side of things before. Now I understand you and our interactions better."
- **Take responsibility.** "I'm sorry I was in a bad mood and took it out on you."

Exercise: Acknowledging the Harmful Consequences: Repair the Relationship

Think about a "stupid" fight: Then read the list above. As you review the list, think of what grade you'd give yourself in your efforts to sort out even an everyday conflict, with the use of acknowledgment. What grade would you give your partner? What grade would you give each other? What can you improve?

Openly acknowledging the fallout of unfairness matters both to the individual and to the health of a relationship. Remember, acknowledgment works best when it's reciprocal. It's not that every injustice is fifty-fifty. But neither is it one hundred/zero. When both partners take their share of responsibility for harm and for healing, they have moved beyond the blame game. Now let's return to Caleb and Leslie to hear how the second step of the repair process might sound. Caleb needs to own up to the harm his unrealistic demand for total respect has caused. His acknowledgment begins to restore fairness and rebuild trust.

CALEB: "Leslie, I'm beginning to understand how awful I've made you feel and how critical I've been over this stupid issue of loading the dishwasher, and just in general. That's my problem. My ideas about respect were straight out of my dad's family. I see how I thought I deserved the same respect, and how I thought you didn't care about what mattered to me. Now I see that how I've treated you wasn't right."

LESLIE: "That means a lot to me for you to say that."

CALEB: "I thought how I treated you was normal, because that's how I grew up, and I was angry that you were letting down your end of the bargain. You know, when I was a kid, I had exactly one chance to do it right, and after that, there was hell to pay. I guess I always thought that was okay—like, what doesn't kill you makes you stronger."

Here, Caleb demonstrates personal accountability, remorse, and compassion. His insight shows his willingness to be responsible and vulnerable. Caleb's validation of Leslie's experience stands in sharp contrast to his old impatient and condescending ways. Caleb explains but doesn't excuse the way his old model of fairness distorted his perceptions and did harm.

Did the balm of acknowledgment work for Leslie? Leslie was surprised and moved by Caleb's regrets and remorse. His honesty about himself made a huge difference in how she felt about him. Leslie then returned acknowledgment, as she also took her share of responsibility for their conflicts, and for their healing.

LESLIE: "I feel so relieved that you see how unfair it was to think I was disrespecting you whenever I didn't do things your way. I guess I never understood that I was also reacting in part to feeling as though I could never please you, just like with my parents. When you corrected me—at first I tried harder, but later I gave up and went on the attack mode. I felt so angry that I refused to do it your way, and then I got the kids to take my side." Leslie hesitated, then added, "I'm not a detail person—you should know that by now. But, I do see your point about the energy savings. Could we call a truce?"

CALEB: "Deal."

LESLIE: "I'm sorry I hurt you, too." Caleb smiled and gave her a hug.

In this vignette, Caleb was able to own up to the consequences of his unfair behavior. But it might have worked out differently. Suppose he could not, or would not, take responsibility? In that case, Leslie would have experienced yet another injustice at his hands. But Leslie, like anyone who has endured unfairness, only has two real choices—exit and voice—and both have risks. With exit, you vote with your feet. You leave the relationship, literally—

physically or emotionally by distancing yourself. Voice is the messier of the two options and involves making a claim for fairness, our next step in repair.

Survival Kit Step Three:
Making a Claim to Restore Fairness

Even if your partner fails to own up to an injustice, it's important to assert what's fair to you. Simply put, stand up for fairness. Making a claim for fair consideration is in your control. It expresses an earned request for consideration on your terms. You can't control your partner's response, but you can translate your idea of fairness into change requests that are meaningful to you. You'll increase your chances of receiving fair treatment when you're able to do this. Let's return to a pre-enlightened Caleb to illustrate how Leslie would make a claim for fairness.

Like many women, Leslie had initially tried silence to cope with her frustration with Caleb. Self-silencing in women is an avoidance strategy that can increase the long-term risk of heart disease and depression. For Leslie, the short-term result was a mild irritable depression. At least by voicing her feelings, and by claiming what she wanted, she had the opportunity to release her pain constructively, and hold Caleb accountable for what was fairer to her. By making a claim, she would also be taking responsibility for changing her part of the unproductive, circular dynamic between them. Remember, each partner has to take a share of responsibility to create a new fairness. Making a claim is distinctly different from unleashing your anger (however justifiable) or getting into a blaming match. The goal of making a claim is to stop the unfair relating by clearly stating what you want, deserve, and expect. Ideally, you can generously include your understanding of your partner's position, even when it has been unfair. With Leslie, this might sound like this:

LESLIE: "Caleb, I've been trying to understand what gets you so upset when the dishwasher is run half empty. I know that you had to watch every penny growing up, and that anytime you see waste, you see red."

CALEB: "Well, if you know it upsets me, why do you do it?"

LESLIE: "Sometimes I'm running pots and pans and dishes that are really crusted over. Sometimes I've run out of silverware or plates or glasses. I'm not doing it to go against you. I can almost feel sorry for how you were treated as a kid, until you treat me the same way, and then my sympathy goes out the window. I need you to change how you treat me, and how you talk to me. If you act like that again, I'm going to say stop it, and walk away! I'm not going to get sucked into explanations of why I'm doing what I'm doing. That doesn't help either of us. I'm asking you to change your behavior."

Leslie was taking a risk. Perhaps Caleb would blow her off, as he'd done in the past. But Leslie had determined that she had more to gain by advocating for herself. Remember, when you make a claim for fairness you're not in charge of the outcome—that's a two-person enterprise. You're only responsible for asking for and offering fair consideration. Asking for fair treatment is empowering, even if at first you don't get the outcome you deserve. Making a claim holds your partner accountable, and fortifies your own reality. If you chronically silence yourself, you may lose track of your own feelings. On balance, the risks are often worth taking.

PLAYING TO THE OUTCOME WITH THE HIDDEN CLAIM

Are there other choices to cope with unfairness besides exit (leaving in some fashion) or voice (making a claim)? Sometimes instead of silence, partners skirt around their true feelings and play to the outcome. When you play to the outcome, you try to control getting what you want without directly asking. The back-door logic is that at least then you're not vulnerable to getting rebuffed. This self-protective (but manipulative) approach intuitively (though incorrectly) seems safer than asking for what you need. Unsurprisingly, this maneuver to avoid negotiation creates more mistrust. Playing to the outcome often has a hidden claim embedded in it.

- Honey, I was thinking that it would be fun to have some people over to see our new deck, so I'm just waiting to hear back from about ten to fifteen friends for this Saturday. (Hidden claim: I want to celebrate, whether you do or not.)
- Oh, didn't I tell you that my son and daughter planned to throw me a sixtieth-birthday party? I thought that would save you the trouble. (Hidden claim: I don't want to have to choose between you and my kids. Let's not get into that again.)
- I couldn't get a flight back from Las Vegas tonight, so I'll see you tomorrow. (Hidden claim: I wanted to stay overnight and go to the casino, but I didn't want to give you veto power.)
- I got a real deal on the flight to spend the holidays with my folks! Isn't that great? (Hidden claim: I want to spend the holidays with my family, and I was afraid you wouldn't, so I made the plans without checking with you first.)

Making a claim is just the opposite of playing to the outcome. You're taking a chance up front by voicing your needs, knowing that you might not get what you want or even deserve. At first expressing and negotiating your needs can feel childishly, irrationally risky. From an early age, you quickly learn that it hurts when needs aren't met, and you learn to avoid that emotional pain. Adults, like children, do their best to avoid the risks of voicing their needs. I encourage you to think of making a claim as empowering yourself through fair relating. Let's convert the examples above from playing to the outcome to making a claim for and negotiating fairness.

- I'd really like to celebrate our new deck with some friends. How would you feel about me inviting people over for a get-together? I know you like to take the weekend to relax, but I'll do what I can ahead of time, so it doesn't all fall to you.

- It's really important to me that my kids get to throw me this sixtieth-birthday party. They really want to do something for me, and I don't want to tell them thanks but no thanks. I know that you don't always see eye to eye with them, so what would you need so that you didn't feel left out? (Making a claim ideally entails a willingness to consider the other person's needs.)

- I've had a tiring business meeting, and I'd like to stay over in Las Vegas this evening instead of catching the red-eye home. I find going to the casinos relaxing. I know you aren't crazy about me gambling, but how about if we agree on a "not to exceed limit"? (Here a claim is made while consideration for the other person's concern is extended.)

- I know that spending the holidays with my folks isn't your first choice, but I hope that we can work it out so that we both get some of what we need from our vacation time.

The rewards of making a claim are self-empowerment and the possibility for a fairer and closer relationship. Making a claim (voice) beats the alternative of letting experiences of mistrust accumulate and destabilize a relationship (exit). By making a claim for fairness—and attempting to negotiate fairly—you stand to gain. At the very least, you aren't shortchanging yourself by self-silencing, and you've left the door open for future change. Who stands to benefit from making a claim to restore fairness? First, you do. Secondarily, your relationships do. Let's return to Leslie and Caleb and see what making a claim and negotiating fairness sound like.

Leslie and Caleb Make Claims

Leslie had often called Caleb a "control freak," one among many choice names. Her anger at his corrections was justified, but she hadn't spelled out what she needed him to change. I encouraged her to write up a list of actions she'd like Caleb to take. Instead of bombarding him with twenty things at once, I suggested that they should start with one item per week. That would allow him to make an effort she would notice, and have time to reinforce it before making another claim. Leslie identified both everyday changes and enduring changes she needed Caleb to undertake. Small changes are obviously easier to implement than personality overhauls, so it's important to break things down into small steps. The short-term goal is to decrease the negatives and increase the positives. The long-term goal is to rebalance fairness, rebuild trust, and restore loving feelings. Leslie's claims were:

- Stop telling me the right way to do things.
- Stop being critical.
- Tell me when you see my side of things.
- Offer compliments.
- Tell me what you appreciate about what I do.
- Ask me how my day was.
- Apologize when you've dumped on me.
- Soften your complaint with warmth.

And what might Caleb fairly claim? You might wonder whether Caleb had any "rights" to ask for anything given his earlier unreasonable demand for respect. While the onus was on Caleb to take the first steps to earn back trust, he deserved consideration, too. Healing through fair relating is always a two-way street. So in turn, Caleb asked Leslie:

- Don't use the children against me.
- Catch me doing something good . . . tell me when you notice my new efforts.
- Give me a hug when I come in the door.
- Help me when I slip up.

Making claims is a significant aspect of the shift toward a new kind of fairness. Every couple needs to identify the particular action steps that will help them restore fairness in their relationship. Listed below are both everyday and high-impact examples of claims:

Making a Claim to Restore Fairness: Sample Action Steps

Everyday Changes
- Ask for my input.
- Greet me with hello and good-bye.
- Don't read the newspaper at the kitchen table during our breakfast.
- Protect our date night from your children's plans with you.
- Ask about my day.
- Ask for a rain check instead of just turning me down for sex.
- Tell me about how you are.
- Ask about how I *really* am.
- Recognize that I'm trying.
- Don't read your e-mails during dinner.
- Give me some credit and appreciation before you point out what I haven't done.
- Let me calm down, and don't regard my cooling off as a rejection.
- Plan a family day with the kids and me.
- Come home for supper.

High-Impact Changes
- Move jobs for my career.
- Put me through graduate school.
- Put the house in my name.
- Stop drinking.
- Put our monies into joint accounts.
- Come to couples therapy with me.

- Split the household responsibilities and child care more evenly.
- Have a child.
- Stop blaming and criticizing me.
- Don't call me names.
- Stop threatening to divorce me when we fight.

EXERCISE: MAKING CLAIMS: REPAIR THE RELATIONSHIP

Identify several "stupid" fights from your relationship. Then think about your own ideas for making a claim for fairer relating. Now, write your own claims beside your "stupid" fights list. Think about how you could make claims for the two or three most important items, in a nonthreatening, even acknowledging way. To be fair, and to make this exercise more likely to yield positive results, explain the process of making a claim to your partner and then ask your partner to do the same—identify "stupid" fights, and think of a claim to make about that example. Work on everyday changes at first. Save the high-impact changes for later.

The circular aspect of true repair blurs the lines between injured and injurer. Each bears some responsibility for injury as well as repair. Clearly, the partner who has done more harm is more in charge of the repair efforts, but each partner must work to rebuild trust.

Survival Kit Step Four: Replenishing Trust

"How do I learn to trust him again? Because right now I can't."
(Zara, married six years to Juan)

"She thinks that she's the only one who's been hurt." *(Juan)*

A powerful indicator of injustice is the loss of trust. When your wants and needs aren't fairly considered, trust gets drained. The very first psychological task in life is the development of basic trust. However, trust, like love and fairness, isn't an entirely stable element in and across relationships. Trust is built up by reciprocity and maintained by the ability to negotiate fairness. When a couple's trust level gets depleted it takes repair work to refill it.

Trust is replenished through all of the repair skills we've reviewed: recognizing an injustice done, acknowledging the harmful consequences, and making a claim to restore fairness. Trust grows when your partner demonstrates care, sincere remorse, and takes steps to prevent hurtful recurrences. Yet you and your partner have to define and negotiate the steps that are most meaningful to each of you to rebuild trust.

As your reserves of trust rise, feelings of love and security flow. Your relationship begins an upward, hopeful spiral. Even when injuries are disproportionate, as they were with Caleb and Leslie, no one partner can replenish trust alone. That's because trust, like fairness, is *between* people. It's more than the sum of its parts.

In Caleb and Leslie's marriage, Caleb had done more damage by his ongoing insistence on a deferential show of respect. To rebuild trust, Caleb acknowledged the harm he'd caused, showed remorse, and took steps to both understand and change his behavior. Therapeutically, it was also important not to overload Caleb with full responsibility for their problems. That would be inaccurate and unfair. Leslie brought her own baggage to the marriage, too. Her unfinished business had left her quite sensitive to feeling unappreciated. Leslie's ability to own up to her part helped Caleb accept the lion's share of the problem. As Caleb became more capable of recognizing injustices he had both endured and served up, he cared more about being fair-minded, and less about being respected or "right." One day he said to me, "You know, it's no fun being right anymore, I don't even want to. What a change. Having a better relationship feels like winning now. I hope my kids can learn from what I'm doing now—and not from what they saw me do in the past."

Who stood to gain from the couple's changes? Their kids, for sure. They saw a calmer, fun side of their dad, and a more lighthearted side of their mom that they'd almost forgotten. Respect was exchanged for negotiating fairness— even with the kids. Their parents and siblings, too, got a secondary benefit, as both Caleb and Leslie began to relate more from truth than respect, more from directness than protective distance. Clearly, more than anyone, it was Caleb and Leslie who gained from their new model of fairness that they created together. For Caleb and Leslie, as for all beginners practicing a new skill, there were times that their new understanding involved a struggle. At times Leslie still felt unappreciated, and Caleb felt disrespected, but with practice they changed a formerly tense and unfair pattern. They learned to catch themselves when they started to have these familiar and painful feelings and do a reality check to see what was really going on. They were able to repair the everyday abuses of fairness before they became an enduring feature of their marriage. Sometimes, they were even able to laugh at themselves.

But how do you make sure happy endings last? You explore your understanding about what a "stupid" fight means to you and your partner. You negotiate a new model of fairness that creates a generous environment of reciprocity, acknowledgment, and a willingness to replace blame with claims. Leslie and Caleb's situation shows that resolving a "stupid" fight can lead to a whole new way of relating fairly.

With the background noise of the small abuses of relationships playing, let's explore the topics of money, children, chores, and sex, when they're not just "stupid" fights but solidly established roadblocks to a couple's growth. You'll see how the skills to repair fairness can be applied to the challenges common to marriage. So, with your new survival kit in hand, let's move on to the growing pains that partners face.

MONEY, CHILDREN, CHORES, AND SEX: RESOLVING FAIRNESS AND THE GROWING PAINS OF LOVE

Couple #1

She said: "I've been reduced to an allowance! Why? I'll tell you why. My husband is totally clueless about how much things cost—the kids' clothes, their sports, their music, the groceries, gas for all the chauffeuring I do! It makes me so crazy there are times I think, this marriage is for the birds!"

He said: "She has no concept of the value of a dollar! She wants a nice vacation at the beach every year, so to pull that off I had to start giving her money for the week, and saving the rest. She'd never save a dime!"

Couple #2

She said: "When the baby was born our relationship went downhill. Suddenly we were locked in these male/female roles. By 'locked,' I mean, someone threw away the key. It hasn't been the same since."

He said: "I come home from a hard day's work, and she won't even let me sit down to read my e-mails. She holds out her arms—to hand over the baby. Now I'm doing two jobs."

Couple #3

She said: "From that first night of our honeymoon it was clear to me that sex was going to be a problem. I wanted it to be romantic and he wanted it to be kind of kinky. We're still hashing that one out."

He said: "It's not like I'm asking for anything weird. You'd think she'd been brought up in a convent the way she treats me."

Being fair in love sounds like a wonderful ideal until it meets up with the commonly experienced growing pains that happen when couples try to decide what's fair when it comes to money, kids, chores, and sex. These are the problems that top the list of what couples argue about. These challenges of marriage require the flexibility to negotiate the shifting needs of both partners. Unlike the idiosyncratic, everyday abuses of fairness introduced in chapter 7, the issues of this chapter are faced by nearly every couple, and require partners to change and grow as their relationship evolves. While each topic has its own particular set of problems, learning to fairly resolve any one conflict teaches you the skills to resolve others. Though the topics of this chapter include almost universally experienced issues, inevitably they take couples by surprise. No matter how many generations before you have juggled the practicalities and inherent tensions that money, kids, chores, and sex bring, you're sorting them out for the first time.

For example with finances, you have to sort out: *Who makes the money, who manages it, who spends it, how do your answers to these questions change over time, and who decides?* Then there's parenting. How do you divide parenting responsibilities if both partners work full-time? *Who raises the children, who decides what's best?* And then there are the career questions. *Whose career "counts" more?* And while everyone is busy with children and careers—the chore wars heat up. *Who's going to do what, and whose job is it to clean the house week after week, do the laundry, chauffer the kids, cut the grass, wash the car, shop for the birthday gifts?* It's impossible to avoid differences of opinion about who does what and when. You also have to decide if your roles are gender defined, or to what extent. *Does that work for each of you? How can things be fair when they aren't even?* And in the midst of this, you're trying to figure out when sex fits in—or if it does.

Sexual desire, as you know, changes, too. Differences in a couple's sexual needs and desires may be a matter of biology, time, or energy. You're left to figure out: *Whose schedule sex is on, with what frequency, and whose preference counts.* The fluctuations of emotional and sexual feelings of attraction to your spouse are also related to how fairly you're navigating all the other demands of life.

With all the demands on partners and changing circumstances, the question for marriage is not, *Will we have challenges,* but, *Will we choose to grow from them?* In my work, I'm always interested in a couple's emotional growth because no one pays much attention to this aspect of adult development until it's off-course or someone's in a crisis. We often think of development as exclusively reserved for childhood; we think we come to marriage fully formed. But couples, like individuals, also have to grow up. Development is a bit like the process when you're born—the losses come before the gains. With birth, you lose the comfort of the womb before you gain the freedom of autonomous life. Losses sometimes come before the gains for growth in couples' relationships, too. The losses may include the loss of a childlike dependency on a partner; the loss of assumptions about love and fairness; the loss of blame as a crutch; the loss of an old, familiar way of relating; the loss of doing things the way you've always done them—and your parents have done them. But the gains for both individual and couple may include an increased sense of freedom that comes with self-awareness and accountability; a feeling of closeness that comes with functioning as a team; an enhanced experience of empowerment that replaces insecurity and vulnerability; a surer footing about what is fair across all relationships; and a solid base of trust and love. There's as much, if not more, knowledge to be mastered in a couple's relationship as in individual development. In fact, the realm *between* people is where there's the greatest possibility for growth. This chapter guides you through the common challenges you'll face—not just what to expect but also how to grow through stress to fairness.

Inequitable But Fair?

Yet, how do couples find fairness when real imbalances of time, money, division of labor and child-care responsibilities exist between them? These growing pains can be even more distressing when partners start with the assumption that their relationship should be equal. The myth in American culture is that things are equal. We are created equal; we have equal rights;

and we are equal partners in marriage. Right? Wrong. The first two rights are protected by law, but marriage has not yet been designated an equal opportunity venture. It's usually inequitable, but it can still be fair—even when it comes to money, children, chores, and sex.

When is uneven or inequitable fair? Social scientists point to the family as an institution that ideally meets each member's needs regardless of their input. For example, I think we'd all agree (if we limit consensus to this culture and era) that it's fair for a child to receive food, clothing, and shelter despite not contributing to his parents financially. This model of family life is fair, though not precisely equitable. If we didn't value fairness, it would be equitable to have a child earn his way. But, of course, you aren't married to a child—although sometimes in exasperation, a spouse will complain that a partner is acting like one. So how does the notion of equity apply to couples?

It's tricky for partners to draw a line between what's fair (even if it is inequitable) and what's inequitable and unfair. One spouse may contribute more money, the other may put in more parenting time, cooking time, and cleaning time. Or one partner (usually the woman) may work as many hours, but still have the other responsibilities of child care, housecleaning, and doctor's appointments—in other words, "the second shift." According to a recent study, women still do about twice as much housework as men, even when they're both fully employed. It's hardly a surprise then that nearly 60 percent of women feel the division of labor is unfair to them, whereas only 11 percent of men feel that way. Complicating things further—an arrangement of responsibilities can seem fair at one time, but unfair at another. A change in circumstances may also require rebalancing what's fair. These transitions include the birth of a child, the illness of a spouse or family member, a change in job responsibilities, a new job, job loss, a change in income, redistribution of household responsibilities, simply getting older, an awareness of the need for something different, or a change in lifestyle. Some of these changes are welcomed—even celebrated. But when they require a renegotiation of what's fair, some couples struggle. It's up to partners to assess whether their expectations are fair or unfair, reasonable or unreasonable, realistic or unrealistic, equitable or inequitable. But how do partners decide?

First you look at the "shoulds." The *shoulds* of a relationship form an important aspect of your expectations (reasonable or unreasonable) for give-and-take with your partner. Role divisions are less likely to be either fair or mutually satisfying when they're unconsciously dictated by the *shoulds*: what you *should* do as a wife, what you *should* do as a stepparent, what you *should* do as a mother, what you *should* do as a daughter. Living a life by *shoulds* is also oppressive to men: what you *should* do as a husband, father, and son, not to mention the *shoulds* of being a good employee and provider for the family. The expectations that you carry for yourself and for your partner are shaped by your gender, cultural and societal expectations, and the historical era. More important, the *shoulds* for who does what in a marriage are formed by each partner's family legacy, values, and loyalty expectations. Partners who impose role divisions and values on each other often end up on a collision course.

One couple I saw several years ago illustrates this problem of the *shoulds*. After their youngest started kindergarten, Janet, who had stayed at home until then, took a sign language class. To her surprise, she loved it so much that she next enrolled in an intensive program that trained interpreters. Soon she was offered a part-time job in a school for deaf children. She happily accepted and reflected, "I felt like I had found myself. I know it's a cliché, but it's true."

Unfortunately, Janet's husband, Eddie, wasn't so thrilled with the new deal. Here's his side of things: "The house is always a mess. She used to do a great job taking care of me and the kids, and the house. It worked for the family. It was what I thought she *wanted*. I don't see what was so wrong with how it was. The times we used to sit in front of the TV and relax are history. I never know if my shirts will be clean, if the kids will get to school with everything they need, or if there'll be milk in the house, or dinner on the table. Could I get my real wife back?"

Their marriage had quickly changed in dramatic ways—and unhappily for Eddie. The question before them, as it would be for any couple, was what are the *shoulds* they both carried? Could they look at their former expectations for reciprocity and find a new way of negotiating what is fair now? The old model had worked well for the family and for Eddie. Eddie had expected

Janet to orient herself exclusively around what he and the kids needed. She had done that for several years but began to feel trapped by her role. Eddie in particular was reacting from some very well-established and comfortable *shoulds*. From his perspective, Janet had pulled the rug out from under his feet. If Eddie couldn't explore his old assumptions, he and Janet would remain caught in this storm and be blown around indefinitely or until one of them simply gave up from exhaustion.

Eddie typifies what happens in a marriage when the deal no longer works for one of the partners. What you can see from this brief slice of life are Eddie's protests at his losses before the gains of a new fairness emerge. But Eddie can't turn back the clock or reinstate their traditional roles by stomping his feet and screaming, "It's not fair!"—as we all feel like doing sometimes. If he and Janet are to get beyond this, Eddie will have to recognize what his old assumptions were, and Janet will need to acknowledge that there are losses as well as gains for the couple. Janet has experienced her individual gains first, but it won't be fair—and it won't work for the couple unless Eddie gains something, too. Beyond the concrete advantage of her income, Eddie might acquire a new appreciation for what Janet had contributed to the family. Janet might better imagine what the workaday world had been like for him, now that she's in it again. They might each juggle child-care responsibilities, and from that share more of the ups and downs of parenting. In this process of creating a new kind of fairness, they'll need to negotiate a deal that works for each of them, *and* both of them.

As you read through the remainder of this chapter, I encourage you to spot and then challenge your own expectations concerning the "right" thing for yourself or your partner to do. I've included an exercise at the end of this chapter designed to heighten your awareness of your *shoulds*. Your enhanced ability to evaluate and possibly revise role expectations allows for greater clarity as you negotiate *what's fair, and from whose point of view*. Let's begin our tour of the inequities of marriage, starting with the chore wars, where the *shoulds* are heavy ammunition.

The Chore Wars: Division of Labor/Parenting

"Marriages with children can't be fair." *(Diane, forty-one-year-old mother of two)*

"Housework? Him? You have got to be kidding me." *(Mary, married nine years)*

One of the commonest developmental challenges for couples arises with the addition of children, which prompts the issue of who *should* do what. Many years ago, when my children were quite young, someone sent me a greeting card for new parents that captured the spirit of all the many tasks at hand. On it was a circle with an arrow to spin. On alternating sections of the circle were the words, "Your turn. My turn. Your turn. My turn." Not only do couples get a new role and identity (parents), but as the chore wars heat up, they also have to redefine child care, household, and work responsibilities.

"The kids were running around like wild animals, and I was in the kitchen, trying to finish cooking, and then I had to change the baby, too. Eli had been home for about an hour. He was just sitting on the couch, with the TV and the computer on, checking his e-mails. I yelled to him in the next room that I needed help. He hollered back: 'I've worked all day, this is your job.' He kept playing on the computer, ignoring the kids and me. I finally got so fed up that I marched into the living room and threw the baby's dirty diaper at him." (Bobbie, married eight years)

Is this an example of women's lib gone wild, or a more serious commentary on how couples contend when the division of labor feels unfair? Remember our chimpanzees that were stuck with nonreciprocating partners? Eventually, they became so angry they hurled their feces at the unfair chimps. Humans aren't that different. We're powerfully motivated by fair—and unfair treatment. Complaints about the day-to-day division of chores and responsibilities reveal very concrete examples of discrepancies between give-and-take. Add children to the mix of responsibilities, and the balance becomes even more lopsided. In my office it sounds like this: *He says*, "All I do is clean up the kitchen and take the kids to the park," and *she says*, "He never helps around the house, and he leaves his dirty socks all over the place! If he'd just clean up once in a blue moon I'd be nicer." *He says*, "She's a shopaholic. She brings home bags of clothes, and I say, 'How much did you save today?'" *She says*, "I'm the external memory drive. Everyone depends on me to remember everything, and then remind them." *He says*, "All she does is nag me to do one more thing on the honey-do list. Then she wants me to woo her. Why should I? We're married." It's not surprising that a recent study reported that the topics of children and housework top the list of issues that women quarrel about, while men more often argue over sex and money. Fairness can seem in short supply with so many demands on time and energy and plenty of responsibilities to go around. But to the mother who adamantly declared: "Marriages with children can't be fair," I would respond that marriages in general aren't equitable. No two partners carry exactly the same burdens or responsibilities. The family is a unique institution where what you put in and what you get out doesn't usually operate on a quid pro quo basis. That's because marriages run at least partly on trust.

But when trust is iffy, couples keep score, and the results can look absurd. One young mother told me about how she "evened up" the time of breast-feeding their son. For every three hours she breast-fed, her husband put in an hour of housework. However quirky their solution seemed, this couple was struggling with a fundamental and important question: How can you trust that things will be fair when your contributions are not (and cannot be) shared, even, or equitable? When the inputs are different, what does each partner get for what they contribute? And how do you decide?

The goal in a family and for a couple is to both consider and strive to meet everyone's needs (but not by an exact marketplace accounting). Yet when there are real inequities, can the seesaw of reciprocity be balanced and fair? That's the challenge each of the couples in this chapter faces, as they use the relationship survival kit to create a new fairness. Let's view a scene from the chore wars to see how one couple, Jennifer and Greg, negotiate the growing pains of an unequal division of labor.

The Chore Wars: Who Does More?

A young professional woman arrived at a cocktail party without her husband, a respected businessman some years her senior. A guest turned to her and asked, "Where's Tony? Is he babysitting the kids tonight?" She replied coolly, "No, he's parenting tonight." *(Christine, age thirty-eight)*

Since the typical family today has two wage earners, the traditional family of breadwinner/stay-at-home mom is now in the minority. And the "who does what" around the house is equally in flux. Jennifer and Greg typify this problem area. When the kids are sick, she takes time off from work. When they need a babysitter, it's Jennifer who spends hours on the phone finding one. When the babysitter needs to reach a parent, or the school has a problem to report, Jennifer gets the call. When Jennifer is late getting home from work, she walks in to the scene of Greg standing in front of the refrigerator, asking, "What's for dinner?" Jennifer is sick and tired of pulling the late shift at home. Yet when she complains, Greg makes fun of how silly she is to argue over who cooks dinner—since he can't cook. Greg and Jennifer need a fairness overhaul in the chore wars before their marriage turns sour.

In their first appointment, I asked each of them to take turns telling about this problem area. Jennifer jumped in first with her side: "We both work, though I usually get home first. I get dinner started, then help the kids do their homework, and later get them to bed. I'm also the default parent on weekends. There I am making the kids' breakfast, and he's reading the paper, and then I'm playing with them or organizing their day, and he's up in his study writing. Greg says he can be interrupted, but that's not really how it is. We all tiptoe around Dad, who's always at his darn computer. And then, in the evening after the kids are in bed, I'm somewhere folding the clothes. I nearly whacked Greg over the head last week when he said, 'But, honey, you like to fold the clothes.' The other week, when I had lunch with a friend, and Greg was home all day, he didn't do a thing to help. When I came home, I felt like throwing plates I was so mad."

Greg mounted a weak defense. "But, Jen, I did watch the kids that day. And I can't help it if you hardly ever take a break. I encourage you to get some downtime, but you never just sit and relax." Jennifer's frustration rose to a pitch, "Einstein, that's because there are still things to do! I'd love to relax, but who's going to cook dinner, do the wash, and fold the clothes? You're in your study or watching goofy TV with the kids. When I got home from my lunch last week it took two hours for me to clean up the house after the three of you. It's hardly worth going out! Besides, once I get home you head straight for your study again." Jennifer's face slowly turned crimson as she made this last point.

Greg, who was now equally aggravated, said, "But, Jen, you really could interrupt me—I'm there if you need me to watch the kids. But you don't like how I do things, because you're so much neater than me. If I don't do it 'your way'—whether it's doing the laundry, or dealing with the kids, or getting takeout instead of cooking, you give me an earful. Listen, if you want to go down the 'look at all I do' lane, let me remind you that I take care of the cars and the yard work and all the money—the checkbook, the savings account, the investments, and the taxes. Sometimes I think you forget how much I have to juggle. Besides, I'm always under pressure to make bonus money, and manage my group of employees. You think when I'm reading e-mail it's for fun? Believe me, it's not fun. It's work!"

Competitive Suffering

Jennifer and Greg are engaged in competitive suffering—the who has it worse game, where there are no winners. Both feel burdened and neither feels appreciated for their contributions. Lapsing into competitive suffering is understandable, but it doesn't restore fairness. In order to assess and more fairly balance responsibilities, I asked Jennifer and Greg to fill out a comprehensive responsibility list, which I've included at the end of this chapter. The list asks who does what and what an ideal distribution of tasks would be. This was their "homework" for the following session.

The next week Greg and Jennifer came in, lists in hand. "We spent about two hours on this darn thing!" Jennifer exclaimed. "After we each checked off the lists individually we compared them. Let's just say we didn't see eye to eye on who does what, but finally, we agreed on what to change and share—at least for the most part. By the end, I have to say, we were laughing at some of it." Their ability to talk with each other and work things out was a good sign. But what exactly did they learn?

Upon completion of their lists, Jennifer and Greg were able to recognize some of the imbalances that burdened Jennifer. Completing the lists also helped them realize how much *each* did. As Greg put it, "I think it's amazing how hard we're both working." The discussion of chores then moved to a deeper level, to the model of fairness and expectations for give-and-take that each brought to the marriage. What Jennifer and Greg needed (long after they stopped seeing me) was the ability to evaluate the meaning of their differences, now and in the future. Then they could transfer those skills to other challenges in the years ahead. They could learn how to recognize injustices not only from their side but also from their spouse's perspective. They could begin to acknowledge any unfair consequences their partner had sustained, and make claims from a new negotiated fairness. Greg and Jennifer took turns talking about their old models that had got them into trouble.

Greg acknowledged that he had held unspoken and unfair expectations (*shoulds*) for Jennifer to be in charge of the household and the kids, because she was the mom. He felt entitled to downtime when he got home—after all, he put in longer hours at the office. But Greg hadn't understood how worn out Jennifer was because she always looked so efficient. Greg struggled with the reality that his model of fairness was based on how little his parents had asked of him, beyond getting good grades in school. There had been very few expectations for him to help out around the house. Greg had unwittingly transferred this model to his marriage. He took a hard look at his subconscious and unfair assumption that being the primary wage earner (he made about 30 percent more than Jennifer) meant that Jennifer should be on the front line at home. After all, she worked, too. Greg told Jennifer that their old deal had seemed fair (and normal), because it so closely mirrored his childhood model of what was expected of him. More important, he acknowledged how the deal was no longer working for Jennifer—or, for that matter, both of them. Jennifer was put in an overgiving position, which in turn made her mad at Greg, which took a toll on warmth, affection, and their sex life. She'd say she was too tired for sex, but underneath her fatigue was her resentment. She was pulling away from him. Jennifer agreed with Greg's assessment. The chore wars definitely had a negative impact on the couple. They both agreed on that.

Jennifer also owned up to her part in how they got stuck. For a few years after the kids were born, she stayed at home. After her return to work, she and Greg never figured out which responsibilities needed to get reshuffled. Jennifer had become the expert on the kids, and the expert on cooking, as well as knowing what was needed to keep the household running smoothly. She realized—and courageously admitted—that in some ways she enjoyed the fact that the kids were closer to her and that everyone teased Greg about the one meal he knew how to make—scrambled eggs.

Jennifer had some deep convictions about what was important, but Greg didn't share them all. Jennifer brought more *shoulds* to the marriage than she'd realized. She had clear expectations of what and how Greg *should* parent the kids. He *should* cook, not order takeout; he *should* play games with them, not watch "goofy" TV shows. No wonder Greg slacked off, when the message he got from her was: *You're not doing it right!* I suspected that Jennifer's limited ability to take time for herself was related to an (un)fair model she learned in her family. When I asked her about that, she confirmed that she tried to live up to her mother's standards for running the household and raising children, despite their different circumstances (her mother had been a stay-at-home mom until her brother was in high school and Jennifer was twelve). Jennifer felt that since her mother was able to maintain "Martha Stewart standards," she should be able to as well.

Once Jennifer started to identify all of the *shoulds* that informed her life, she saw that some of them were the very things that kept her stuck and angry. She realized that she had to be willing to share her role as expert. If Greg was to do meals on certain evenings, Jennifer had to relax her standards about what the kids ate. She had to stop expecting Greg to defer to her on kids' issues and let him parent them in his own way (she was strict, while he was lax; she allowed them to watch only educational TV while Greg liked to watch "junk" TV with them). In addition to giving up some of her chores, Jennifer also gladly gave up the role of taskmaster and drill sergeant for the kids. In order to share the minuses, Jennifer also had to share the pluses of her parental role. She had wanted to give up feeling so resentful and overwhelmed, but she hadn't bargained on letting go of feeling that special closeness that comes from being supermom, and the preferred parent. Now Jennifer recognized that it would be fairer to everyone, including the children, for Greg to be a real presence at home, rather than the figurehead (and the recipient of her resentment). Maybe they could all become closer and have more fun together.

As Jennifer and Greg gave up their competitive suffering and stopped taking each other for granted, their hard feelings drained away. They each made claims and jointly came up with a plan to implement the agreed-upon changes. Everyone, including their children, benefited from the conciliation created by the new fairness. Jennifer's initial loss of her special role as primary parent to their children was eventually replaced by the joy that she got from seeing Greg more involved, as well as the gratification she got from pursuing more of her own interests (in her newfound downtime). Near the end of our sessions together, Jennifer announced that "the kids are so excited—they see the difference in us. Our eight-year-old used to tell me that I was working too hard. Now she looks forward to playing a board game with me at the end of the evening." Greg and Jennifer had created a new deal for give-and-take that even a kid could see was fairer.

The chore wars are full of inequities. The couples stuck in them are often overwhelmed by demands on their time, energy, and finances. In order to grow through these times, it's crucial to stretch your imagination for what fairness might look like for each partner, as Jennifer and Greg did. At the same time that women complain most about child care and division of labor, men more often take a stand over money and sex. Let's turn our attention to these concerns next, as we learn how to be fair despite inherent gender differences.

Money: Who Makes It,
Who Spends It, Who Decides?

Money disagreements are a major source of tension for many couples and one of the growing pains that pose a challenge to being fair. A recent Gallup poll showed that couples questioned about money management reported being most likely to fight over "spending too much and saving too little." No doubt they interviewed Sam and Nettie for that poll. Sam opened their first session with this statement: "We should still be in our honeymoon phase. It's only been six months, but things aren't going so well. This may seem crazy, but we're here over a ninety-dollar hat." Nettie asserted, "But I got it on sale." Sam retorted, "You think you saved us money because it was on sale? You *spent* money, not *saved* it—apparently, a foreign concept to you. You can be such a spoiled brat." Nettie bit back, "Well, you're a maniac and totally neurotic about money." Why were these newlyweds off to such a rocky start?

Both Sam and Nettie work full-time, so generally money isn't a big worry to them, but how it's spent is. Nettie is impatient to take out a loan to remodel their house. Sam agrees that the house could use some work but drags his feet about taking on more expenses. He objects to how Nettie charges small and large extravagances—from her upgrades on their honeymoon to her morning latte—especially since they don't have any savings. Sam can see the day coming when they'll have kids and only his income. "We both make good money," she shrugs, "why not enjoy it while we're young?" Sam takes the opposite point of view: "We need savings in case something bad happens." Both believe that of all the things to argue about, it shouldn't be money. Sam continues, "I love Nettie, but she just can't seem to see my side at all. I'm not asking her to take a vow of poverty—I know she likes her trips to the mall—but this is going to be a starter marriage if she doesn't change. I can't take feeling so stressed out about money!" Nettie looks startled. "That sounds like a threat. You mean you'd dump me over a measly ninety-dollar hat?"

Sam sees their money conflict as a make-or-break issue. He worries that he'll spend his life paying for Nettie's standard of living. He sensed it was a problem when they were dating, but he figured things would settle down once they were married. Sam thought he'd be able to reason with Nettie and have a bigger influence on her. He fears: "Won't things get worse when we have bigger money responsibilities with kids? Or one of us loses our job?" Sam isn't sure he wants to find out.

Nettie thinks Sam has an anger problem, and is cheap on top of it. She's fed up with his temper. To avoid having the same fight over and over again, she now hides her purchases in the back of a closet, cuts the price tags off, and lies if found out. She's sick of his constant griping about her spending. She makes money, too, and feels entitled to spend it. She didn't get married to have him count her pennies: "Bad enough that he's always acting like it's the last twenty cents in his pocket, but he can keep his nose out of my business."

They're both discouraged. Their disagreement has revealed a distressing inability to negotiate fairly. Underlying the couple's "stupid" fight over a hat is the important task of fairly balancing their divergent values about money. Sam's worry over her spending has caused him to lose trust in Nettie, given her unwillingness to see his side of things now, or even give an inch on something so important to him. They each come to the marriage with very different approaches to finances and meanings attached to money. Neither approach is intrinsically right, nor intrinsically wrong. But such differences do test the commitment and the ability of couples to understand the underlying meaning of a problem, stop their recurring fights, and in the process learn to be fair. If Nettie and Sam don't resolve this growing pain, it will poison their well of trust. Let's begin to understand how their positions have been shaped by their families' financial legacies.

How you value money is typically related to whether your parents and extended family struggled, or were well off; whether they invested in the stock market or hid money under the mattress. Your take on money is based on your family's legacy with its values, its meaning, and its expectations for how much money you need (or don't need), what you'll do to get it, and what you'll do with it once you have it. You bring that emotional charge to your marriage. Your task then is to sort out the baggage each partner brings, so it's possible to negotiate fairly. What histories and experiences were fueling Sam and Nettie's disagreement?

Sam's father likes to tell the story of how Sam's grandparents managed during the Great Depression. They took in boarders, drank "blue" (powdered) milk, and pinched pennies just to scrape by. It took another generation to work their way up to the middle class, and send a son to college. That son was Sam. As a ten-year-old, Sam vividly remembers one morning when his quarter for school lunch milk rolled under the baseboard at home. He felt sick about it, and was afraid to tell anyone he'd lost it; he just went without milk that day. Sam worked from age twelve, first with a paper route, and later as a waiter to help defray his college expenses. Sam and his family live by the motto: "If you need more money, spend less." For Sam, money is about cutting back and holding on.

As if in another universe, Nettie's family has been prosperous for generations. Nettie has fond recollections of saving her allowance, buying comic books at the drugstore, and taking summer vacations on Martha's Vineyard. Nettie is the third generation of college graduates. Her family mandate regarding money is: "If you need more, make more." In Nettie's family, "cutting back" was not part of their vocabulary.

These differences have led Sam to feel misunderstood and uncared for by Nettie, and for Nettie to feel defensive about her spending and dismissive of Sam's concerns. Sam is guilty of calling Nettie a spoiled brat. Nettie retorts that Sam is just totally neurotic about money, and needs to get over it. Their maturation as a couple depends on their ability to thoughtfully negotiate these differences. Respectful acknowledgment must be part of any successful negotiation that yields fair consideration. Unfortunately, neither partner is demonstrating emotional flexibility, nor trying to see the other side of things. Neither offers any acknowledgment of the very real basis of their partner's perspective. Such recognition and acknowledgment has to come before either of them can make a claim for a change in the status quo. Right now Sam and Nettie are stuck in a negative loop.

The Dance of Fairness

Because money is both about current practical realities and also about the meaning you attach to it, there is no absolute right answer to help you reach consensus. We know you can't decide what's fair by calling names, as Sam and Nettie have done. Being fair calls for finding the truth in both sides, and then creating a new truth. Both partners must get beyond their naive and self-serving notion that each holds the moral compass to the truth. Both Sam and Nettie need to explore their preconceptions from their family playbooks about money. Neither of their family's values is wrong, per se—it's just wrong to impose your values as if they were the only thing that's right. Nettie's experiences don't make her a spoiled brat any more than Sam's make him neurotic. Nettie doesn't *make* Sam anxious about money—he came to the relationship that way. To get to fairness, each must take responsibility for the tilt his (and her) own model is adding to their standoff. They need to reevaluate their learned models and assumptions. This important step will help them grasp and respect each other's reality.

Next, both partners need to own up to the harm they've done and do damage control. Sam has to resist the urge to blow up and engage in name-calling, while Nettie has to stop mischaracterizing Sam as neurotic. Sam needs to realize that he can't sway Nettie by his logic alone, and certainly not by attacking her. Sam has felt justified in blowing up: "Why doesn't she get it?" Because it's not just the hat, it's the pattern of disregard for him that triggers his explosion. However justified he feels, Sam needs to acknowledge that his angry contempt is counterproductive and destructive. It diverts the couple from the task of figuring out the meaning that spending has for each of them, and results in the loss of hope, mistrust, and an ever-widening distance between them.

Nettie has hurt Sam, too. She's dug in her heels and brushed off Sam's distress as neurotic. But his worries aren't just in his head. Nettie's spending habits and Sam's family's hard times were lived—they're real. Nettie can't shame Sam out of his worry. That strategy only sidesteps her responsibility and fuels the argument. If Nettie isn't compassionate, how can she expect Sam to give her understanding when she needs it? Nettie needs to acknowledge the fact that her spending pattern has left them with no savings, despite a healthy income. Nettie has minimized the harm she's done, because nothing catastrophic has happened—yet. So far, the damage has been more to their relationship than to their pocketbook. Yet Sam has a point—the forecast isn't good.

What else needs to happen? Both need to make claims for fairness on their terms. Again, a claim is different from a complaint. In a claim, you counterpropose rather than accuse. You substitute self-righteous certainty with a commitment to both ask for and offer reasonable consideration. Claims are often explicit requests as well as broader appeals to change a way of relating. The partner who experienced the most harm is entitled to make the most claims. Making and responding to claims sets a positive feedback loop in motion.

What could Sam claim? For starters: return the hat. Nettie could demonstrate her goodwill by this gesture. Or keep the hat, but make an agreement for the future to talk about purchases over a certain dollar amount, before making them. What other reasonable claims could Sam make? Put away the credit cards; make automatic deposits into an IRA, and into a savings account; hold off on any major loans until they've reached a savings goal. Live on a cash basis—with a budget for discretionary spending. Stop calling me neurotic. Some of these claims would be easier for Nettie to accept than others. All would be in the direction of fair consideration.

If Nettie made any of the changes that Sam might request, she would earn trust. In turn, what claims would Nettie make? Don't judge my purchases if I stay within our agreement. Designate an amount of weekly "mad money." Call a contractor for the home renovations after we've met a savings goal. Stop calling me a spoiled brat. Get your anger under control.

When partners are able to negotiate new terms for fairness by making and responding to claims, then closeness, openness, and loving feelings return. What's at stake, in any one dispute, is not only the resolution of that particular issue but also, and even more important, learning new skills to fairly manage whatever the future holds. In the dance of fairness, it's crucial to avoid repeated missteps, the sour notes of mistrust that become a motif of emotional and even physical distance. As Sam and Nettie learn this new dance, they'll be able to negotiate future conflicts more fairly and, in the process, build trust.

Nettie and Sam illustrate the complexity that the merger of two families brings when it comes to a charged content such as money. Imagine the progression of difficulty when you begin with different values about money, and then add a divorce, a second marriage, and stepchildren into the mix. That's the story of our next couple.

Money: Separate, Equal, and Unhappy in a Second Marriage

TERRELL: "You think you can dictate what I spend money on for my two kids? Let's see you tell them—that because of you, their stepmother, I'm not going to pay for their colleges!"

LILLY: "Fine! You pay for their colleges, and I'll just take myself on vacations, and maybe I'll meet someone who isn't married to his children!"

While figuring out money issues is challenging enough in a first marriage, as the even higher divorce statistics for second marriages tell us, people aren't learning how to fix problems just by changing partners. The complexities of remarriage often include stepchildren. This reality adds the dimension of balancing the competing financial needs of children from prior marriages with the needs of the couple.

Some couples manage their money separately in an effort to avoid financial disputes. This strategy often arises in a second marriage where there are many more variables, such as prior assets, past debts, the request for prenups, postnups, the support of children from a former marriage, and, in fewer instances, alimony. The separation of assets can work as long as partners follow a guideline not to keep anything secret and to share and contribute to the same financial goals. However, this separate but equal strategy can run amok when spouses aren't functioning as a team. This is more likely to occur when their values, their incomes, or their histories entering marriage are dissimilar. With different financial expectations, couples may be in danger of not feeling cared about or protected by their partner. That's the story of Lilly and Terrell.

Lilly and Terrell have been married just over three years, she for the first time at age thirty-eight, he for the second time at forty-two. Terrell has two teenage daughters from his first marriage. Lilly agreed with Terrell's request not to have children together, since she'd never had a burning desire to have children. Still, she felt prepared to take on the role of stepmother. Terrell's daughters stay with them on most weekends. They're polite, but keep their distance from Lilly—partly out of loyalty to their mother, who didn't want the divorce and hasn't remarried, and partly because Lilly just doesn't "feel" like family. Lilly tried hard at first to engage the girls, but she was easily rebuffed and offended by them. Terrell plays peacekeeper. Terrell hears complaints from both sides, while trying to smooth over hard feelings that seem impervious to his efforts.

Their disagreements almost always center on money. Terrell feels like it isn't a real marriage because Lilly doesn't want to have a joint checkbook. Lilly contributes half of the mortgage and utilities, but she refuses Terrell's repeated request to join their monies and checkbooks, and to pay for their cars, gas, clothes, and any incidentals. Lilly objects to Terrell's spending any extra for his daughters, since he already pays child support. They also have heated discussions about his plan to help his daughters pay for college. Lilly asks, "Wasn't this going to be our money—used to relax and travel? You're putting your daughters ahead of me! This isn't the deal I signed up for."

Terrell complains that Lilly "nickel-and-dimes" him. "She makes as much money as I do, but she never offers to reimburse me. I pay for everything around the house. She pays one-quarter of the groceries, down to the penny. But she doesn't count the fact that her health and life insurance comes out of my paycheck. The nerve of her telling me not to help my kids through college! I feel like she doesn't care about me or the kids, just about herself. When she didn't have much money, early on, I was very generous with her. Now that she can afford to be generous, she isn't. She keeps her accounts a secret and won't tell me how much she spends on herself. It's just wrong; it's not fair."

Lilly counters: "I don't have to share that information—it's my money—I earned it. I don't work to pay for your children and your ex. You'll spend on the kids and then we don't have enough left over for even a week's vacation. I think you just charmed me at the beginning. I thought you were a generous guy, not a cheapskate. You can forget me putting my money into the pot. I'll take care of myself. I don't want you telling me what I can and can't spend. The last thing I want is to feel beholden to you over money. So you pay for my health insurance? Well, you save a lot of money because I cook for you and your kids, not that anybody's grateful. While you're calculating how much I owe you, shouldn't that get counted?"

You can hear in their cross fire the sounds of hurt feelings and resentment, as simple irritations become corrosive. Terrell feels the loyalty pulls between his daughters and Lilly. He's scared that he's headed for a second divorce. Prior to their marriage, neither of them anticipated how Terrell's child support would be a problem. Terrell earned a little more than Lilly, and since he'd been managing on his income and a no-frills lifestyle, they figured they would be better off with two incomes. They hoped to add travel and vacations to their life together—something Terrell couldn't afford before.

Lilly and Terrell's arguments over money have devolved into daily digs with a threatening undertone. Neither Lilly nor Terrell trust that they'll be fairly treated with regard to their financial priorities. Instead, they've substituted a structural solution of very separate monies because they can't negotiate fairly. Their stalemate now threatens to destroy their marriage.

Looking back, Terrell realizes that he gave too much in the relationship early on. He paid for Lilly's last year of nursing school and her living expenses. He believed that if Lilly loved him enough she would similarly put his needs ahead of hers when she could help out, and that fairness would simply happen. To become fairer, Terrell first has to evaluate his old model of fairness and own up to his reasons for overgiving. Terrell came from a family where it was considered selfish to think about your own needs. If someone else had an obvious need, you met it in order to be considered a good person. You got extra points if you could guess what others needed, before they asked. Terrell had transferred this way of relating from his family onto his relationship with Lilly.

Lilly had also made a mistake—she took too much. Lilly loved how bounteous and effortlessly generous Terrell had been in their courtship. At that time, she felt protected and cared about. In many ways their earlier relationship had parent-child overtones: Lilly felt protected and expected that her needs would always come first. Without recognizing it, Lilly had taken too much from Terrell, not only literally for her nursing school tuition, but also in an emotional sense. Terrell often deferred to what Lilly wanted; he prided himself on being the flexible one. Lilly wrongly believed that since she was a caring person, her take on things was usually fair. Initially, she believed that nothing would get better unless Terrell changed. She had no clue that her childhood traumas—her father's early death, which left her alone with an alcoholic mother—had anything to do with the couple's distress now. Lilly had done so much emotional caregiving for her mother that she longed for a man to sweep her off her feet and protect her the way her father had. She had a rude awakening when Terrell made claims about how they had to make sacrifices for his daughters. Lilly hadn't recognized her baggage. She just expected that their "deal" in which Terrell took care of her would continue despite their realistic financial limits and the needs of his children.

How can this couple find fairness in the midst of their hard feelings and deepening distrust? What do they need to change to solve their problems and turn mistrust into fairness? First, I asked Terrell and Lilly to recognize the fact that their early unspoken deal was neither fair nor realistic. Terrell had overgiven, and it had boomeranged. I asked Terrell to acknowledge that it wasn't fair to "give with strings attached." If he was going to give, it truly had to be a gift, and not a chit that he secretly held for later collection on his terms, when Lilly was asked to pay a higher price than she'd bargained for. I also asked Terrell to recognize that he could never repay Lilly in kind for the contributions she made toward parenting his children. She cooked their favorite meals, took the girls shopping on occasion, and was the chauffeur as often as Terrell was. Despite her efforts, they didn't warm up to her. To Lilly, it wasn't much of a return—she was doing all this for Terrell's sake.

In turn, I asked Lilly to examine why she'd felt so entitled to be on the receiving end from the very beginning of their relationship. Due to her childhood losses, she deserved more parenting—just not from a partner. To heal her unfinished business, Lilly had to grieve her father more completely, and make a claim for her mother to care about how she'd neglected Lilly. Lilly went to her mother to seek reconciliation. Her mother, now sober for many years, was deeply remorseful about the past.

As Lilly made progress, she saw how her past experiences had colored her relationships with Terrell's daughters. Until then, she'd viewed her stepdaughters as she had her own mother—selfish, self-centered, and needy. The healing process with her mother helped Lilly develop more tolerance and compassion for Terrell's daughters. After all, like Lilly, they had also lost their intact family, but to divorce, not alcoholism and death. Lilly's shift in attitude slowly allowed her to develop a warmer relationship with her stepdaughters, who sensed that she no longer resented them.

With the recognition of imbalance and the crucial acceptance and acknowledgment of personal accountability each took, Terrell and Lilly were finally able to create a new and fairer deal. Terrell asked Lilly to join their monies and put an end to the ungenerous nickel-and-dime economy between them. Lilly made a claim for them to save a certain amount for their vacations and retirement travel. Because each could see the other was trying, they were able to make compromises. Terrell was able to balance the needs of his daughters and his loyalties to them and to Lilly, with the couple's goals of spending time together and saving money for the couple's vacations. Lilly agreed that Terrell would pay a certain amount for his daughters' college educations, but also ask them to work in the summers and take out student loans.

As these changes occurred, Lilly became more trusting that Terrell would take care of their priorities as a couple, too. The money tensions that had gripped their marriage, eased. Learning to be fair to each other promoted a more generous spirit of give-and-take between them. They no longer felt the need to keep score of everyday expenses, or keep a secret of any separate monies. The couple's emotional economy was now full of trust, that they could balance the children's financial needs and also protect their future hopes. They now understood that while money, or any other growing pain, had its own significance, their happiness and longevity as a couple depended on their ability to fairly manage their differences. I trusted that their new-found abilities would hold them in good stead.

The seesaw of second marriages adds more players and complexity to the balancing act that partners need to keep. But at the same time that couples are sorting out all the other growing pains—financial stressors and child-care and household responsibilities—they're also trying to maintain a sex life. This rather stressful combination has been referred to as "mating in captivity." That's how Nick and Danielle felt.

Jealousy: "Valentine, You're Swell"

Their argument seemed like the kind that should've blown over. Danielle had received a Valentine's Day card from the principal—her boss Steve—with a candy heart inside stamped "Valentine, You're Swell." Danielle defended it: "Nick, try to remember that we work in a school, where all the kids give out these cards and candies. Steve was just being funny." Nick was hurt that Danielle blew off his concern about her boss's flirtation. Before this, they joked about how her boss liked women with short skirts and long legs. But this was no joke for Nick. Danielle reluctantly conceded that Steve had been out of line a few times before. But what was Nick thinking, telling her to report Steve for sexual harassment? She indignantly refused. She had worked hard to be in her position of vice principal. She wasn't going to ruin her job and her career because Nick was jealous or because her boss was a flirt. She could manage him.

To make things worse, what began as a stupid disagreement became a long-running argument. The longer it played out, the cooler their sex life became. Danielle wondered if the good times of the past had been an illusion.

Would someone find the switch and beam her husband back to earth? Of course, Nick felt the same way—if only Danielle would come to her senses. The couple's original conflict had mutated into a true threat to their marriage. Would Danielle pull back from the relationship with her boss? Should she? Would Nick calm down and accept Danielle's "take" on the friendship? Should he? What's fair in this situation? Could Danielle and Nick grow from this crisis, or would their marriage crumble under its weight?

Sexuality: Needs, Expectations, Desires, and Loyalty

Sexuality in marriage is based on many things, such as physical attraction and your personal sense of security, which helps you tolerate temporary rejection. Sexuality can be an expression of passion and mutual love, or it can be a negative demand. But for all couples, sexuality is an arena where desire sometimes collides with differing needs and expectations. As you might guess, as problems persist, whether over money, career, parenting, or chores, sexual desire falls.

When you're no longer subject to the mad rush of neurochemicals giving the brain a good washing during early love, desire settles into a routine. With mature love and commitment, partners often need reassurances that they'll continue to be desired. You need those reassurances, because, after all, it's easy for your partner to be attracted to someone else, especially when your flaws are magnified by day-to-day life, while a stranger's flaws are obscured. As a result, most of us experience jealousy at some point. For some couples it's a fleeting feeling, and for others it's a more constant theme. Jealousy reveals the uncertainty and insecurity about whether your partner will choose you over past partners and the world of possible partners. Jealousy functions to secure the boundaries of the relationship and protect it from sexual interlopers—*you're mine and no one else's*. Jealousy is most often an early stage or premarital issue. While domesticity often provides some relief from jealousy, it can emerge or reappear whenever the relationship is

scxually threatened. Now let's return to Danielle and Nick as jealousy com-
busts with the day-to day demands of a couple and their unfinished business
from the past.

Jealousy: Choose Me!

What started as a Valentine's Day argument has lasted for months. Married
for nine years, they've never really fought like this before. Danielle is starting
to think that the fun guy she married is turning out to be more and more like
her controlling father. Nick liked the fact that Danielle was coolly self-
sufficient. Now they've lost the ability to laugh or coolly deal with just about
anything.

Nick is alternately hurt and furious that, despite his pleas, Danielle is still
on such friendly terms with her boss. Nick wants Danielle to limit the time
she spends with Steve. No more after-work dinner meetings, no more phone
calls at home. Nick is more and more desperate to convince Danielle that
she's wrong about Steve—he's after her. To prove it, Nick has spied on her
e-mails; he's asked her to show him her cell phone calls (which she's refused
to do); he's checked up on her when she's supposed to be out with friends;
he's argued with her. He's pressed her to be close and sexually available—
instead, she's colder and more rejecting now. Danielle says that having sex has
become something she does just to shut Nick up.

Danielle is deeply insulted that Nick mistrusts her, and defends her right
to have a friendship with Steve. "It's innocent," she protests. "Sure, Steve's
my boss, but he's a work friend, too." But eventually she concedes—"Okay,
okay, he's a flirt. So what? Besides—what am I supposed to do—quit my
job?" Yet Danielle is in denial about the extent to which she has contributed
to Nick's distress, and about the fact that her friend is not a friend to their
marriage.

Both Danielle and Nick believe that if only the other would change, then
the problem would be solved. Danielle tells Nick to get a grip on his jealousy;
Nick retorts that Danielle is clueless, cold, and uncaring. Each is predictably

defensive and neither budges. It took several tense sessions to begin to un-tangle the ongoing argument about Danielle's boss. Both remained angry and hurt during this time. On their third visit to me, Nick angrily charged that despite all that he did to help Danielle—by working from home to be available to their three young children, and by sacrificing his career chances so that she could pursue hers—she showed no appreciation and no remorse about the damage she was causing. He burst out, "You're so selfish! You're screwing up as a wife and as a mother. I don't know many husbands who would put up with this. I do so much for you, and you thank me by spending more time with him than with me. You don't make it home to put the kids to bed, but you have dinner with him at work. I need you to pay attention to me! You say you're sorry, but you don't act like it. Nothing has changed. If things don't change I'll consider divorce."

Danielle responded defensively: "I'm sorry that you took this so hard and that your feelings were hurt. I do pay attention to you. You've had women friends. I've never tried to stop that. You have a big jealousy problem. You've blown this so out of proportion."

While accusing each other of being unreasonable, neither is taking a good enough look at their own unfair behaviors. It's always easier to focus on the injury you've sustained than the injury you've inflicted. It's easier to blame your partner than to hold yourself accountable. How do couples arrive at fairness from such different starting points? As is true of many couples in dis-tress, Nick and Danielle's arguments have become destructive. Danielle's first attempts at restoring calm was a sham apology of the highest order: "I'm sorry that you took this so hard and that your feelings were hurt." I told Danielle that her sham apology was tantamount to saying to Nick: "I'm sorry that you're crazy." It shirked her responsibility and sent the underlying mes-sage, "It's your problem, not mine." She hadn't yet offered to meet Nick partway, to find a fairer way to address her threatening male friendship.

I also held Nick accountable for attacking Danielle verbally: "You're so selfish. You're screwing up as a wife and mother." This was sheer destruc-tion. Expressing anger may be cathartic, but it's often just punishing, and typically doesn't get you what you truly need, which is for your partner (whom you're attacking) to care about your pain. I asked Nick to resist his urge to attack, and constructively express his feelings of sadness, anxiety, loss of control, and, of course, injustice, that were fueling his diatribe. Like most couples, Nick and Danielle hadn't identified their problem as a fairness dilemma. They presented their situation as marital strife and jealousy. As soon as I underscored the underlying aspect that neither felt fairly heard or treated, Nick immediately declared: "That's it! It's not fair! The other is just the stuff we argue over." When jealousy occurs, it's never only one person's problem. It's always a problem between people, a relationship problem. Let's take a look at how Danielle and Nick each created this flavor of unfairness between them, by first examining the beast of jealousy.

Jealousy signals an individual's insecure feeling of exclusivity. However, that insecurity may also have a factual basis between partners. While feelings of jealousy can arise unreasonably in an overly insecure or controlling person, they can also arise from the *fact* (as well as the feeling) of not being preferred. When one person feels jealous, it needs to be acknowledged and dealt with by both partners. It was unfair of Danielle to dismiss Nick's jealousy and hurt. It was unfair of her to put "the right" to have her male friendship over her husband's concerns. Her loyalties were misaligned and left her choosing the friendship with Steve over her primary commitment to Nick. Danielle charged that Nick was simply insecure and overly controlling—his problem. Although at this point Nick was insecure, he didn't start out "neurotically" insecure (out of proportion to the problem). His insecurity grew in proportion to Danielle's denial of his reality. From a fairness perspective, it's reasonable for your partner to have their loyalty priorities straight—and prefer you and choose you over another's company. It's fair for a spouse to pay more attention to your reasonable needs, than to someone else's, friend or not.

I helped Danielle recognize that her unfinished business with her father had a distinctly negative charge on her marriage. Danielle described her father as rigidly controlling, cold, and unemotional. She felt proud that she had learned to cope by "not needing Dad." In fact, she rarely spoke with him, and only saw him on family holidays because she wanted to see her mother, brother, and sister, too. She married Nick because he seemed warm and funny—just the opposite of her father. Danielle determined early on in her life never to be dependent on a man, to never let herself be too vulnerable—she wasn't going to repeat her mother's mistakes. What she hadn't realized was that the very way she dealt with her father's repressiveness had become the way she handled Nick's displays of distress, by becoming more and more emotionally inaccessible. Danielle hadn't resolved her problems with her dad; she was still captive to them, and now she was repeating them.

What was Nick's share in their problems? At first, Nick was convinced that "she was selfish—it was all her fault." I challenged him to stop painting things as either black or white, with shades of gray viewed as an excuse. Slowly Nick saw that his way of framing blame created more distance and made his marriage vulnerable to the kind of "just friends" relationship that was now threatening it. He had learned a blaming style from his mom, who directed her put-downs mostly at his dad, but at the kids, too. Nick brushed aside my initial attempts to be more specific about what happened in his household. "Hey, my mom was really great—you just wanted to stay out of her way when she was in a bad mood." He seemed uncomfortable discussing his family's "dirty laundry," as if he were committing high treason, and so gave only vague responses. His loyalty was getting in the way of understanding himself better. His focus was on how screwed up Danielle was. I scheduled an individual session, on the hunch that he was worried that Danielle would use anything he revealed about his family as ammunition to turn the focus back on him.

In his individual session he spoke more freely. "Don't get me wrong, I love my mom, and it's gotten better over the years, but she could be pretty intolerant. When I used to cry as a kid, she'd say, 'Now, just cry me a river,' to get me to buck up. Or when I was mad, she'd drag me into my room and tell me to stay there until I could act like a human being. But like I said, mostly she was good with me. She wasn't too thrilled with Dad, though. I remember her saying things to my dad, like, 'You call yourself a man?' What she meant was, he didn't measure up to her sisters' husbands. They were more successful; they had married up, and she hadn't. Or she'd go out of her way to put him down to the repairmen who came to the house: 'If my husband was at all handy we wouldn't need to call you.' My dad was such an easygoing guy, he just took it. But what's this got to do with Danielle and me?"

I helped Nick see that he had subconsciously resolved never to be rolled over like his father. Nick had never seen his father stick up for himself or for Nick, either. So Nick was going to do a 180-degree turn from his father's passivity. Nick half-expected to be steamrolled by women. When Danielle butted heads with him, he was ready, and escalated defiantly. He needed to recognize that this way of relating was now hurting his marriage.

In order for Danielle and Nick to repair the damage between them, each had to take actions to restore fairness and rebuild trust. At first, no one wanted to "go first." When couples are in a standoff, they often try to avoid the one-down feeling of taking the first conciliatory step. It helps to agree to a process where there will be mutual turns of accountability. To assist Nick and Danielle, I assured them that I would ask each to take a turn owning up to their share of the problem and taking their fair share of responsibility. I reasoned with them: "If you want a fair hearing you have to offer one. At least you can move the ball out of your court." Danielle went first.

Danielle finally admitted the harm she'd done. She dropped her justifications, and acknowledged that Nick's claims to change the nature of her friendship were reasonable. She agreed to stop after-work phone calls or dinners with Steve; and she did. She agreed to make Nick and the girls a priority in the evening; and she did. But she drew the line at Nick's request to view the hundreds of work e-mails she got in a week. Danielle promised to stop any nonprofessional exchanges but told Nick that he had to trust her on this. Nick didn't like this, but he accepted it, and felt reassured, overall, by what Danielle was doing. Danielle showed remorse about hurting Nick. She admitted that she recognized early on that Nick had a valid point about Steve. "But once I was really angry at Nick, it was hard to go in reverse. It took on a life of its own."

Nick, in turn, made his claims for fairness from a vulnerable position rather than an attacking mode. He acknowledged that his insecure eavesdropping, questioning, and accusations had been a result of his feeling out of control, and were only pushing Danielle further away. He understood that his fierce determination not to be "rolled over" made it harder for Danielle to compromise without feeling that she was being squashed, as she had been by her father.

Over time, they not only regained their warmth but also learned repair skills that would be useful to them in the future. Their newfound insights and skills enabled them to give each other a fair hearing and to explore their relationship challenges rather than react defensively. Would they have conflicts down the road? Of course. Conflict is a by-product of change and the accompanying need for growth and development. Hopefully, they now had the tools to negotiate fairly and prevent their disagreements from becoming major breaks in trust.

As the couples in this section reflect, sexual tensions are often a symptom of an unfair pattern of relating. A healthy sex life benefits from a couple's insights, fairness skills, and the courage to risk emotional vulnerability. With these elements in play, eroticism can happily coexist with domesticity.

The couples in this chapter had different kinds of problems, but to resolve any one, each couple had to learn skills for becoming fairer. Learning to resolve one problem area can provide couples with the ability to overcome other obstacles and the future growing pains that all marriages encounter. When you learn to negotiate fairly, then the inevitable inequities in relationships don't give rise to unproductive attacks, stalemates, or the loss of trust.

But what if trust has been shattered, or drained for so long there's almost nothing left? Next, I'll show you what happens to individuals and their marriages when everyday unfairness and the growing pains that test relationships are compounded by the crises created by abuses of power, affairs, and addiction. Crises of this proportion threaten the life of a marriage. You'll learn how these gross injustices can occur *to* good people, and *by* good people. And you'll learn how relationships can both survive and renew themselves in the aftermath of a monumental injustice.

EXERCISES FOR CHAPTER 8

EXERCISE: DISCOVERING YOUR *Shoulds*

Exercise 1-A: This exercise helps you identify your *shoulds*. Some *shoulds* are reasonable—you should pay the bills on time, you should have food in the house for the kids, you should teach your children right from wrong—but other *shoulds* are unfair. Those *shoulds* come to the surface when you're angry with your spouse for some small infraction (a real or perceived slight). Over the next week when you feel angry or annoyed at your partner because he didn't do something you wanted (or did something you wish he hadn't), make a note of what the aggravation was and your critical *should*. Then make a more benign explanation. Don't assume your spouse's slipup is intentional. Take it at face value—as a mistake. Recognize that you'll get farther by making a claim for what you need, rather than preaching your *shoulds*. For example:

THE AGGRAVATION	YOUR CRITICAL *SHOULD*	YOUR FAIR CLAIM
1. Left dirty breakfast dishes in the sink for me to come home to.	Everyone *should* be responsible for his own mess.	Make a claim for a clean sink to come home to. But remember: we all have our "slips."
2. Didn't drop the letters into the mailbox at the corner like I asked.	You *should* get it right the first time, and be more thoughtful.	Ask if she'd be willing to make a special trip.
3. Forgot Mother's Day and I got zilch!	He *should* just remember these things, if he loved me.	Try not to take it so personally, but ask him to get a better system to jog his memory in the future.

(continued)

| 4. Spouse wrote three checks and failed to record them. | You *should* be more careful. | Speak with your partner about a method for recording checks, or offer to take over the check writing. |
| 5. Let the three-year-old go to nursery school with her hair uncombed. | Children *should* look neat to make a good impression. | Be aware of your oversensitivity to other people's opinions. |

Now look at the second column to see what you can learn about *yourself*. Don't use this exercise to attack your partner for failing you. Its purpose is to help you discover the *shoulds* you have at work in your life. Your next task is to figure out what claim you can make.

Look at Aggravation #3 above. What did this wife learn? She learned that her options were to be hurt, feel devalued, and complain, or to make a claim for her absentminded husband to do a better job remembering events. She decided to send him an e-mail once a week for three weeks to remind him of upcoming occasions. That worked really well, since her husband's family hadn't celebrated what they called "Hallmark holidays." And what did her husband learn? He learned to take more seriously the occasions that were important to his wife, rather than forget them because he thought these holiday remembrances were frivolous.

In Aggravation #5, this wife learned that she had a great sensitivity to what other people thought of her. She was mad at her husband for letting their daughter go to nursery school with messy hair. What could she do? Take some responsibility for the fact that it was other people's opinions of her as a mom that bothered her so much. And with that in balance, ask her husband to take that into consideration (without the expectation of perfect compliance). And what did her husband learn? He learned not to take his wife's upset so personally. It really was her issue. Knowing that, he was able to stay in neutral, rather than responding defensively.

EXERCISE: WHO DOES WHAT? THE RESPONSIBILITY LIST

After a couple has taken stock of imbalances, it's time to make adjustments. As you review the "who does what" list, think of what items you'd like to change in your relationship. It's unrealistic to think that all items on a list can be shared, or divided down the line. Despite differences in absolute number of items per spouse, if both partners agree on how to share tasks, they're much more likely to feel that things are fair.

The following list initially appeared in a workshop given by Dr. John Gottman, a world-renowned authority on marriage. It is reprinted with his permission, including the introduction. Following his list are additional items I have introduced. Please skip over items that are not applicable.

EXERCISE: NEGOTIATING MARITAL POWER: WHO DOES WHAT IN THE MARRIAGE?

This exercise is designed to help couples negotiate their ideas about gender roles in marriage. There is no right or wrong solution. The important thing is the perception of fairness. The issue is respect and being a team. This is a revealed differences exercise, in which people fill out the following questionnaire individually, and then again through discussion, trying to arrive at consensus. Sometimes therapists like Peggy Papp have couples read books like Arlie Hochschild's *The Second Shift*, which is about gender inequality, for purposes of discussion.

Instructions: For the following items, please describe your perception of how things currently are handled (*now*), and then how you would like them to be handled (*ideal*).

(continued)

Running errands to the cleaners	Now:	Ideal:
Washing windows	Now:	Ideal:
Planning the food menu	Now:	Ideal:
Going grocery shopping	Now:	Ideal:
Cooking dinner	Now:	Ideal:
Setting the table	Now:	Ideal:
Cleanup after dinner	Now:	Ideal:
Cleaning the kitchen	Now:	Ideal:
Cleaning the bathrooms	Now:	Ideal:
Putting out clean towels	Now:	Ideal:
Keeping counters clean	Now:	Ideal:
General tidying up	Now:	Ideal:
Getting the car serviced	Now:	Ideal:
Putting gas in the car	Now:	Ideal:
Sorting incoming mail	Now:	Ideal:
Paying the bills	Now:	Ideal:
Balancing the checkbook	Now:	Ideal:
Writing letters	Now:	Ideal:
Taking phone messages	Now:	Ideal:
Returning phone calls or e-mail	Now:	Ideal:
Saving money	Now:	Ideal:
Taking out garbage and trash	Now:	Ideal:
Recycling	Now:	Ideal:
Doing the laundry	Now:	Ideal:
Folding the laundry	Now:	Ideal:
Ironing	Now:	Ideal:

Putting the clean clothes away   Now: Ideal:

Sweeping kitchen and eating areas   Now: Ideal:

Vacuuming   Now: Ideal:

Washing and waxing floors   Now: Ideal:

Changing lightbulbs   Now: Ideal:

Repair of appliances   Now: Ideal:

Making the beds   Now: Ideal:

Defrosting and cleaning refrigerator   Now: Ideal:

Shopping for clothing   Now: Ideal:

Planning travel   Now: Ideal.

Home repair   Now: Ideal:

Remodeling   Now: Ideal:

Home maintenance   Now: Ideal:

Buying furniture   Now: Ideal:

Redecorating home   Now: Ideal:

Buying items for the home   Now: Ideal:

Buying new appliances   Now: Ideal:

Sewing and mending   Now: Ideal:

Straightening kitchen cabinets   Now: Ideal:

Yard and garden work   Now: Ideal:

Lawn, tree, shrubbery maintenance   Now: Ideal:

Errands to the bank   Now: Ideal:

House, plant care   Now: Ideal:

Straightening and rearranging closets Now: Ideal:

Getting house ready for guests   Now: Ideal:

(continued)

	Now:	Ideal:
Party preparation	Now:	Ideal:
Buying children gifts	Now:	Ideal:
Taking children to school	Now:	Ideal:
Picking children up from school	Now:	Ideal:
Child care after school	Now:	Ideal:
Child meals and lunches	Now:	Ideal:
Spending time with kids	Now:	Ideal:
Family outings with kids	Now:	Ideal:
Pediatrician	Now:	Ideal:
Dentist, orthodontist	Now:	Ideal:
Child homework	Now:	Ideal:
Child baths	Now:	Ideal:
Child discipline	Now:	Ideal:
Bedtime with kids	Now:	Ideal:
Dealing with a sick child	Now:	Ideal:
Handling child crises	Now:	Ideal:
Dealing with a child's emotions	Now:	Ideal:
Teacher conferences	Now:	Ideal:
Dealing with the schools	Now:	Ideal:
Special kid events	Now:	Ideal:
Kid birthday and other parties	Now:	Ideal:
Kid lessons	Now:	Ideal:
Kid play dates	Now:	Ideal:
Shopping for kids' stuff	Now:	Ideal:
Getting people presents	Now:	Ideal:
Keeping in touch with kin	Now:	Ideal:

Preparing for holidays	Now:	Ideal:
Planning vacations	Now:	Ideal:
Planning getaways	Now:	Ideal:
Romantic dates	Now:	Ideal:
Planning quiet evening at home	Now:	Ideal:
Planning weekends	Now:	Ideal:
Planning a special meal	Now:	Ideal:
General conversation	Now:	Ideal:
Planning a romantic evening	Now:	Ideal:
Initiating lovemaking	Now:	Ideal:
Planning dinner out	Now:	Ideal:
Family outings, drives, picnics	Now:	Ideal:
Financial planning	Now:	Ideal:
Major purchases (cars, etc.)	Now:	Ideal:
Managing investments	Now:	Ideal:
Talking about the relationship	Now:	Ideal:
Get-togethers with friends	Now:	Ideal:
Keeping in touch with friends	Now:	Ideal:
Doing the taxes	Now:	Ideal:
Legal matters (e.g., wills)	Now:	Ideal:
Family medicine	Now:	Ideal:
Drugs and other health areas	Now:	Ideal:
Exercise and fitness	Now:	Ideal:
Recreational outings	Now:	Ideal:

(continued)

The following additional items are not in the Gottman inventory. Some items are tasks, others represent emotional caretaking. Beyond the perception of fairness, the purpose of the exercise is for partners to assess the balance of give-and-take between them.

Organizing the kids' clothes and rooms	Now:	Ideal:
Being the family chauffeur	Now:	Ideal:
Organizing schedules	Now:	Ideal:
Responsibility for remembering	Now:	Ideal:
Scheduling appointments for others	Now:	Ideal:
Missed time at work for a child's illness	Now:	Ideal:
Arranging play dates for the children	Now:	Ideal:
Planning kids' summers	Now:	Ideal:
Keeping track of the school holidays	Now:	Ideal:
Taking care of the pets	Now:	Ideal:
Buying gifts for other family members	Now:	Ideal:
Remembering birthdays	Now:	Ideal:
Remembering special occasions	Now:	Ideal:
Taking kids to extracurricular activities	Now:	Ideal:
Being the parent on call after school	Now:	Ideal:
Being the parent on call for weekends	Now:	Ideal:
Researching school choice	Now:	Ideal:
Providing consistent limits for the kids	Now:	Ideal:
Setting logical consequences	Now:	Ideal:
Religious education	Now:	Ideal:
Being the primary wage earner	Now:	Ideal:

Worrying about money	Now:	Ideal:
Taking an extra job to make more money	Now:	Ideal:
Juggling credit card debt	Now:	Ideal:
Setting aside money for taxes	Now:	Ideal:
Saving money for vacation	Now:	Ideal:
Saving money for college or retirement	Now:	Ideal:
Keeping the social calendar	Now:	Ideal:
Taking care of an elderly or sick parent	Now:	Ideal:
Emotional tasks of the couple	Now:	Ideal:
Staying calm when there is a conflict	Now:	Ideal:
Appreciating efforts	Now:	Ideal:
Asking how your partner is "really" doing	Now:	Ideal:
Actively repairing hurt feelings	Now:	Ideal:
Being responsive	Now:	Ideal:
Being sensitive to a partner	Now:	Ideal:
Staying neutral, not blaming	Now:	Ideal:

Once you and your spouse have completed the responsibility list, discuss it with each other. If you decide to redistribute tasks, start small, with one or two items, and then add more over time. The main purpose of this exercise is to begin a dialogue with your partner about what feels fair.

ENDURING INJUSTICE: TO THE BRINK, AND BACK TO FAIRNESS

"The only woman who ever took care of me I cheated on and divorced."
(Karl, married five years, divorced three years)

Happy families are all alike; every unhappy family is unhappy in its own way.
—LEO TOLSTOY

Tolstoy's observation about unhappy families was first published in 1876. While the formal study of families has a recent history, writers, philosophers, and couples have long mulled over why certain families are happy and others aren't. Through the lives of three unhappy couples we'll explore the paradox of what leads spouses to both perpetuate and endure injustice, and the possibilities for the renewal of fairness and love. What distinguishes the couples in this chapter from the couples in the previous chapters are traumatic (whether one time or ongoing) breaches of fairness that result in the near total loss of trust. You'll meet Sasha and Andreas, who are dealing with an abuse of power throughout their entire marriage; Kate and Tim who have endured years of fallout from Tim's addiction; and Lois and Josh, who are dealing with the impact of a midlife crisis. People often think of the worst betrayals as onetime events, such as the searing damage of an affair, the discovery of a second family, or a duplicitous and ruinous financial debt. However, we know from studying childhood resiliency that frequently the chronicity of neglect, or a pattern of poor treatment, repeated day after day, yields the more lasting harm. In my experience, the same is true for the emotional distress created by ongoing patterns of unfairness between partners. But unlike a onetime betrayal, the long-playing drama of injustice, with some happy times interspersed, lulls a partner into feeling sometimes hopeful, sometimes loved, and gradually acclimating to the slowly worsening conditions of the relationship.

In a climate of injustice, the effects of time or the crushing weight of betrayals make the path to restoring fairness even more challenging, and put a couple at a much higher risk of divorce. The nature of enduring injustice is that neither partner knows how to repair the relationship, if repair is even desired or possible. In these circumstances, creating a new model of fairness and rebuilding trust typically requires a longer recovery process. The journey from treachery to trust resembles a bumpy car ride in a minefield, fraught with hidden dangers. But this passage, which requires couples to peer into the abyss of their relationship, offers the best possibility for true healing. Before we meet our three couples, let's first glimpse scenes from the minefields, where you'll feel the depth and breadth of the pain, mistrust, and injustice that hold these couples captive. For these couples, the journeys may be deadly.

Scenes from the Minefields

SCENE 1

Him: Do you think it's fair that I started my day taking my mother to the ER, and then I drove two hours for an important meeting, then I drove back and put in a full day's work, and when I got home, on a day where you had help with the children, you were drunk? Do you think that's fair? Well, it's not!

Her: I was not drunk! I had taken my sleep medication and only had one glass of wine. And what am I supposed to do since you're out so many evenings? And even when you're here you're so cold to me.

Him: That glass of wine must've been a "grande." But let's stick with the facts for once. You don't seem to recognize I'm cold because I'm so furious with you for your drinking that I can either withdraw or go into a rage at you in front of the children. And I think you've done enough damage to the kids already without my adding any.

Her: Yeah, you always hide behind the kids. It makes you sound like such a good guy. Frankly, I could care less what you think.

SCENE 2

Her: Where you and your kids are concerned, my opinions don't count. I knew you had two kids when we met, but they were older, and I figured things would work out. I've never felt welcomed by your family. I got blamed for your divorce. Everybody loved your first wife—except you. Right after we were married you had your kids for five straight weekends. It felt like your place, not mine, not ours. You invite them to dinner without even letting me know; I wind up doing all the holiday meals and I'm supposed to be sweet about it. You think I hate your kids? No, I hate how you let them treat me.

SCENE 3

Her: I've tried to please you and your family all these years. I hauled my pregnant self to their houses to watch our kids while you drank yourselves stupid. I put you to bed when you were too drunk to stand up. I hosted your mother and father and put up with your selfish brother and sister all these years. I put them ahead of my own family. I didn't get what I deserved. Now it's payback time—big-time.

SCENE 4

Him (confiding to a therapist): My wife had an affair. According to her it's my fault because I wasn't "there for her." I work hard to support her and the family, and this is what I get. She even brought the guy to our house. The night I found out I went from sobbing to wanting to hurt the creep. I left for a few days because I couldn't stand to look at her. Now it's two years later, and we're still together, but I'm still strung out over it. I was too humiliated to tell anyone. Things seem back to normal with us, but I can't shake this awful feeling. I wonder if I'd be happier just starting over with someone else?

SCENE 5

Her (confiding to a therapist): I just don't like him anymore. I don't respect him, and I don't love him. If he would only be kind, I could put up with the fact that he isn't successful. If he would only be nice to me I could forgive him for the fact that all he seems to care about is sex and playing poker with his friends. Once in the middle of the night, I woke up because he was taking me—having sex with me while I was asleep. But the killer is, I found out that he spent a lot of money on a hooker in Vegas. I can't stand it anymore.

SCENE 6

Her (telling her sister): I'm a terrible person from all his abuse. Some days I just hope he'll drive his car into a tree and never come home. We could live off his life insurance—at least I could count on that. We'd all be better off. I hate who I've become.

These are the sounds of partners in despair. In despair, there's plenty of blame to go around, and little personal accountability for harm done. None of these couples thought this is where they'd wind up years down the road. But when injustices pile up over time with no healing, relationships are stretched to the breaking point.

The Paradox of Enduring Injustice

As you read the scenes above, you might have thought to yourself not only: "Can this marriage be saved?" but also "Should it be saved?" Remember, no one is obliged to remain in a relationship that is chronically unfair. Why would anyone even bother to try to save such a damaged marriage, one that's hanging by a thread? Let's take a minute to think about the paradox of enduring injustice. The phrase itself defies logic. If you experience injustice—why hang around until it becomes enduring? Why tolerate a grievous onetime injury, much less a series of them? On the other side of the question—why make a travesty of love and hurt your partner, not only once, but over and over again? The statistics on the timing of divorce shed some light on these questions. Breakups have peaks at years five to seven, and years eighteen to twenty. The earlier breakups most often represent volatile marriages that crash and burn from the sheer destructive energy of fighting. These may be intractable situations in which abuses to fairness dictate a safe exit. The later breakups most often result from partners being on autopilot, knowing that there are problems, but sweeping them under the rug. On average, there's a five-year interval between the emergence of significant marital problems and when a couple first seeks help. Why do couples wait so long to get help? At one level, people are often afraid that therapy is a death knell—it means that things are so bad the marriage might end. And of course, the longer they wait and the worse things become, the greater that likelihood is. But there's a more benign reason for the delay. Couples hope that love will conquer all, without doing the work to repair fairness.

Couples are captive not only to injustice and pain, but also to hope and longing that things could be as they were, or as they had once imagined they would be—that they could love and be loved again. Partners often try to let go of the past, only to have their trust broken again. Each time hope is dashed it becomes harder and harder to keep trying. Cycles of injustice are often interrupted with a promise to do better, which leaves a couple feeling temporarily closer and more hopeful. This is what I call "the morning-after effect." "We had a bad night, but tomorrow morning we make up and we're going to be OK." There's a promise of love, an extension of trust, until the promise is broken, and the cycle comes full circle, only to start again. When partners haven't healed on their own, they need more than promises. Yet it may be years before one of the partners seeks help or decides to leave. If a marriage is to survive, both partners must own up to their share of the problems. Otherwise, injustice will prevail and unravel the fabric of a relationship.

While early needs (the six entitlements of childhood) mold your ability to be fair in intimate relationships, your unevaluated model of fairness clouds your ability to see new ways to relate. Your unfinished business shapes your current reactions, your expectations for reciprocity and fair treatment, and precipitates the enduring injustices of marriage. Obviously, none of these problems prevents people from falling in love, marrying, having children, and even divorcing and remarrying. An unhealed past simply makes it more likely that old learning will be transferred and repeated in a way that deepens injuries and creates lasting damage. The injurer is often in denial about how much pain he or she has caused, while the injured party may be blind to what he or she deserves. Paradoxically, it's often in the midst of a crisis—in the midst of anger and mistrust—that pain can be a catalyst for healing. At that defining moment, new possibilities for growth can emerge.

For the three couples in this chapter, the enduring injustices are compounded by the accumulation of many smaller abuses of fairness that have accrued over time. By taking an inside look at their relationships, you'll learn what meaning each partner attaches to these injustices, and what wounds as well as resources lie hidden even from them. You'll see not only the presenting symptoms, but also the hope and the remembrance of love past that creates the paradox of enduring injustice. Finally, and most significantly, you'll see how they begin the hard work of repair and attempt to resolve the mistrust that now characterizes their marriages. Let's start with Sasha and Andreas. You'll see the unfinished business from their families worsening the enduring injustice of Andreas's abuse of power in their sexual relationship.

The Buildup of Injustice: Sexual Coercion

Couples often *do* sex better than they talk about it. Even in my office, discussions about sexuality tend to come up after everything else because dissatisfaction with your sex life is often a by-product of other troubles. But occasionally a couple's sexual relationship is the breakdown issue. For Sasha, coercive pressure in sexuality was the straw that broke the camel's back.

Andreas called me in a panic. His wife of seven years told him out of the blue that she wanted a divorce. How could this be? Andreas thought everything was going great. He was just about to get a terrific job, they had two kids in preschool and their third child had just turned two. Life was getting better. Andreas begged Sasha to come to couples therapy before separating. Sasha told him she didn't have much hope, but she agreed to come—once.

Sasha was a dark, lovely twenty-eight-year-old woman, and Andreas a tall, ruggedly featured man. Andreas began the first session frantically addressing Sasha: "I know I used to be a jerk. I wasn't nice to you, I didn't do my share of child care; I thought you were supposed to do everything, because I was working so hard to get ahead. But I've changed. I think you can see that I do so much more around the house than I used to. I love you. Please tell me what's going on?"

Sasha calmly and sadly replied: "Andreas, I don't know if I ever loved you. We had a great summer fling when we first met. Then, before we even knew what we wanted, my parents jumped in. They were so thrilled that you were Greek Orthodox. It was so important to them for me to follow the religion and pass on the traditions to my children. So despite my doubts early on, I married you. Remember, we've talked about this before. You even agreed that my parents seemed at least as excited as we were about getting married. And I do love you, but as a friend. You've really hurt me over the years and I can't keep trying in a relationship that feels more like a friendship—but with all the pain added in."

"What kind of pain?" Andreas asked without taking his eyes off Sasha. "Whatever it is, I'll do anything to make this up to you."

Sasha responded: "In the beginning of our marriage you compared me to your other girlfriends when you didn't think I was being sexually adventurous, or when I didn't want to have sex every day. You made me feel really terrible about myself. You wanted sex so much more than I did that I felt like you were putting a gun to my head. When I told you no, you'd just get angry. I can predict that if we haven't had sex in two days, you'll be nasty to me. I've kept track in my journal—it's like clockwork."

"But, Sasha," Andreas said with a look of confusion on his face, "I thought this was going well. Don't you remember the last time you came on to me?"

Sasha spoke clearly and to the point. "Did you notice that I drank first? I knew that you were expecting us to have sex, and if we didn't, you'd be mad at me, and I wouldn't get any sleep. I usually have a couple of drinks first so I won't feel as angry with you."

Andreas's shoulders drooped and he asked, "Oh, my God, Sasha, all this time? For seven years?" There was silence, and then Sasha responded, "Yes, Andreas, all this time."

They both stared sadly at each other. In this first appointment, Sasha described a cycle of put-downs, pressure, and emotionally coercive sexual comments by Andreas, accompanied by his anger, and then numb retreat on her part. Andreas's coercion took the form of insistence on sexual contact much more frequently than she wished. When she turned him down, he was predictably mean to her afterward. Sasha concluded that she'd left a chauvinistic father for a chauvinistic husband. In her family, her brother was favored, though her parents denied this. Andreas had a similarly traditional family, in which the females pampered the male family members, and the wife was expected to wait on the husband. This was true despite the fact that both his parents worked. Andreas had gone into marriage expecting the same deferential treatment from Sasha. Fair give-and-take or negotiating was an unknown to both of them. Life was governed by role expectations. Their crisis was years, and even generations, in the making. It was a crisis of trust with Sasha's no vote for their future.

The remarkable turnaround took place quickly and began that first session with Andreas's immediate recognition of the injustice and pain he'd caused Sasha. When Andreas called himself a jerk, he began to own up to the many ways that he'd been unfair. He named some of the earlier imbalances, the responsibilities he'd dumped on Sasha: expecting her to be the parent on call morning, noon, and night; leaving her entirely responsible for raising the children; keeping in touch with his family; taking the kids to see his parents every week; paying the bills; mending his clothing; planning social events; running the household—from cleaning to cooking. More personally, he acknowledged "not being nice," and often commenting on how Sasha could improve how she was doing things—from how she dressed to how she "did" sex—rather than showing any appreciation for all that she did do. Andreas now begged Sasha to tell him what he could do to make these years up to her. Sasha agreed to three evaluation sessions before she declared their marriage dead. Between sessions, I asked Sasha to write down the consequences she'd experienced from those years in which the emotionally sustaining climate of fairness was missing.

Sasha came to the next session with five single-spaced, handwritten pages. As she read her account of the manner and instances in which she felt disrespected and taken for granted, pressured, and coerced sexually, Andreas slumped lower and lower in his chair. When she finished, his hands were hiding his tears. He responded by saying how sorry he was for the very real ways he'd hurt her. He acknowledged the consequences of his actions. He clearly felt very ashamed of himself for taking so much from her. Andreas didn't try to defend himself or shift any responsibility to her. He was sad and full of regrets. Sasha passed him a box of tissues and said that it helped her to see how deeply remorseful he was. His sorrow and shame made her feel a bit more trusting of him. But there were all those years of pressure and hurt and the buildup of her mistrust. Could he really change? Could she truly love him? Did she want to love him at this point? Both Andreas and Sasha were asked to go home and talk about how their marriage would need to change, and how that would be different from their parents' models. Sasha was asked to list all of the things she would need in order to know that Andreas's contrition was genuine.

When they returned, Sasha began by asking for a different division of household responsibilities, so that she could go to night school to complete her education. Andreas agreed to be responsible for the dinner, kitchen cleanup, and children those evenings. When they visited their parents, she wanted Andreas to help her. No more holidays with the women cooking in the kitchen and minding the kids, too, while the men sat around eating nachos and drinking beer while waiting to be served dinner. Sasha needed Andreas to show her and their families that they were changing things.

In the area of sexuality, Sasha needed Andreas to reflect on why he wrongly felt entitled to be mad at her when she wasn't interested. She asked him to grapple with the fact that they could have different needs without his responding as if she were maliciously rejecting him. She asked for talk before touch. I suggested that for the next period of time, Sasha should be the initiator of affection or any sexual intimacy—if there was any—so that she could begin to gauge her own level of desire. I also suggested that she think about the ways her desire manifested itself when she wasn't reacting to Andreas's demands.

Three sessions turned into seven months of therapy. Over that time, Andreas and Sasha continued to reinforce the new patterns they were establishing. Sasha learned to trust Andreas's resolve to pay attention to what felt fair to her. Andreas worked on earning her forgiveness as well as forgiving himself for what he had done, and that he hadn't known better. Their crisis of fairness, focused on sexuality, proved to be a turning point for them individually and as a couple.

Sasha had experienced injustice—and endured it. Why did she tolerate such egregious behavior for a day, much less for seven years? Sasha's kindness, intelligence, and, yes, her beauty struck most people who met her. So why, of all people, would she put up with what Andreas did to her?

One day when Andreas couldn't make it to a session, Sasha made a comment that stuck with me. "You know, I kept hoping that the Andreas I loved the summer we met—when we were young and in love—would reappear. I prayed that he hadn't been just a figment of my imagination, and that I hadn't been a complete fool. That the Andreas of that magical summer, the Andreas who held doors for me and brought me flowers—was the man I married. Now, I'm beginning to believe that maybe he was for real. I'm still not sure. But he's starting to win me over." In that moment, Sasha explained, in her own words, why she had endured so much. She had held on to a little hope.

Andreas and Sasha were able to address their problems relatively quickly. This is unusual for couples that have experienced enduring injustice. For the next two couples, rebuilding fairness and reestablishing trust reserves was painstakingly slow. Our next couple reveals the toxic and far-reaching effects of alcohol on a marriage.

Enduring Injustice: Alcoholism

A soul is never sick alone, but always through a betweenness,
a situation between it and another existing being.
—MARTIN BUBER

At the end of a holiday weekend, I picked up a voice mail saying: "Hi, my name is Kate. My individual therapist referred me to you for marital counseling. My husband's an alcoholic. He's been sober for nearly four years, so it's no emergency. But now that he's sober, I'm depressed. He's better and I'm worse. Please call back." In my return call, Kate said, "Seems like I should have been depressed all those years when Tim was drinking." She hesitated and then added with a note of resignation, "For the first time in our marriage, I've pulled away from him—in every way. It scares him and, honestly, it scares me, too." There was a long pause before she continued. "Tim's frightened that my request for couples therapy means I want a divorce and I'm trying to break it to him gently. To tell you the truth, I'm not sure that he's off the mark." I hoped that Kate wasn't coming to therapy just to say she'd tried everything. I was about to find out.

Early on a cold and rainy Monday morning, Kate and Tim arrived for their first appointment. Kate's round, freckled face was framed by frizzy, auburn hair. They'd been married for twelve years, but she could have passed for a college student. Tim, angular and nearly a foot taller, was as intense looking as Kate was soft. Tim sat fidgeting as Kate began: "We're really very blessed. We have two healthy kids, a nice house, and good friends. But I can't shake my depression, even with medication. I should be feeling better now that Tim's been sober for so long, but I'm not. I guess you'd say our life is happy, but we're not." Tim immediately corrected Kate: "*You're* not happy, Kate, and *I* can't fix your depression. Remember, this was your idea—you and your therapist's. I feel like no matter what I do, it's not enough to make up for the past. I can't hit the redo button." Kate nodded as if in agreement but looked simultaneously mad and tearful. Tim was to learn that until fairness is restored, there is no putting the past behind you.

Recently, and for the first time, Kate had begun to express her anger about Tim's drinking years. "I don't know why it's coming out now. Maybe it's because I'm depressed. Maybe it's because we had a bad past." At this, Tim jumped in again: "It's a shame that Kate can't seem to be happy. She's always looking back and not forward. It's like she can't let go of the past." That was Tim's analysis of Kate's depression. Then he asked me testily, "Why do I need to go to therapy for her problem?" I said simply, "Because you owe it to her and to your marriage." Tim sat back, stared at me for a long moment, and said, "You're right, I do." I knew then that they had a chance.

Before I could help them understand the here-and-now realities of Kate's depression, her anger, Tim's defensiveness, and the consequences of Tim's alcoholism, I needed some history. Not ancient history, but a search for clues to the still active, dynamic patterns that shaped their capacity for fairness. I needed to assess whether Kate's depression was only her individual problem, or a sign of a relationship sickness. I also needed to search for now-hidden strengths they might draw on to try to find a fairer, more loving balance.

Their early years were good. Kate and Tim had dated for four years in college and married a week after graduation. Tim started graduate school that fall and Kate worked full-time to support them. "Life was easy—and we were best friends," Kate recalled. "But the honeymoon didn't last long. It's a blur, but things slid downhill fast. At the time, I excused a lot, though I didn't see it that way at the time."

In a voice brimming with sadness, Kate recounted the eight painful years of Tim's alcohol abuse. She described incident after incident of Tim's emotional outbursts—most aimed at her. He was demanding and often expressed his disappointment in her. "Once, in front of our friends, he hit me with a pillow he'd hurled across the room, yelling, 'You know better than to ask me to take an afternoon walk.'" When I asked how she responded, Kate said, "I guess I did what every good victim does. I put my head down, and took it. I didn't realize—not at that point anyway—that his drinking was out of control." I was struck by Kate's analysis of herself at that time in her life—a "good victim."

Tim interjected: "She always brings that up. It was a damn pillow, for God's sake. You'd think I'd beat her up the way she tells it." Here was Tim's denial and defensiveness on display in their very first session, just as Kate had lived it for years. But for Tim to begin to trust me, he had to be reassured that I would treat him fairly, too. I told Tim that he would get a turn to tell his side. I acknowledged that there are always at least two versions of any couple's marriage, but for now it was important for him, and for me, to understand and acknowledge Kate's painful experiences. He sat back, and Kate, though a bit rattled by his protest, continued.

"What was even worse for me was how Tim 'took off' when I needed him most—like when our first child was born. I had gone through a long labor by myself all day, alone, and I was scared. I couldn't reach Tim. That evening, after Catherine's birth, I made more calls to Tim's friends and his department. Finally someone got him to the phone. He was a ten-minute walk from the hospital but he said he couldn't come then." Her voice dropped to a near whisper. "He said he was playing bridge with his grad school friends. He said he'd be there 'in an hour or two.'" Kate hesitated and then added: "His exact words were, 'I can't stop right now. I'm winning.'" Kate took a deep breath as tears streamed down her cheeks.

Tim had sunk down in his chair. He moved his glasses back and forth on his nose as if he were studying what to say next. Somberly he said, "I was not a stellar human being. I was so sick from alcohol that I probably did what Kate says I did. I don't have many memories of that time. I think she exaggerates a bit, but she's probably right." Tim turned and looked directly at Kate: "But I didn't mean to hurt you. I was trying, too, you know. I worked, I went to grad school, and I was a new father. You don't seem to understand that I felt all this pressure. It was hard for me, too!" In this first session, Tim's defensiveness and difficulty acknowledging Kate's side made it clearer to me why four years of sobriety hadn't gone farther toward healing them. Alcohol wasn't the only culprit; fairness had been imbalanced for years. Kate had given too much, and Tim had taken too much. How had this happened?

Over the first four years of their marriage, Tim slid from being a heavy social drinker to craving alcohol on a daily basis. He hid most of his drinking from Kate while "studying" at night when she was asleep. By the time their daughter was born, Tim was drinking heavily nearly every night. As his al-

cohol consumption increased, his responsiveness to Kate's needs decreased—
to the point that he missed Catherine's delivery altogether. At that time, Kate
had no idea how much havoc the alcohol was wreaking in their marriage. She
didn't understand that Tim's drinking was largely responsible for his irritability, his unreliability, and his poor treatment of her.

Kate felt herself drifting away from Tim. But she chalked it up to having
a baby, tight finances, exhaustion, and the pressure of his studies. Fifteen
months after Catherine's birth, Kate was pregnant with their second child. As
the pregnancy progressed, Tim's behavior became even more erratic and difficult. Kate never connected the dots of his foul moods and irritability with
the near toxic amount of alcohol he was consuming until one defining moment after Todd's birth. "I was sick with a bad cold and asked Tim to do the
midnight feeding so I could sleep. Around one a.m. I woke up because Todd
was crying. After about fifteen minutes I couldn't take it anymore and got up.
I was sick and half asleep and annoyed with Tim. When I walked into the
hallway what I saw scared me to death: Tim was teetering at the top of the
steps with Todd in his arms. Todd was crying and flailing his arms and legs.
Tim could barely hold on to him. I was terrified for Todd, and in that exact
same moment I understood. I finally, finally understood what was going on.
Tim was a drunk."

At this, Tim jumped in—and nearly out of his chair—"I was just sick
from alcohol! I really didn't know too much of what was going on. Kate
makes it sound like I did this on purpose. I didn't! I was stressed! I had to
teach and take classes, write a thesis, and work in the summer. I had to hustle.
I did a lot of bad things. But it was the alcohol. Kate wants to blame it all on
me, but it was my disease!" Once again, Tim attempted to minimize his responsibility. For their marriage to have a chance to heal, Tim would have to
learn to empathically hear her pain, acknowledge his responsibility, and take
steps to rebuild trust.

Then there was Kate's part to consider. Why had she put up with so much
for so long? She wasn't responsible for Tim's alcoholism, but was she only
his victim? While Tim certainly came across as the victimizer, the "saint and
sinner" marriage is rarely, if ever, the whole picture. To get that picture in fo-

cus, we had to sort the baggage that Kate and Tim brought to the altar. Their familial fairness models combined with Tim's alcoholism were a volatile mix that took their marriage to the brink.

Tim's Baggage

Tim initially thought he'd had an ideal childhood that had no bearing on his drinking or his marriage. But he humored me by giving a thumbnail sketch: "I was an Eagle Scout, excelled in school, and had loads of friends. My parents were really proud of me. I went to a good college, graduated with honors, and then got my master's degree." What took Tim much longer to acknowledge was the pain and loss below the surface of his apparently idyllic childhood. The childhood he tried not to think about was the one where he learned to detach emotionally and later numb himself with alcohol. His pain had to do with his mother and Ben, his beloved older half-brother. Ben's mother died in childbirth, and was raised by his maternal grandmother until Tim's father married Reva, when Ben was three. Ben, an introverted, creative boy was always at odds with his stepmother. He was no match for her very high expectations. "I grew up watching them go after each other on a regular basis." Tim recalled many times he hid in a closet to keep from seeing them fight, though he couldn't drown out their yelling. "It just never stopped. Never."

Tim's father, gentle and caring, didn't stick up for the boys when his wife was on the warpath, which was often. "Keeping my mother happy was the name of the game in our house." Tim overachieved to please his mother and avoid run-ins with her. "I could do it; Ben never figured it out." By age fifteen Tim was drinking to get drunk. Alcohol dulled Tim's adolescent (and later adult) pain, sadness, and anger, and constant sense of needing to please his mother. Later in his marriage, Tim did to Kate what his mother had done to him: demanded perfection, used anger to cover up more vulnerable feelings, and failed to take personal responsibility. Slowly Tim connected the dots of his alcoholism and his childhood. It relieved him to see that there was some reason for his drinking. He wasn't just "a bad person."

Kate's Baggage

Kate, like Tim, had experienced both love, as well as fair and unfair treatment by her parents. The fourth of five children in a traditional Irish-Catholic family, she recalled that "it was pretty good, my childhood. We didn't have any extra money, but I got what I needed." But as we delved more deeply, Kate saw that, like her mother, she had learned to quietly tolerate unfair treatment in the name of love. "My father was the silent type—to put it politely." Kate's father used silence to punish his wife, sometimes going for up to a month at a time without speaking to her. Kate felt like a disappointment to her father. "I didn't measure up in my father's eyes. He thought I was stupid. And I believed him. I was told I was dumb in a lot of ways. I'd make a mistake and my father would roll his eyes and say to Mom, 'She's your daughter!' I pretended, as much as I could, that he was just joking. But it hurt."

Kate's early experience left her with a low sense of deserving, particularly from men. Instead of recognizing the injustice of her father's judgmental, distant, and rejecting behavior, she tried to make up for what she saw as her flaws—particularly not being smart enough. She worked hard at being compliant and "good." Because Kate expected to be judged, she tolerated Tim's judgment, criticism, and anger. And just as she'd done with her father, she dodged Tim's bad moods, and tried harder to please him. When she was unhappy with her marriage, she wondered what she was doing wrong—just as she'd done as a girl. Her low entitlement, forged in childhood, contributed to her depression and codependent behaviors. From a fairness perspective, codependency means a person who overgives and underexpects. In other words, someone like Kate, who feels unentitled to fair treatment. The baggage she brought to the marriage was a perfect fit with Tim's baggage—a sadly matched set. Now they needed to heal.

Repair and Rebuilding Trust

Tim and Kate had many changes to make. To bolster her low sense of entitlement to one that realistically matched the facts of give-and-take, I encouraged Kate to state the facts more strongly. When Kate made comments like, "I *feel* like I was abandoned by Tim," I would interject, "No, you *were* emotionally abandoned—you didn't merely *feel* abandoned." Kate needed Tim to validate the very real consequences she had suffered with him, and stop being impatient with her process. After all, she had endured years of mistreatment; he could offer months of patience.

Eventually, Tim was able to listen without defending himself or his actions. For the first time, he offered heartfelt apologies for all the ways he had abandoned her in the years of his drinking, as well as through his criticisms and his tendency to retreat emotionally. Slowly, Tim started to trust that if he could give Kate a fair hearing, he would earn the right to ask Kate for one, too. At this point you might be asking yourself why Tim deserved any hearing at all. Because it's fair. Tim had a side, too. He wasn't just the "bad guy." It would be a disservice to both Kate and Tim (and to their children) to remain locked in their roles of victim and victimizer.

With Tim's accountability, Kate was able to acknowledge her part. Kate now realized that her low self-esteem predated Tim's mistreatment of her. She had to stop her sacrificial tendency to put other people's needs first. She had to learn to stand up for herself. While she wasn't responsible for Tim's drinking, her selfless stance had contributed to her depletion. Now, she wanted a marriage in which love was built on fair relating. She was sick (depressed) and tired of being a doormat. The couple's next step in healing was for Kate to ask for a fairer balance of give-and-take.

Kate needed to claim something more for herself. Kate's first claim had been for Tim to join her in couples therapy, despite his resistance. She later made claims to redistribute parenting responsibilities and division of housework. Kate made a claim for a "one cooks, one cleans," split on the kitchen chores. Until then, she'd done it all. She asked Tim to take a full day each weekend to spend time with the family. Kate also asked for Tim to drop three evenings of AA meetings. For the four years of his sobriety he'd gone to AA meetings every night of the week. She was tired of being a single mom, an AA widow. This was a tricky claim, as Tim depended on the AA meetings for his sobriety. But he agreed that he could go to lunchtime meetings instead. As a result, Tim got to know his kids better and develop a closer relationship as a father, as well as becoming a more supportive husband.

Kate had one more claim to make—she wanted to quit her part-time job and explore what she really wanted to do in her life. She had always dreamed of becoming a teacher, but it had seemed impractical until now. Tim responded in a truly generous spirit. He reassured her that they could afford to live on his salary; and encouraged her to take the time she needed. Kate was elated. Tim felt proud that he could finally do something that Kate wanted, that clearly demonstrated his love for her. He wanted to be on the giving end of things to make up for the harm he'd done. It helped him to experience himself as kind and loving. As Tim gave and she received, Kate felt truly cared about and loved. They were rebalancing their seesaw of reciprocity. As these changes occurred, Kate's depression slowly lifted. She reduced her antidepressant medications and spoke with more emotion, force, and enthusiasm.

Tim's alcoholism and the long period of injustice are a part of the tapestry of their marriage forever. There is no redo button for Tim to make the right choice to be present for Catherine's birth. But out of his despair that he couldn't change the past, Tim learned that taking responsibility for the hurt he caused, and making a commitment to become fairer, was healing in itself.

Toward the end of their therapy, Kate arrived first one day for an appointment. As we waited for Tim, Kate recalled a defining moment from an earlier session: "My heart softened as I imagined Tim as this scared little boy hiding in the closet—not the brave Eagle Scout, the Ivy League know-it-all. I saw him, for the first time in a long time, as a hurt little kid. That was the moment—if there was just one—that allowed me to see him again as the man I loved and married—the person who was my friend. Now we aren't our pasts anymore. We have each other again."

This was one of those privileged moments that strengthens my belief that couples can find unexpected and life-giving trust reserves when they set out to rework fairness. Josh and Lois next tested my conviction, with a midlife crisis, more than twenty years in the making.

Injustice at Midlife

Lois called me requesting couples therapy. She reported that she and her husband, Josh, were in a terrible crisis. They were in their early forties and had been married for twenty-one years. Later that week, I met them in my office. Lois was a petite, well-dressed brunette, with a wide smile and piercing blue eyes. Josh was a tall man with a dark beard and thinning hair. Josh worked as an architect in a large firm, where he was a partner. Lois was a human resources trainer. They had two teenage children, one doing well at college, and the other in high school. If looks could tell the story, here was a couple that "looked like" they should be happy—attractive, successful in their careers, about to be empty nesters. But appearances, seemingly so important, mean nothing when love, marriage, and your future are all up for grabs.

In their first session, Lois reported bitterly, "This was supposed to be the time to look forward to, to enjoy our lives. But I can't go on like this. I don't know what's wrong, but for months he's been mean, he's cold." Lois then accused Josh of having an affair. He angrily denied it. She pressed on, asking why he was so late coming home from an after-work function. He gave a credible excuse of helping a female coworker who'd had a flat tire. Lois confirmed that Josh had called to let her know he'd be late on that account. She tearfully added, "But not three hours late." Josh accused Lois of being "jealous, overly emotional, and paranoid." He further declared that he was sick of how clingy and dependent she was.

Crying, she asked me, "Why has he changed?" I asked them to give me a bird's-eye view of their relationship, starting with any recent losses or events. They looked momentarily puzzled and then Lois spoke: "Well, my father died a couple of years ago. I'll always miss him, but it's not as bad as it was the first year. Our son left for college last year, and our daughter will be leaving this fall. We're very proud of them." Then Josh casually added, almost as an aside: "And about a year ago, I had a brain aneurysm repaired. It was discovered by accident—I hit my head when I crashed my racing bike. I never lost consciousness, but I was really dazed for about fifteen minutes. The ER checked me out with an MRI of the head. I was okay from the fall, but that's when the aneurysm was found. It was scary at first, since when you hear the words 'brain aneurysm' from a neurosurgeon you think, 'I'm a walking time bomb; it could burst and I'd die.' But, hey—here I am to tell the story. I got it coiled, my recovery was fast, and the docs say I should be fine. Other than that—just life as usual." Lois nodded, as if to say, "What's this got to do with anything?" But I was playing detective, and I needed as many clues as I could find.

To fill out the picture, I asked them to tell me about their families. Since her father's death, Lois often checked in on her mother, who lived nearby. Their relationship was good, though Lois acknowledged that she was sometimes worn out from juggling the needs of her mom, the kids, her work, and the home. Josh reported that his parents were still living, but had their share of troubles—his father gambled too much and his mother was the "dependent type." He kept up with them more out of obligation than closeness. Next, they described their marriage as having had its ups and downs, but nothing significant. Josh thought Lois was too busy with the kids and her mom. He complained that she took the kids' side most of the time, and sometimes he felt undermined as a parent. Lois thought Josh was a workaholic, and often irritable and dismissive of her. But even with these rumblings, they still had fun sometimes. They didn't expect marriage to be perfect.

With this sketch to go on, my mind started churning on possibilities. I wanted to learn more about their early courtship, and more about how they'd managed Josh's brush with mortality. They'd glossed over so much about their families; I wondered what they weren't aware of, what fairness models they worked from, what unfinished business each had. I started to find answers to some of my questions in their follow-up sessions.

Their courtship was marked by parental disapproval about interfaith issues. Lois was Protestant and Josh, Jewish. Neither family was happy to think that their child might abandon their religion. Lois and Josh struck a compromise—they would raise children with both faith traditions, while they each observed their own. This met with grudging acceptance. But what did it mean that Josh's parents still kept in touch with Dee-Dee, his longtime high school girlfriend, whose parents belonged to their synagogue? Lois accused Josh of never standing up for her to his parents. If he had, they would've stopped their contact with Dee-Dee years ago. Lois still felt twinges of jealousy, knowing that she was the rebound girlfriend after Dee-Dee. Dee-Dee's return to their neighborhood, following her divorce, only heightened Lois's insecurity. Finally, there was the puzzle piece of Josh's medical threat.

Josh had handled his medical crisis very matter-of-factly. After the first neurosurgery consult, Josh told Lois that he didn't need her to go to other appointments—that would feel more upsetting to him. He almost superstitiously refused to redraft their will or make a health care directive. He reasoned that the odds for the procedure he'd need were in his favor—an 8 percent chance of incapacitating problems, less for mortality.

I paid close attention to Josh's flat, almost scientific reporting of his medical scare, and thought, "Okay, we have the triggering event for 'a lost possible self.'" A lost possible self is what psychologists call the rethinking many people do (not always at midlife) about what their lives "might have been." It's a "what if" scenario. In experiencing the possibility of his own mortality, Josh had begun to rethink his life, including wondering what life might have been like if he'd married someone else. This rethinking at a crisis point can precipitate an affair. I would have to check out my hunch in an individual session with Josh, because he was flatly denying the affair that Lois was accusing him of.

I assured Josh of the confidential nature of our individual session, and asked him to level with me about whether he was having an affair. If he couldn't be honest with me, he was wasting their time and money. Josh disclosed the truth. He'd been having an affair with Dee-Dee for ten months. The flat-tire story was just a cover-up to spend time with her. There were a multitude of cover-ups over the last many months. Josh and Dee-Dee rekindled their relationship a month after his aneurysm diagnosis. He hadn't intended to have an affair. He e-mailed Dee-Dee to tell her what was happening to him (and maybe say good-bye). It had just seemed important to Josh to have the closure he'd never had with her. He got her e-mail address from his parents. I asked if he'd been thinking of separation or divorce prior to his affair. Josh adamantly denied this. But now he wasn't sure that he wanted to stay married to Lois. He vaguely stated that he'd begun to feel cold toward Lois, angry and resentful of her neediness and dependency on him, particularly over the past few years.

In that individual session, Josh said he thought he was in love with Dee-Dee. She seemed strong and independent and fun. And what a turn-on to be desired again. With Lois he often felt as though she was just servicing him— pity sex. I cautioned him to separate the exciting fantasy of an affair from what real life would later reveal. I told him that he owed it to himself, to Lois, and to their kids to make a rational decision, and not allow himself to be swept up in the tidal wave of emotions that an affair brings. He told me he didn't know what a rational decision would look like. I explained that at a minimum he needed to understand what individual as well as marital issues had led him to this point. Other than his amorphous anger at Lois, Josh initially had little insight into his own reasons for starting an affair. Josh's angry and blaming stance toward Lois was characteristic of an unfaithful partner justifying an affair. I knew that his anger didn't necessarily mean that his marriage had been bad before—just that it was bad now, as any marriage would be when threatened by an affair. But if the marriage hadn't been bad before, it had been vulnerable to an affair. The couple would need to learn why.

At the moment, though, Josh was stuck in an angry, defensive, first stage that often precedes repair. While Josh recognized the injustice of the affair to Lois, he displayed little remorse. I suggested to Josh that if he could understand the layers of meaning behind his affair, he would have a better shot at making that rational decision. "Saving the marriage" would be a by-product of the couple's mutual efforts to refill their reservoir of trust that had been drained by his affair, and probably by both of them before that, too, for reasons no one yet understood. Their progress would also depend on their willingness to work on the issues that made the marriage vulnerable to an affair.

The goal of the therapy was to slow down enough to find fairness in this noxious mix of anger, mistrust, and hurt, rather than abandoning the marriage in despair. It would be premature to make any decision to leave the marriage at this point, just as it would be premature to predict that the marriage could be salvaged. It would be months before they had more certainty about what was possible between them again. Another goal was to help the couple address prior imbalances and injustices, so that they could see what each had contributed to the current breakdown. Then, and only then, could they begin to understand whether a new fairness could take the place of their old, broken model.

Josh asked me if there was another choice, besides slogging through this painful process with Lois. I told him that in my experience, if he didn't rework these problems, he would take a similar dynamic into his next relationship—with Dee-Dee or anyone else. Not only would the same issues follow him, but also any new relationship would have the additional burden of the legacy of his infidelity. That much was nearly guaranteed. I also challenged him to recognize that the fantasy of the perfect mate was just that—a fantasy. If he thought the current challenge of day-to-day hassles with Lois was daunting, I asked him to imagine adding to that picture the volatile mix of trying to establish a life with his affair partner, while not only Lois, but also his teenage kids, were furious with and judging him. Josh agreed to continue couples sessions with the goal of understanding how he and Lois had gotten to this point. Josh said he probably wouldn't do therapy except for their kids' sakes. I told him that his ambivalence was understandable and even expectable. Whatever the outcome, he could regain some of his integrity through this process. Too much was at stake to do otherwise.

With his decision to do couples therapy, Josh knew his next step was to tell Lois the truth. It wasn't fair to her to distort reality and make her feel like she was crazy for having suspicions. Josh was understandably worried about what Lois would do when he told her. That was a risk he had to take. He couldn't rebuild trust by continuing to lie. It would be a long road through the minefields. This was the first hard mile.

Josh admitted his affair to Lois in the next session. As Josh feared, Lois was wild with anger and sick with grief. "How could you love me and betray me like this? You must hate me to have done that. Are you trying to destroy me? How long has it gone on? You've never stopped loving her, have you? How could you have sent me that beautiful anniversary card just a few months ago? How could you have done this? Who are you?" Lois pounded Josh with question after question. Then she turned to me: "How can I ever trust him again? Should I even try?" Then Lois sobbed uncontrollably for nearly five minutes. When she calmed down enough to hear me, I affirmed that she deserved answers to all her questions. That would be the work of their therapy. The first step to healing, painful as it was, had taken place. Josh had told Lois the truth; Lois had begun to absorb the meaning of it.

While Lois would continue to have questions for many months, right now she needed Josh to make significant changes. He owed her that. Her first claim for restoring fairness was to ask Josh to stop all contact with Dee-Dee—the secret liaisons, the e-mails, the texting, the phone calls, everything. Lois couldn't tolerate it, nor should she. I watched Josh closely because I was uncertain if he was committed enough to the process of therapy, let alone to Lois, to make such a move. Josh nodded his head slowly and agreed to end the affair. Unlike his previously belligerent behavior, he appeared solemn, perhaps sad. I didn't know what, if anything, had changed for him, but he appeared to be trying to give therapy—and his marriage—a chance.

Over the course of the next month, he acquiesced and provided Lois all that she asked for: open access to his e-mail accounts, and his cell phone, writing Dee-Dee a good-bye letter (which Lois, with my encouragement, edited and watched him send). This was not a friendly letter—no "Dear Dee-Dee," no mistaking the business tone. In it he stated that it was over, that he loved his wife, and that he was going to work on his marriage. This declaration of finality was more than he felt prepared to say at the time, but he acceded in the spirit of his commitment to make a genuine effort. In return, Josh asked that Lois refrain from telling their children. He feared they might hate him for his infidelity. I backed Josh up—not because Lois necessarily felt like sparing Josh any indignity, but because it wouldn't be fair to burden their children with this information at this time—especially in its raw, undigested form. They could decide later whether it made any sense for the children to know. Despite his good faith efforts that first month, Josh was still largely unrepentant and occasionally lashed out at Lois. At times I wondered if he was just a cold, uncaring man. But I knew the truth had to be more complicated than that.

Neither of them was very hopeful about a good outcome. Lois felt equal parts angry, scared, confused, sad, and certainly, betrayed. She had a number of seemingly unanswerable questions:

- How could Josh have loved her and hurt her this much?
- Why had this happened?
- Did he in fact love her?
- Even if they worked on their marriage in therapy, could she ever truly trust him again? And if not, what was the point of continuing?
- What was wrong with Josh?

Questions that were unasked but crucial were:

- Why was the marriage vulnerable to an affair?
- What harm had Lois (in addition to Josh) done in the marriage?
- What model of fairness did each bring from their family of origin?
- What were the past imbalances in fairness?
- Was Lois simply Josh's victim, or how else could she understand it?
- Was there a more sympathetic way to look at Josh?
- What did they each owe themselves and the other, and their children?
- What actions were necessary to restore fairness and rebuild trust?

Colliding Injuries

In order to answer these questions, we had to understand the meaning and the prior histories of unfairness that left the marriage so vulnerable. As you've seen before, oftentimes couples identify their current problem without connecting the dots between how they treated each other, and their unfinished business. Only through this exploration could we answer Lois's question, "Why did this happen?" If they chose to stay married, this journey would help them build a more solid foundation for their future. We set some ground rules so that each would have a turn speaking about their injuries, and acknowledging the other, as best they could. For Lois, who was so betrayed, this in itself would be challenging. But she wanted to move forward.

Lois opened with her account of how ill-treated she felt even before Josh's affair. "Last year I got a promotion at work. I had worked hard to get it, despite the politics and the pressure to do more. And Josh knew all that. So I bought a bottle of champagne on the way home from work. I was excited— and I wanted to celebrate. But the first thing Josh said was, 'So does it pay more, or is it just an "atta girl"?' I felt humiliated admitting that there was just a tiny increase. I've supported Josh for his accomplishments, but never felt that he did the same for me. Whatever I'm doing, according to Josh, I could've done it better. He acts like I'm an irresponsible kid, always on the verge of screwing up. I'm sick of feeling like a disappointment. Now, I'm angry with myself for putting up with his foul moods and critiques." Since his diagnosis, Lois noticed that Josh's fuse was even shorter. "But [she glared at Josh] I gave you the benefit of the doubt. I wrote it off to your stress from all that was going on. I didn't know the half of it."

Now the ball was in Josh's court. Could he begin to acknowledge the pain he'd caused and move the healing process forward—or would he become defensive once again? He spoke in a calm, thoughtful voice. "Lois, I had no idea I'd hurt you when you got your promotion. It was more my way of complaining about your company. I guess I'm better at finding fault than I am at recognizing what people do well, or how what I say feels to someone else." I took Josh's response as a hopeful sign. The fact that he could listen and take some personal responsibility showed an ability to acknowledge her side and a willingness to be fair. Whether they stayed together or not, it was important that Josh and Lois learn to relate more fairly, even if only for the sake of their children.

I asked Lois if she had any response or other thoughts. Lois continued, "Okay, well I'm glad you can see you hurt me. I've needed more support because the last couple of years have been really hard on me. First my father died, and I 'inherited' my mother. Then my son left for college, and my daughter is getting ready to go. Josh was used to me being independent, and then poof, I was sad and leaning on him more. Maybe I didn't pay enough attention when Josh had his medical problem, but he didn't want me to." She added bitterly, "Apparently he wanted his girlfriend there for him."

She hesitated and then said to Josh: "And your parents—they've never approved of me. His parents wanted him to marry a Jewish girl, not a shiksa like me." Josh rolled his eyes and clinched his jaw but remained silent and let Lois go on. "And Josh never stuck up for me. I guess I was insecure about things, but who could blame me? His parents were always catching him up on how Dee-Dee was doing." Lois scowled at Josh, then said, "Your father is depressed, and hard to please. No matter what, he finds the negative side to things." She looked at me and asked: "You know the glass being half-empty or half-full? My father-in-law has never seen a half-full glass in his life. He gambles to enjoy life and picks on his wife. I think that must have something to do with why Josh is so hard on me. And Josh's mom never stuck up for herself, much less Josh. She did the opposite: she leaned on Josh."

Josh responded: "Lois is always blaming my parents—because she thinks they don't accept her. For God's sake, it's been over twenty years of this." Despite Josh's defensiveness, Lois's interpretation had a ring of truth. It would, however, take Josh some time to stop being the loyal defender of his parents. He'd first need to recognize that his upbringing had blinded him to how dismissively his father treated his mother, who then turned to Josh for comfort. Josh had felt too responsible for his mother, yet excused his father. As a result, Josh couldn't tolerate women who seemed needy to him. He felt first burdened by his mother, and then by Lois. At the crucial moment when he needed to be on the receiving end, when his life was on the line, he went outside the marriage rather than turn to Lois. Being in love again with Dee-Dee felt like the antithesis of dying, the antithesis of vulnerability. Now the affair began to make sense.

But Josh had a different spin to add. Fueled by what he took as a shot at his parents, Josh retorted: "Lois comes across, or likes to come across, as the strong, independent one. But with me, she's not. She puts on kind of a show. And I fell for it. I'm sick of Lois's dependence on me. Granted, she has a demanding job, makes good money, and is well respected, but that isn't who she is with me." Lois's body stiffened as Josh spoke. The pain of his affair was still overwhelming, and hearing Josh's criticism was too much for her at this point. But to her credit, she stayed glued together, closed her eyes and continued to listen. He gave an example to illustrate his point about Lois: "Many days when Lois comes home from work, she frets endlessly about whether her training has gone well, whether she'll get positive feedback, whether her boss will be impressed. No matter how much I reassure her, it never sticks. The next night it'll be the same thing. But to the outside world, she's great. She looks good—the clothes, the calm voice—but inside she's a bundle of nerves and self-doubt. Nobody else sees how overwhelmed she gets." Josh then turned to her angrily with this parting blow: "Yea, I didn't want you with me at the doctor's because I would've spent too much energy reassuring you that I was going to be okay. I didn't need that on top of a brain aneurysm." The color washed from Lois's face—she began to cry.

The scrutiny of injustice in a relationship changes kaleidoscopically, with shifting views from each person's perspective. Josh and Lois's realities, seen through their own personal prisms, provide a deep, but narrow landscape of their relationship. Neither has a broad perspective, an encompassing view of the realities of his side, her side, and the reality between them. When partners hold such different perspectives and both feel unfairly treated, how do you determine what's real? What are the truths in their two perspectives? How do you restore fairness and then intimacy to a marriage that has such obvious and enduring injustices? The next step relies on understanding the validity of each person's perspective.

Josh's Side

In an individual session, Josh reported always being super-responsible. First it was to his father—to achieve—and then to his mother—to be strong for her. Later he felt responsible for boosting Lois's sagging self-confidence. "At the start of our marriage I thought that my support would change her—well, at least help her. But as time went on and her struggles didn't seem to get better, I got tired of it. I couldn't help, and I felt worn out." Looking back on the timing of the affair, Josh realized that he had been frightened, not only about his aneurysm, but also scared that maybe he'd blown his one chance in life to be really happy. He wondered what his life might have been like if he and Dee-Dee had worked it out. "You see, Dee-Dee got pregnant at the end of high school. She wanted the baby, but I didn't. She got an abortion, and then broke up with me. I felt so guilty. I've never told anyone about this secret till right now." The relief on his face was quickly shadowed by panic. "You won't tell Lois, will you?" I reassured him that his session was confidential, but I knew that we'd need to return to this last secret for him to gain closure.

Josh met Lois soon after the end of his relationship with Dee-Dee, and dedicated himself to beating back the past. He tried hard to be successful and hold things together, but what had it gotten him? To his way of thinking, just burden and resentment. It seemed to Josh that only Dee-Dee really cared about him. He wondered aloud one day during an individual session, "Wouldn't Dee-Dee be better for me, or is that just an illusion?" Josh still wasn't sure what he wanted.

Why did Josh feel so crushed by responsibility, so resentful of Lois? Initially, Josh was dismissive of Lois's interpretation about his parents' share of the problem. "You're just trying to shift the blame," he told her. His loyalty to his family prevented him from recognizing the truth in her observations. Relationally, Josh was operating on the basis of several common but incorrect beliefs about love and fairness. For instance, he believed that the past had nothing to do with their marital dissatisfactions. Josh also thought that the only way things were going to improve was if Lois changed, or if he left. He thought her insights were "just making excuses." But as he debunked his old beliefs, Josh began to understand that love also depended on fairness. He had felt destructively entitled to act out by having an affair, because he hadn't felt fairly treated. But where did that feeling begin?

Josh's Baggage

Josh was the oldest of three, with a younger brother and sister. He never had any doubt that his parents loved him, though his parents weren't the warm and fuzzy kind you turned to when things were hard. "You just had to handle your own problems, take charge, and keep going." Mostly, that had worked for him. As the oldest, he was responsible for helping his mom, who relied on him in many ways. Looking back, he thought it was probably a good guess that she had been depressed off and on—probably about his dad's gambling. The family had a car repossessed once to pay off some of his bad bets. Josh remembers that his dad also worked a lot, often getting home after the kids went to bed. Josh reflected that he and his dad were more alike—very driven, and not easy to get close to.

As Josh slowly started to accept the premise that his past could impact his present, I asked him to review a list of crucial childhood experiences. As he scanned the list he became quieter, visibly lost in thought. When asked to flag the key experiences that can impact fairness, he marked several items. At first he described his positive experiences that promoted his sense of family loyalty:

- feeling nurtured;
- feeling loved;
- feeling special;
- feeling competent to give back to his parents;
- feeling proud of his accomplishments.

No wonder Josh was such a staunch defender of his family. They had given him a very important sense of love, purpose, and identity. Their evi-

dent love made his recognition of his painful experiences feel disloyal. I encouraged him to think about loyalty as something he both owed his parents,
but also owed himself. He didn't owe it to his parents to shrink from the truth
of the parenting he'd been entitled to, even if they hadn't been able to give it.
Josh became noticeably sadder as he described the experiences that had inhib-
ited his growth and unfairly shaped his relationship with Lois. This is my
summary of what Josh said:

- feeling valued for achievement only;
- feeling too much was expected of him;
- feeling parental to both parents and younger siblings;
- feeling as if he needed to perfectly meet his parents' expectations;
- feeling there was no emotional advocacy for him;
- feeling there was no one to turn to.

Josh recognized that he only felt valued if he was successful academically
(which he was). At home, he felt that too much was expected of him. "My
mom depended on me a lot, but there was no such thing as asking for what
you needed or wanted. You just did what you were told to do, whether it
seemed fair or not." He recalled that he frequently picked up slack for his
younger siblings so his mom or dad wouldn't yell at them. They loved and
admired Josh, but never imagined that he had any problems. Neither of his
parents felt emotionally safe. "Nobody would get hit, but you'd have 'hell to
pay' in attitude—my parents backed each other up, even when they were
wrong. I realize now that I was good at taking care of people, but it was way
too much." And his dad? "You could hang out with my dad at the poker
table—he taught us all how to play a hand." Josh continued in a voice that
was both dispirited and thoughtful: "I was the kid nobody had to worry
about. The one time they had to worry, they blew it. I never told them what
happened between Dee-Dee and me about the pregnancy. But I kind of hinted
around. I told them a good friend was going through something like that. My
father almost took the roof off. 'Well, you better damn well be sure no girl

ever traps you. You've got a life ahead of you, and college.' So I never told them. And I kind of bailed on Dee-Dee. I didn't go with her to the clinic for the abortion. Then she broke up with me. My freshman year I met Lois. I'd never dated outside my religion before. The relationship didn't feel that serious at first. Lois was a person I really liked and trusted, though I probably half dated her to get back at my parents—I knew they'd be displeased about her religion, but I didn't care. Yea, I knew they kept up with Dee-Dee. I guess I sort of wanted to know how she was doing. I brought a lot of baggage to Lois, didn't I?"

As Josh recounted this story, he also defended his parents. "You know, I don't want you to get the wrong idea—they really loved me. So how can I say things were unfair? I know they were just doing the best they could do, raising a teenager, wanting more for me than they'd had, not wanting me to screw up my chances for college." But Josh finally recognized that these hurts, the old emotional injuries and unmet fairness needs, had cost him something. Josh had learned that being vulnerable left him open to being both burdened and disappointed by others.

His family history propelled him toward being independent, not wanting to need anything from anyone. He purposely kept his issues—both good and bad—to himself, which eventually resulted in his depletion. Because he wasn't able to lean on his parents, he hadn't learned how to make a claim for himself. He became self-sufficient and competent to a fault. He appeared not to need anything from anyone. Everyone leaned on him. His experiences created a default way of relating—seeking distance when he felt unfairly treated by those closest and most important to him. He had repeated this pattern with Lois. Getting close to her resulted in his being loaded down by her expectations and needs—just like in his family.

In all of his relationships Josh felt that he was loved conditionally—loved for what he could do for someone. With Lois, he was tired that it was always about her needs. But he didn't know how to change it. If Lois really loved him, wouldn't she just do what he needed without his having to ask? He longed for Lois to automatically know how to love him. To Josh, Lois had become just one more person who expected the world of him, another person he had to please, who took him for granted—who thought he was the person no one had to worry about. Then he contacted Dee-Dee.

Josh came to understand that his affair was a very indirect as well as a very destructive way of holding Lois accountable for how skewed he felt things were. It was complicated by the lost possible life with Dee-Dee, the child they hadn't had, and the immature search for closure through an affair. He also realized that his lopsided way of relating preceded even knowing Lois. Josh didn't know there was a difference between love and fairness. To avoid the risk of losing the love of his parents, he tried to be perfect. He complied with their needs, even when it was unfair to him. Fairness wasn't part of family talk. Love, yes. Expectation and obligation, certainly. But fairness? That was the missing link.

Josh then transferred his childhood model of relating onto his marriage, without consciously knowing that these pathways of emotional behavior were being deeply laid. What he knew at the time was that he felt wronged and used by Lois. Like many spouses, he made the mistake of not recognizing his childhood distortion in fair relating, and then compounded the problem by holding Lois primarily accountable. This unconscious maneuver loyally protected his parents at the expense of his marriage. But this displacement was actually disloyal to himself and unfair to Lois. This confusion made Josh more susceptible to the romantic illusion that the new love of an affair would enable him to sidestep his task of learning how to rebalance fairness with Lois and with his parents, with whom he already had deep, if imperfect, relationships. To heal, Josh had to make direct claims for fairness in all of his primary relationships, rather than acting out his distress. That was Josh's reality. What was Lois's?

Lois's Side

Between the two families, Josh and Lois had always enjoyed spending more time with Lois's parents—they were easier to get along with, especially her father who was affectionate, warm, and funny. He was an architect, too—he and Josh had a lot in common. Josh got the closeness from her father and family that he hadn't gotten from his own. And unlike in Josh's family, when there was a problem, no matter how small, the family talked out everything. Then Lois's father died, and things changed dramatically. Lois's mother fell apart—she'd never been on her own before. Lois looked in on her mother daily, and had her over to dinner twice a week. It was a strain, but of course they needed to help out. Despite these challenging circumstances, how could Lois's childhood, which she recounted in glowing terms, have had any negative influence on her or her marriage?

At the outset, Lois clearly believed that she was the only injured party. But while no one deserves to be betrayed by an affair, or have their partner justify infidelity by blaming them (as Josh had initially done), it's still imperative that the wounded partner recognize that it's counterproductive, as well as unrealistic, to believe that responsibility between any two partners is unshared. A marriage heals best when each partner is accountable. Lois's challenge was to discover her part. Her childhood provided important clues.

Lois's Baggage

Lois was the youngest of three children, with siblings, six and three years older. Her mom reentered the workplace when Lois started elementary school. Lois recalls that she was particularly clingy when her mom returned to work. "I loved being the baby of the family. I was indulged by my parents and my siblings." This was evident in many ways. While her older siblings recall their father as being very strict and stern, Lois never had that experience of him. She was "Daddy's little girl." And more than her siblings, Lois turned to her mother when she was upset. Later on, Lois called her parents daily from college, sometimes talking to her mom more often—tearfully describing a recent breakup with a boyfriend, frustration over a bad haircut, or flubbing a test. Nothing was too small to take to her mother. Her mother calmed her down in a way Lois couldn't do for herself. This pattern of seeking reassurance continued into adulthood.

Until she married Josh, Lois lived at home. Her parents didn't need the money, and so they didn't ask Lois to contribute toward her living expenses. Sometimes her father would slip her extra cash to pay for an overcharged credit card, just to help her out. "It was really the perfect childhood. That's why it feels hard to be critical. I owe my parents. I owe my family for giving me the kind of life I had, the kind of attention I got. They were so loving. And when Josh and I married, they accepted him into the family with open arms. He was another son to them."

The problem, as you might discern, is that Lois's childhood lasted too long. It had lasted into her marriage. Lois's parents had erred by giving too much. Lois hadn't learned from her family what a reasonable amount of give-and-take in a relationship looked like. She had never had the experience of anyone leaning on her. She had seldom been asked to reciprocate. Instead she had a false sense that since she was a good person, her take on things was fair. But because Lois had taken so much with little expectation for return, her sense of fairness was skewed, and perpetuated her major mistake of expecting and taking too much. She was a kind and loving person; that much was true. Her parents adored her and she knew that. She had benefited in many ways from this unconditional love. But her parents hadn't helped her grow up with an accurate take on fairness.

Through her therapy, Lois eventually recognized that it was inherently unfair to expect Josh to replace her mother as the source of her confidence building. It wasn't reasonable or fair to transfer her expectations for unconditional love and support of a parental nature onto her husband. Josh felt relieved that Lois had finally acknowledged this pattern. While all marriages hopefully provide each spouse with a "port in the storm," when one partner is always in the storm, and the other is always the port, the relationship can't be reciprocal. It can't be fair. The lopsided dynamic between Lois and Josh was one factor that made their marriage vulnerable to Josh's affair. Lois had implicitly asked Josh to function *in loco parentis*. After her father's death, Lois turned to Josh more and more, as now Lois was the support for her mother. To repair things on her side, Lois had to become more accountable, as well as acknowledge how she had burdened Josh.

Healing a Monumental Injury

With such significant blows to basic fundamental fairness, you only have two choices: you can try to understand the underlying meaning of the fairness imbalances in order to heal, or you can more simply devalue your partner. A partner can be reduced to a cheater, a gambler, an alcoholic, a tyrant, an abuser, or a manipulator. These representations may recognize *a* truth. But typically in relationships, there are multiple truths. There is the truth of the injured party, there is the truth of the injurer, and there is the truth between them. There are multiple layers of truth, and many factors that create imbalances between partners.

For Josh and Lois, the path to refilling their reservoir of trust began with recognizing the injustices, small and large, between them. What had begun as a simple story of Josh's infidelity had grown more complicated with their understanding of the legacies and models of fairness they brought and then transferred onto their marriage, with near disastrous results. Next, they were encouraged to take an inventory of the consequences of how their unfinished business from childhood was transferred into marriage. What did they discover?

TRAJECTORY OF FAIRNESS ISSUES: FROM CHILDHOOD TO MARRIAGE

EXPERIENCES FROM CHILDHOOD	CONSEQUENCES TO THE MARRIAGE
Josh	
Only felt valued for achievement	Overfunctioned
Parents failed to recognize his needs	Met Lois's needs, then felt depleted, angry, resentful
Never learned to make a fair claim	Depended on Lois to know what he needed
	(continued)

Emotional hurts never acknowledged	Buildup of resentment and sense of entitlement to act out to get his needs met
Closeness = vulnerability = danger	Felt more powerful to be critical and angry
Lois	
"Babied" in childhood with loss of autonomy	Overreliance on Josh to make her feel okay
Expectation that she would be on the receiving end	Hadn't learned to have reciprocal give-and-take
Parental love was an unconditional one-way street	Love wasn't expanded to include the concept of fairness

Next, Josh and Lois were asked to identify what fair give-and-take in the present would look like. Trust couldn't be rebuilt unless each fundamentally changed a former pattern of relating. For Lois, that change would entail a form of growing up. She had to learn the difference between a legitimate need for support, and a burdensome dependency on Josh for a type of parenting. To learn this, she needed to explore the roots of her unfair expectations. For Josh, it meant learning how to make a claim instead of critical distancing or acting out. He also needed to make peace with the lost possibility of a life with Dee-Dee.

Lois hadn't anticipated that for their marriage to heal, she'd have to make some changes, too. After all, one of her original questions in therapy had been "What's wrong with Josh?" At first, she was understandably angry with me for suggesting that she had work to do, too. This is a common response to being betrayed—the belief that what the marriage needs is for the *spouse* to change. And there's some truth to it, just not the whole truth. Even though Josh had drained most of the trust by his affair, Lois had made some significant withdrawals herself. Once she understood that no one was accusing her of being a bad wife, or of letting Josh off the hook for having an affair, she was able to give up her defensiveness, and think about what she could do differently. Lois would have to relinquish an old way of relating. She had to come to terms with the fact that having the favored spot of being the baby in her family actually cost her something important. It came at the expense of her self-reliance, and Josh's respect. It cost Josh something, too. It unfairly burdened him with unrealistic expectations for what a partner could continuously provide. Lois owed it to herself and to Josh to risk a new and fairer way of relating.

For Josh the first challenge to repair required him to stop justifying his infidelity (Lois was too needy so his feelings had changed) and start being accountable in a more complicated way. He had to stop defending himself and take the risk of recognizing painful truths about himself and about his growing up. He had to accept the fact that his mode of overfunctioning was his responsibility to stop. No one else could do this for him. He had to know when to say enough is enough rather than lashing out at Lois. He had to identify what changes he needed Lois to make. Instead of blaming Lois for not meeting his needs, Josh had to replace blame with claims. Key to this change was Josh's insight that his old belief about unconditional love was misguided. Underneath his apparent anger at Lois was a childhood longing to be so well known and loved that his needs would be met automatically.

Yet Josh still worried that making claims would make him vulnerable to being rejected; vulnerable to feeling foolish for asking. That was a possibility, but he was more likely to get his needs met if he made a claim, which would empower him regardless of the outcome. Another challenge for Josh lay in figuring out what to ask for. He'd never had much practice recognizing his feeling states and his needs. Josh had to learn that when he felt angry, it was usually because he was hurt and needed something. To Josh it felt more powerful to be angry than needy, but he slowly realized that he was better off translating angry feelings into constructive claims. For example, instead of resenting Lois for asking him for confidence building, he could give her a few minutes, and then tell her that while he hoped she'd feel better, he needed to change the subject, or even have them relax and have fun at the end of the day. Josh had to discover what he needed, and make himself, his feelings, his hopes, wishes, desires, and expectations known. In the crucible they forged between them they would sort out what was fair. But Josh first had to supply the basic ingredients of self-knowledge. His old pattern of selflessly complying with what Lois wanted usually flamed into an angry outburst later. He could consider her, but still ask for his terms of consideration. He learned that caring about another is different from caretaking another. As he took these steps, he gradually and simultaneously experienced remorse for how he had truly hurt Lois. His regret and empathy for her replaced his anger. They began to be able to joke around and have fun again. They commented that they felt closer to each other in a new way than they'd experienced before. Parallel with these changes, Josh found himself attracted to Lois again. Now that he didn't feel so burdened by and resentful of her, their sex life improved. Now that he wasn't so impatient with her, her desire for him rekindled, too.

Rebuilding trust has many action steps. In addition to the ones mentioned above, Lois and Josh decided to talk with their parents about their childhood experiences of the imbalances in give-and-take. They wanted to understand the context of their lives better by inviting their parents to respond. This is different than a blame convention; rather it's a genuine attempt to be closer by repairing past unfairness. For Josh, this meant letting his parents know how he had struggled to feel valued for anything other than his accomplishments and being a good caretaker. He decided to talk with his parents about how he could never turn to them. He wanted to talk with them about Dee-Dee's abortion when he was in high school, but first, he needed to take another risk and tell Lois about it. He was quite apprehensive, but he was tired of having secrets, tired of never feeling fully lovable unless he hid his shameful and imperfect self. He hoped that the efforts he had made to rebuild trust would hold them together in the fallout of his last painful secret.

Josh gathered his courage and told Lois about the secret of Dee-Dee's pregnancy and abortion. At the same time, he reassured Lois that he no longer had any ambivalence. He felt closer to Lois than he ever had, he loved her, and wanted to recommit himself to their marriage. While Lois reeled from his disclosure at one level, at another, it helped her understand why Josh had had such a hard time letting Dee-Dee go. Now Josh's lack of closure with Dee-Dee, and why he let his parents stay in touch with her made sense. It wasn't simply because Dee-Dee was his high school girlfriend, but also because Josh felt terribly guilty, fearing that he had screwed up Dee-Dee's life. He had taken his father's advice, but his conscience wouldn't let him forgive himself. His long-held secret had made it that much harder for him to be emotionally vulnerable with Lois. Now there were no more secrets, and no more shame. While Lois didn't anticipate it, shortly after Josh confided in her, she felt more secure and closer to him than ever. Finally, she felt that *they* were the couple. Having told Lois his deepest secret, Josh was prepared to tell his parents about this critical juncture in his relationship with them.

Josh's parents were stunned when he told them about the abortion, now almost twenty-five years later. "Dad and Mom, I tried to tell you but Dad scared me off. I was just a kid really, and I couldn't tell you—always afraid of disappointing you. Well, look what being strong has gotten me—screwing up my marriage, distant from you. I can't do it anymore." His mother moved to put her arm around him. "Josh, you were always there for me. I'm sorry I wasn't there for you, honey." His father hung his head and said, "I really messed up, huh? I'm sorry, son." His parents didn't know what else to say, but their sad silence spoke for them. Josh then made a claim: "I know you love me, but I can't stay stuck in that old role anymore. I need you to do something for me." "Sure, anything," they promised. "Stop your contact with Dee-Dee. I never put my foot down, and it's been wrong and hurtful to Lois. She deserves better from all of us." Josh's mother started worrying right away: "But won't that hurt Dee-Dee's feelings? What will we tell her parents?" But Josh's father "got it" immediately: "Josh is giving us another chance, and he's the most important person to us. None of the rest matters." They agreed to end their relationship with Dee-Dee.

When I saw Josh the next week he was hopeful—nearly buoyant. "You know, I feel better about seeing my parents again. Not that it will be perfect, but maybe we could have a closer relationship. The thing with my father is, he really heard me." Josh smiled, appearing lost in thought. When I asked what he was thinking, he said, "I just keep playing my father's words over and over again, '. . . he's the most important person to us.'"

For Lois the new fairness meant she had to stop parentifying Josh. She had to learn a better balance of give-and-take. She decided to have a heart-to-heart talk with her siblings and mother, too, about how the problem with being the "baby" in the family had only changed when her father died. Lois's mother and siblings knew immediately what she was talking about. They had been actors in the same play and were relieved to talk about it so openly. Her siblings admitted that they had resented Lois for her privileged position. They hadn't imagined that it had cost her anything. Lois told them that part of her marital problems arose because she had carried this pattern into her marriage. Another shift for Lois came in the loyalty department of her marriage. It wasn't helping that Lois thought of her family as superior to Josh's. Now that Josh had evaluated his family's fairness model, and she had challenged hers as well, the couple had more appreciation for both the upside and downside of each family. Each set of parents had brought their own blinders to parenting, as well as their evident investment and love. Josh and Lois had truly created a new fairness model for themselves. It wouldn't be perfect—but it would be fairer.

Josh and Lois knew that the work of fairness would be ongoing. They had taken many risks and were willing to be surprised by what they learned about themselves and each other. Their crisis had precipitated both stress and growth. They had challenged their former way of relating, and become more loving because they were fairer. Over time, their trust deepened. Although neither will ever forget Josh's affair, their new insights, the awareness they gained from their ordeal, and their determination to find fairness in the midst of tremendous pain, strengthened their marriage. A couple of years after our last session, I was surprised to receive a holiday card from them. Enclosed was a vacation photo of Josh and Lois in ski gear with their grown children. Inscribed was the greeting: "We just celebrated our 25th anniversary! Happy New Year!" I celebrated, too.

What can we learn from the paradox of enduring injustices, from the couples that stay together despite serious breaches of fairness? I think more than any other lesson, there is a second paradox in the fascinating and complex lives of couples. In the midst of injustice, in the minefields of mistrust, resentment, and even despair, a new model of fairness can emerge and take root to bring about healing. Emotional pain can motivate couples to evaluate their old beliefs, their distortions in give-and-take, their misaligned loyalties, and their destructive ways of relating, and create a new fairness. While documenting the many ways that enduring injustice leads to unhappiness, chapter 9 also provides a blueprint for the restoration of fair relating and healing, or to put it in Tolstoy's words—happiness.

APPLYING YOUR
FAIRNESS TOOLBOX

I began this book with the notion that there are two major puzzle pieces to finding happiness. One is relatedness, and the other fairness. Yet, as you've learned, you don't simply stumble on fairness because you're a good person, or because you have a strong conviction about right and wrong, or even because you love or are loved. Fairness takes work. Fortunately, most couples can learn to be fair. The preceding chapters have introduced you to the many facets of fairness in an intimate relationship. You learned that your instinctive sense of fairness makes you better at protesting *what's not fair*, than defining *what is*. You learned that your intuitive take on fairness lulls you into believing that you "know" what's fair, rather than understanding that models of fairness are largely learned in our families. Yet your family model is only one among an infinite number—as many models as there are families. You also learned that your assumptions about love and fairness need to be thoughtfully evaluated, so that you can create a new kind of fairness *between* you and your partner, one that better serves both your needs. I think of fairness as a precious resource to be mined. Sometimes fairness is in abundance, sometimes obscured and buried under mounds of hurt, misconceptions, and competing perceptions. However hidden, fairness can be discovered with the right skills and tools.

Before we end, I want to tell you one last story. This story isn't about a couple, but about all couples. And it's true. Friends of mine were in Washington State many years ago on a vacation. They decided to visit the Mount Saint Helens volcano site following its eruption in 1980. At that time, the entire country and the world watched their television sets in horror, fascination, and disbelief as southern Washington and northern Oregon were covered by ash from this massive eruption. Homes were destroyed and people lost their lives. As my friends approached the Visitor's Center of Mount Saint Helens, park rangers stopped them. My friends explained that they had lived in the Pacific Northwest when the volcano erupted and they simply wanted to see what it looked like some seven years later. With a grin on his face, one ranger said, "If you want to see some really good destruction, take the main road east and then south." Later, my friends laughed at the idea of a park ranger—a protector of the environment—suggesting they might want to see "really good destruction."

What my friends found that day at Mount Saint Helens was, yes, some *really good destruction*. But what was most surprising to them was how much vegetation had returned to this recently desolate landscape. Among the burnt and twisted remnants of trees and gray ash, was new growth. In fact, ecologists and geologists were amazed by the resiliency of the vegetation in the aftermath of such destruction. And that brings us to the reason for telling this story: it's a story of renewal, of the ability to find the resources of strength and resiliency where it's least expected so that new growth can take place.

While I see the destructive aftermath of partners' injustice in my clinical practice, more hopefully, I also see couples' courage and resilience to renew their relationships. Paradoxically, unfairness can be harnessed for the sake of new growth. I wrote this book to offer you, the reader, the ability to create the new growth from fairness in your relationship. In that spirit, let me remind you of the tools you now have.

First, you can learn to be fair. Start by reevaluating the model of fairness that you bring with you from your family. Look at both the benefits and the burdens of how your parents transmitted their expectations about give-and-take, and their assumptions about love and fairness. The ability to do this will enable you to take an honest look at your own model of fairness. Hopefully, you've seen that one person's model isn't necessarily better than another's—just different. You may want to keep some facets of your fairness model, but other imperfections—the misconceptions, loyalty binds, imbalances in reciprocity—may best be smoothed away. When two people are willing to honestly and openly evaluate their models for fairness, they can learn to be fair.

Second, let go of the supreme advantage of a one-sided perspective. You have to let go of having only "your story" running through your brain's playback machine. Your internal monologue, cataloging the wrongs against you, is an obstacle to fairness. A one-sided perspective is susceptible to blaming the other. With just one version of the truth, there is no complicated context to consider, just black or white, right or wrong—where you'll miss what might be true for the other person. Being fair asks you to try to see it your way, my way, and then, the truth *between* us.

Third, practice what you've learned. While no one is obliged to remain in a marriage that is chronically unfair, you can first do your part to make it fair. In any intimate relationship, it takes two to rebuild fairness and restore trust. If one partner refuses to take responsibility, you may not be able to overcome this obstacle jointly. But *you* can initiate and attempt all of the repair steps, even with a resistant partner, even when you don't get the outcome you want, or even deserve. You can decide what other options remain, such as rebalancing give-and-take by giving less if you can't get more of your needs met; or setting reasonable limits to buffer harmful consequences instead of accepting a life of codependency. You can continue to speak up for what's fair to you, while giving credit where credit is due. Being fair is your choice. You'll know that you've done what's within your control. That knowledge can relieve you of a future sense of regret or self-doubt. So, ask yourself: "What can I fairly offer as well as claim? What can I be responsible for?" If you don't make enough progress on your own, try to get your partner to see a couples therapist with you. If your partner's initial response is no, go for your own sake. See what you can learn. It only takes one person to change the system. A therapist trained in couples' relationships can often provide a balanced and nuanced perspective, help you see your own blind spots, and offer suggestions for new and fairer ways of relating.

Fourth, improve the relationship skills you learned in childhood. You bring the same relationship skills to marriage that you learned in childhood (unless you have thoughtfully examined and revised them). Your childhood skills include how major or minor differences and unfair experiences were handled between you, your parents, and other family members. Whatever you didn't resolve is the unfinished business that burdens you now. With extra baggage weighing you down, it may be impossible to even imagine how to repair problems in your marriage. You may expect that letting time pass, going back to acting nice, having makeup sex, or letting it go will put things back together again. When the injustices are small and not repetitive, these can be workable strategies. But often, you need more than childhood know-how to bring to the vital work of marriage. Most people hope that love will allow them to leave the past behind. What is truer is that we are the past as we act on the present.

Fifth, let go of anger—risk being vulnerable again. Anger can be quite pleasurable, and fairness difficult. Despite the fact that expressing anger often leads to more aggression, people choose to be angry and stay angry for the same reason they eat chocolate. It's gratifying. Anger lights up the same delicious part of the brain that eating chocolate does. When partners convert injustice into ongoing anger, they often feel more powerful than hurt. While anger itself is a helpful and naturally defensive emotion, ongoing anger is pathological and destructive. It feels good, but it's not good for you or your relationship. Entrenched anger represents a power position and a significant obstacle to fair relating. Staying angry and not repairing a relationship may make you feel stronger and less vulnerable. Yet retesting fairness and rebuilding trust gets you more than anger or revenge.

Sixth, remember—repair is a two-way street. Too often, partners think that it's all up to the other person to change and make it right. Yet to grow through the pain of injustice, each partner must work to become fairer. Repair is a process, earned *between* two people, not simply the result of one partner's change or another's gift of forgiveness. For healing, like fairness, depends on the hard work of understanding each other's side, making reparative efforts to replenish trust, and from that mutual endeavor you've created a new kind of fairness.

My clients sometimes wonder as they prepare to leave therapy, how they'll do without my support. I reassure them that the tools I've shared with them, to live fairer, freer lives are now their tools, not mine. I also remind them that the work of finding fairness in marriage is an organic, ongoing process. While learning to be fair and learning how to heal the experience of injustice is a challenging and messy choice, it's also a hopeful and powerful resource. Finding fairness is work you do for your own sake. Hopefully you'll be rewarded by an outcome worthy of your effort: a happier relationship. But at the very least, you'll grow, and gain an enhanced sense of individual freedom that is both more empowering and freer of feelings of regret. You're likely to realize a better sense of what you deserve to receive, as well as what's fair to give. Finding fairness is now your paradigm for a healthy and lasting marriage. Fairness is both a way of relating and a way of life that strengthens one of the most important bonds in your life—the bonds of love.

APPENDIX

Beyond Self-Help

Sometimes self-help isn't enough to solve problems, especially those that have gone on for several months. You may need a specific treatment for an individual problem such as substance abuse, anxiety, or depression—and couples therapy to improve your relationship. Dozens of studies throughout the world have shown that couples therapy can help a relationship. Although it's also true that some relationships aren't helped, and others may experience symptom relief followed by a relapse. Still, the majority of couples benefit from couples treatment.

A good way to find a therapist is by word-of-mouth referrals from a friend, family physician, or minister. Another approach is to contact your community mental health service or local hospital. Many hospitals have excellent psychiatry/psychology/counseling departments. Again, just double-check that you're seeing someone well trained and qualified in couples psychotherapy.

Questions to Ask

Try to speak with a therapist before you set up an initial appointment to get a "feel" for the person—his or her style and approach, and whether you feel comfortable with the therapist. You can also often obtain information through a practitioner's Web site. Here are basic questions to ask:

1. What kind of training have you had in couples or family therapy? You'll want to know if a therapist has graduated from an accredited doctoral or master's degree program and if the person is licensed or belongs to an accredited organization for couples and family therapy.
2. What percentage of your practice is with couples or families?
3. How do you work with a couple so that each person feels it's balanced and fair?
4. When a marriage has serious problems, do you suggest divorce? When and why?
5. Have you worked with couples in my particular situation?
6. In your experience, what makes the difference between couples that improve and couples who don't improve?
7. What is your thinking on medications to help address depression and anxiety? Today, clinicians recognize the added benefit of psychiatric collaboration and pharmaceutical help when an emotional illness is impacting an individual, and often his or her relationships. If you're concerned about the need for medication, you may need a referral for a psychiatric consult.

Internet Resources

AUTHOR'S WEB SITE
B. Janet Hibbs, Ph.D., Contextual Therapy Associates of Philadelphia
www.drbhibbs.com/

PROFESSIONAL ORGANIZATIONS
American Association of Marriage and Family Therapists. The accrediting body for doctoral and master's prepared clinicians with licensure or specialty training in couples and family therapy.
www.aamft.org/

American Family Therapy Academy. An interdisciplinary group of psychiatrists, psychologists, and social workers who teach, supervise, and/or do research in couples and family therapy.
www.afta.org/

American Psychiatric Association. A professional organization for board-certified psychiatrists.

    www.psych.org/

American Psychological Association. A professional organization for licensed psychologists.

    www.apa.org/

National Association of Social Workers. An association of licensed social workers.

    www.naswdc.org/

RESOURCES FOR MENTAL HEALTH CONCERNS

The sites below provide information on the more commonly experienced mental health disorders.

Anxiety Disorder Association of America

    www.adaa.org/

National Alliance for Mental Illness

    www.nami.org/

National Institute of Mental Health

    www.nimh.nih.gov/

National Institute on Alcoholism Abuse and Alcoholism

    www.niaaa.nih.gov/

National Institute on Drug Abuse

    www.nida.nih.gov/

Substance Abuse and Mental Health Services Administration

    www.samhsa.gov/

There are many other available resources—books, support groups, and Internet sites, some of which can be found on my Web site.

NOTES

Introduction:
Why Being Fair Will Make Your Relationship Stronger

5 One of these is relatedness. Haidt, J. *The Happiness Hypothesis*. New York: Basic Books, 2006.

5 Interpersonal conflict makes us unhappy. Haidt, J. *The Happiness Hypothesis*. New York: Basic Books, 2006, p. 94.

5 Negative stressors can also contribute to heart disease, depression, and a lower rating on that elusive goal of "happiness." Eaker, E., Sullivan, L., Kelly-Hayes, M., D'Agostino, R., Benjamin, E. "Marital Status, Marital Strain, and Risk of Coronary Heart Disease or Total Mortality: The Framingham Offspring Study." *Psychosomatic Medicine*, 69, July/August 2007, pp. 509–513.

8 ... ancient wisdom that reflects an innate aspect of the moral code that makes us human. Wade, N. "Is 'Do unto others' written into our genes?" *The New York Times*, September 18, 2007, p. F1.

8 ... with non-reciprocating chimps became so angry that they hurled their feces at their unfair partners. Graham, S. ScientificAmerican.com. "Chimps' sense of justice found similar to humans." January 26, 2005. From Sarah Brosnan & Fran deWaal, Feb. 7, 2005, Proceedings of the Royal Society B: Biological Sciences.

8 Neuroscientists have traced our intuition for fair dealing to the right prefrontal cortex of the brain, which shows up as an electromagnetic pattern. Hotz, R. "Scientists draw link between morality and brain's wiring." *The Wall Street Journal*, May 11, 2007, p. B1.

8 ... recent studies that there is a fairness "organ" in the brain—by which they mean a strong system for tracking give-and-take. Cosomides, L., & Tooby, J. "Knowing thyself: The evolutionary psychology of moral reasoning and moral sentiments." *Business, Science, and Ethics*, 2002, pp. 91–127.

8   . . . participants will punish a group member who isn't playing a game in a cooperative manner—
     even when the punishment disadvantages the avenging player. Begley, Sharon. "Vengeance Is
     Mine, Sayeth the Lord—But Scientists Differ." *The Wall Street Journal*, Science Journal, October 15,
     2004, p. B1.

9   The understanding of what you owe your family is called *loyalty*. Böszörményi-Nagy, I., & Spark, G.
     Invisible Loyalties: Reciprocity in Intergenerational Family Therapy. New York: Harper & Row,
     1973.

19 After all wherever you go, there you are. Kabat-Zinn, J. *Full Catastrophe Living*. New York: Delta,
     1990.

19 . . . breakups occur as often due to chronic, unresolved fairness issues as they do to volatile dis-
     ruptions. Gottman, J., with Silver, N. *Why Marriages Succeed or Fail: And How You Can Make
     Yours Last*. New York: Fireside (Simon & Schuster), 1994.

19 . . . significant rise in divorce occurs when couples have been married 16 to 18 years (the first rise
     is before year five—in highly volatile marriages). Gottman, J. "Scientifically-based marital ther-
     apy." Clinical presentation, King of Prussia, Penn., May 7–8, 1999.

19 It's a surprising statistic, but explained by the fact that 100 years ago the primary cause was death;
     today it's divorce. Glick, P. "The future of the American family." In J. G. Wells (ed.), *Current Is-
     sues in Marriage and the Family* (3rd ed.). New York: MacMillan, 1983, pp. 289–301.

19 Divorce has become a functional substitute for death. Stone, L. *The Family, Sex and Marriage in
     England 1500–1800*. London: Weidenfeld & Nicholson, 1977.

20 Dr. Iván Böszörményi-Nagy and his colleagues, which focuses on the ethical nature of family re-
     lationships. See Böszörményi-Nagy, I., & Spark, G. *Invisible Loyalties: Reciprocity in Intergenera-
     tional Family Therapy*. New York: Harper & Row, 1973.

PART ONE
UNDERSTANDING FAIRNESS

Chapter 1. Recognizing Your Blind Spots and False Assumptions

25 The catch is, perceptions and expectations about love and fairness are similar to color-blindness.
     Shainess, N. *Sweet Suffering: Woman as Victim*. New York: Bobbs-Merrill, 1984.

27 Automatic thoughts and accompanying distorted beliefs such as these have been well studied by
     cognitive therapists. Burns, D. *Feeling Good* (2nd ed.). New York: Avon, 1999.

28 D. W. Winnicott calls "the good enough parent," who like the weatherman, gets it right about half
     the time. Winnicott, D. W. *The Maturational Process and the Facilitating Environment*. New York:
     International UP, 1965.

31 Hillel, an ancient religious scholar of the first century BCE, summed it up best:

     If I am not for myself, who will be?
     If I am only for myself, what am I?
     And if not now, when?

     See Marcus, Y. (Rabbi). *Pirkei avot: Ethics of the fathers*. Library Binding: 2005.

31 ". . . includes both one's own and other's needs." Thompson, L. "Contextual and relational mo-

rality: Intergenerational responsibility in late life." In J. A. Mancini (ed.), *Aging Parents and Adult Children*. Lexington, Mass.: Lexington Books, 1989, pp. 259–260.

34 "Asking for what we want can be as caring an act as responding to someone else's apparent need." Krasner, B. "Towards a trustworthy context in family and community." Unpublished paper presented at Villanova University, Villanova, Penn., July 1983.

34 Jerome Kagan, a well-respected psychologist, writes that "humans are selfish and generous, aloof and empathic, hateful and loving, dishonest and honest, disloyal and loyal, cruel and kind, arrogant and humble." Kagan, J. *Three Seductive Ideas*. Cambridge, Mass.: Harvard University Press, 1998, p. 191.

36 That's because there's an appetite and biological drive for justice, just as there is for food. Rosen, I. "Payback time: Why revenge tastes so sweet." Cited by Carey, B. *The New York Times*, July 27, 2004, pp. F1 and F6.

38 James Hollis, a noted Jungian analyst, put the dilemma this way: "If we forever see our life as a problem caused by others, a problem to be 'solved,' then no change will occur." Hollis, J. *The Middle Passage: From Misery to Meaning in Midlife*. Toronto: Inner City Books, 1993.

41 Beyond insight, personal and relationship growth also requires endurance and action. Jung, C. G. *Letters* (Bollingen Series XCV), 2 vols., vol. 1, p. 375. Trans. R.F.C. Hull. Ed. G. Adler, A. Jaffé. Princeton, N.J.: Princeton University Press, 1973.

Chapter 2. How Fair Are You?

55 Interpreting another person's unfair behavior is an innate human impulse, which has its origins in stone throwing. Zaslow, J. " 'It's All Your Fault': Why Americans Can't Stop Playing the Blame Game." *The Wall Street Journal*, September 14, 2006, Personal Section: Moving On, p. F1.

Chapter 3. Defining the New Fairness

66 ". . . What relationships do I need and want? What relationships do I have to keep, even when I don't feel like it?" Krasner, B., and Joyce, A. *Truth, Trust, and Relationships: Healing Interventions in Contextual Therapy*. New York: Brunner/Mazel, 1995, p. 18.

67 With fairness, the whole is more than the sum of its parts. Bertalanffy, L. von. *General System Theory*. New York: George Braziller, 1969.

68 Robert Trivers, theorist and biologist, calls "reciprocal altruism"—people taking turns being nice because they know the other will return the favor when they can. Trivers, cited in Pinker, S. "The moral instinct: Evolution has endowed us with ethical impulses. Do we know what to do with them?" *The New York Times Magazine*, January 13, 2008, Section 6, p. 32.

68 Evolutionary psychologists would tell us this is because our interests are yoked, or our genes are linked. Pinker, S. "The moral instinct: Evolution has endowed us with ethical impulses. Do we know what to do with them?" *The New York Times Magazine*, January 13, 2008, Section 6, p. 32.

70 *Earned entitlement* creates the future right to ask the receiver for care in return. Böszörményi-Nagy, I., and Spark, G. *Invisible Loyalties: Reciprocity in Intergenerational Family Therapy*. New York: Harper & Row, 1973.

70 A person on the receiving end (here the man at the top of the seesaw) incurs indebtedness. Böszörményi-Nagy, I., & Spark, G. *Invisible Loyalties: Reciprocity in Intergenerational Family Therapy*. New York: Harper & Row, 1973.

72   In a couple's invisible but powerful relationship ledger, reciprocity is the balancing act, that see-saw between care given weighed against care received. Böszörményi-Nagy, I., & Spark, G. *Invisible Loyalties: Reciprocity in Intergenerational Family Therapy.* New York: Harper & Row, 1973.

72   Failures of reciprocity lead to mistrust, resentment, and the depletion of energy to invest in the relationship. Böszörményi-Nagy, I., & Spark, G. *Invisible Loyalties: Reciprocity in Intergenerational Family Therapy.* New York: Harper & Row, 1973.

75   This kind of taking is called *destructive entitlement.* Böszörményi-Nagy, I., & Spark, G. *Invisible Loyalties: Reciprocity in Intergenerational Family Therapy.* New York: Harper & Row, 1973.

77   Dr. Iván Böszörményi-Nagy, psychiatrist and preeminent family theorist, first noted that loyalty dynamics shape the family's model of expectations and the give-and-take of relationships. See Böszörményi-Nagy, I., & Spark, G. *Invisible Loyalties: Reciprocity in Intergenerational Family Therapy.* New York: Harper & Row, 1973.

77   . . . child's early and growing recognition of parental care and prompts a child to care in return. Böszörményi-Nagy, I., & Spark, G. *Invisible Loyalties: Reciprocity in Intergenerational Family Therapy.* New York: Harper & Row, 1973.

84   "Acknowledgment refers to the willingness of one person to recognize and 'give credit' to the other." Karpel, M., & Strauss, E. S. *Family Evaluation.* New York: Gardner, 1983, p. 34.

87   That's the powerful scientific finding on the salutary effects of the validation of your reality. Fruzzetti, A. E. *The High Conflict Couple. A Dialectical Behavior Therapy Guide to Finding Peace, Intimacy & Validation.* Oakland, Calif.: New Harbinger Publications, 2006.

88   There's your story, your partner's story, and the story that an outside observer might tell. Christensen, A., & Jacobson, N. S. *Reconcilable Differences.* New York: Guilford Press, 2000.

89   On the other hand, when you withhold acknowledgment the result is a stingy, deprivation model for relating. Karpel, M., and Strauss, E. S. *Family Evaluation.* New York: Gardner, 1983.

100 As trust fluctuates, so does closeness. Abrams Springs, J., with Michael Spring. *After the Affair: Healing the Pain and Rebuilding Trust When a Partner Has Been Unfaithful.* New York: Perennial, 1996.

100 . . . you'll see trust visualized as a well between people. Buhl, J. Personal communiqué, 2006.

100 They're relating from the early glow of passionate love, with its surge in brain chemicals that produces the "falling in love" experience. Carey, B. "Watching new love as it sears the brain." *The New York Times,* May 31, 2005, pp. D1 and 6. Cites Aron: Aron, A., Fischer, H., Mashek, D., Strong, G., Li, Haifang, Brown, L. L. "Reward, motivation, and emotion systems associated with early-stage intense romantic love." *Journal of Neurophysiology,* 94: pp. 327–337. First published May 31, 2005. See Carey, B.

Chapter 4. Balancing Give-and-Take

109 . . . "generous economy" in relationships. Karpel, M., and Strauss, E. S. *Family Evaluation.* New York: Gardner, 1983, p. 186.

111 . . . when you give, you earn the entitlement (the "right") to receive. Böszörményi-Nagy, I., & Spark, G. *Invisible Loyalties: Reciprocity in Intergenerational Family Therapy.* New York: Harper & Row, 1973.

115 "The truth about intimate relationships is that they can never be any better than our relationships with ourselves." Hollis, J. *The Middle Passage: From Misery to Meaning in Midlife.* Toronto: Inner City Books, 1993, p. 47.

118 . . . he's trying to collect from the wrong person (sometimes a partner, sometimes sadly, a child).

Böszörményi-Nagy, I., & Spark, G. *Invisible Loyalties: Reciprocity in Intergenerational Family Therapy*. New York: Harper & Row, 1973.

119 . . . couples typically wait at least five years after the first signs of trouble to go to a couples thera-pist. Gottman, J. "Scientifically-based marital therapy." Clinical presentation, King of Prussia, Penn.: May 7–8, 1999.

125 problem of infantilization. Böszörményi-Nagy, I., & Krasner, B. *Between Give & Take*. New York: Brunner/Mazel, 1986.

124 Indebtedness is a by-product of childhood need. Hibbs, B. Janet. "The context of growth: Rela-tional ethics between parents and children." In L. Combrinck-Graham (ed.), *Family Contexts: Perspectives on Treatment*. New York: Guilford Publications, Inc., 1989.

128 "We don't see things as they are; we see them as we are." Nin, A. U.S. (French-born) author and diarist (1903–1977). (Quote widely attributed but unsourced.)

Chapter 5. The Baggage You Bring to Relationships

131 Your odds for divorce rise if your own parents were divorced (anywhere from a 50–100% rise). Amato, P. "How You Interact with Your Kids Today Can Affect Their Future Romantic Lives." Cited by Sue Shellenbarger, WSJ Online, Work and Family, July 13, 2006.

135 . . . it's an unfair pattern of relating, repeated over a long time. Kagan, J. *The Nature of the Child*. New York: Basic Books, 1984.

136 "I've been here before." Hollis, J. *The Middle Passage: From Misery to Meaning in Midlife*. To-ronto: Inner City Books, 1993, p. 13.

137 "More" for some can mean justice-seeking taken to the point of vengeance. Carey, B. "Payback time: Why revenge tastes so sweet." *The New York Times*, July 27, 2004, pp. F1 and F6.

139 These positive factors are predictive of a long and loving marriage. Collins, W. A. "How You Interact with Your Kids Today Can Affect Their Future Romantic Lives." Cited by Sue Shellen-barger, WSJ online, Work and Family, July 13, 2006, p. F1.

140 These dysfunctional patterns include: 1) inappropriate parent-child boundaries—such as the kind of poor limits that put kids in the middle of parental problems; or topsy-turvy roles where the child has adultlike responsibilities or worries; 2) uninvolved or emotionally disengaged parents; 3) criti-cal parent-child interactions; 4) harsh, inconsistent parental discipline; and 5) poor conflict-resolution skills. Collins, W. A. "How You Interact with Your Kids Today Can Affect Their Future Romantic Lives." Cited by Sue Shellenbarger, WSJ online, Work and Family, July 13, 2006, p. F1.

141 You are entitled to the preservation and protection of your parent-child relationships. Böszörményi-Nagy, I., & Spark, G. *Invisible Loyalties: Reciprocity in Intergenerational Family Therapy*. New York: Harper & Row, 1973.

149 Her drinking could be seen as an angry revenge exacted on herself for not being loved uncondi-tionally, either by her parents or Rafael. Rosen, I. Cited by Carey, B. "Payback time: Why re-venge tastes so sweet." *The New York Times*, July 27, 2004, pp. F1 and F6.

150 As you recall from the last chapter, *infantilization* occurs when parents don't hold children ac-countable for age-appropriate behavior or responsibilities. Böszörményi-Nagy, I., & Krasner, B. *Between Give & Take*. New York: Brunner/Mazel: 1986.

153 On the other side of the fairness fence is the situation of *parentification*. Parentification, as the word suggests, is a topsy-turvy role assignment in which the parent leans on the child in an age-inappropriate, adultlike way. Böszörményi-Nagy, I., & Krasner, B. "Trust-based therapy: A contextual approach." *American Journal of Psychiatry*, 1980, pp. 137, 767–775.

162 ". . . the hand that hurts can be the hand that heals." Cotroneo, M. "Women and Abuse in the Context of the Family." In *Journal of Psychotherapy and the Family*, vol. 3, no. 4 (Winter 1987), p. 86. Full Article is on pp. 81–96. The journal was published by the Haworth Press, Inc.

163 Psychologist Leslie Greenberg reminds us that people overlearn emotional pain in order to avoid repeating it. Greenberg, L. *Emotion-Focused Therapy*. Washington, D.C.: American Psychological Association Press, 2002.

PART TWO
REPAIRING EVERYDAY INJUSTICES
AND BREACHES IN FAIRNESS

Chapter 6. Family Loyalty Conflicts:
The Ties that Bond and Bind

180 ". . . innate moral predispositions." Haidt, J. *The Happiness Hypothesis*. New York: Basic Books, 2006.

182 "Well, my Daddy always did it with us, and nothing bad ever happened." Lauer, M. "I know I'm a good mom" (MSNBC.com) *Dateline:* "Interview with Britney Spears," aired 9 p.m., June 15, 2006.

Chapter 7. "Stupid" Fights: How the Relationship
Survival Kit Helps Day-to-Day Unfairness

214 She's burning money on the cell phone, time to misplace it. Carey, B. "Payback time: Why revenge tastes so sweet." *The New York Times*, July 27, 2004, pp. F1 and F6.

220 "It may seem natural to suggest that others do things the way you would do them, but that is taking account only of the message." Tannen, D. *I Only Say This Because I Love You*. New York: Ballantine Books, 2001, p. 19.

220 And it's even more frustrating when you try to talk about what you believe they implied and they cry literal meaning—denying having "said" what you know they communicated. Tannen, D. *I Only Say This Because I Love You*. New York: Ballantine Books, 2001, p. 19.

221 These are the ". . . small events in everyday life that can look insignificant until they touch some old conflict, some longstanding betrayal or shame the person." Rosen cited by Carey, B. "Payback time: Why revenge tastes so sweet." *The New York Times*, July 27, 2004, pp. F1 and F6.

224 Research on marital arguments has shown that criticism, contempt, defensiveness, and stonewalling are the four most destructive factors in a fight. Gottman, J. with Silver, N. *Why Marriages Succeed or Fail: And How You Can Make Yours Last*. New York: Fireside (Simon & Schuster), 1994.

224 Restoring fairness while repairing harm done is the single most important factor in creating and maintaining a healthy and enduring marriage. Gottman, J. with Silver, N. *The Seven Principles for Making Marriage Work*. New York: Three Rivers Press, 1999.

231 You're more likely to remember what caused you to return fire than recognize the damage you've caused. Gilbert, D. "He who cast the first stone probably didn't." *The New York Times*, July 24, 2006.

239 But Leslie, like anyone who has endured unfairness only has two real choices—Exit and Voice—
and both have risks. Gilligan, C. *Exit-voice dilemmas in adolescent development*. In A. Foxley,
M. McPherson, and G. O'Donnell, eds., *Development, Democracy and the Art of Trespassing: Essays in Honor of Albert O. Hirschman*. Notre Dame, Ind.: University of Notre Dame Press, 1986,
pp. 283–300.

239 . . . heart disease and depression. Parker-Pope, T. "Well: Marital Spats, taken to heart." *The New
York Times*, October 2, 2007, p. F1.

241 If you chronically silence yourself, you may lose track of your own feelings. On balance, the
risks are often worth taking. Parker-Pope, T. "Well: Marital Spats, taken to heart." *The New York
Times*, October 2, 2007, p. F1.

247 The very first psychological task in life is the development of basic trust. Erikson, E. *Childhood
and Society*. New York: Norton, 1963.

Chapter 8. Money, Children, Chores, and Sex:
Resolving Fairness and the Growing Pains of Love

252 . . . the losses come before the gains. Kegan, R. *The Evolving Self: Problem and Process in Human
Development*. Cambridge, Mass.: Harvard University Press, 1983.

254 This model of family life is fair, though not precisely equitable. Hibbs, B. Janet. "Intergenerational justice: An intergenerational approach to fathers who seek child custody." Dissertation:
Bryn Mawr College, 1984, p. 42.

254 If we didn't value fairness, it would be equitable for a child to work for his food, clothing, and
shelter. Hibbs, B. Janet. "Intergenerational justice: An intergenerational approach to fathers
who seek child custody." Dissertation: Bryn Mawr College, 1984, p. 42.

254 . . . "the second shift." Hochschild, A., & Machung, A. *The Second Shift*. New York: Penguin,
1989.

259 Men more often argue over sex and money. Eaker, E. Cited by Parker-Pope, T. "Marital spats,
taken to heart." *The New York Times*, Health Section, October 2, 2007, p. F1.

267 A recent Gallup poll showed that couples questioned about money management reported being
most likely to fight over "spending too much and saving too little." Chu, K. "Many marriages
today are 'til debt do us part." Gallup Poll, March 2006, conducted in conjunction with *USA Today*/CNN, *USA Today*, pp. 1–2.

274 While figuring out money issues is challenging enough in a first marriage, as the even higher divorce statistics for second marriages tell us, people aren't learning how to fix problems just by
changing partners. Carey, B. "Watching new love as it sears the brain." *The New York Times*,
May 31, 2005, pp. D1 and 6.

289 "Mating in captivity." Perel, E. *Mating in Captivity: Reconciling the Erotic and the Domestic*. New
York: HarperCollins, 2006.

289 . . . neurochemicals giving the brain a good washing during early love, desire settles into a routine. Aron, A., Fischer, H., Mashek, D., Strong, G., Li, Haifang, Brown, L. L. "Reward, motivation, and emotion systems associated with early-stage intense romantic love." *Journal of
Neurophysiology*, 94: pp. 327–337. First published May 31, 2005. Cited by Carey, B.

301 Dr. John Gottman, a world-renowned authority on marriage. It is reprinted with his permission,
including the introduction. Gottman, J. *Clinical Manual for Marital Therapy*. The Gottman Institute, 2005.

Chapter 9. Enduring Injustice: To the Brink, and Back to Fairness

306 . . . published in 1876. Tolstoy, L. *Anna Karenina*, translated by Joel Carmichael. New York: Bantam Books, 1981.

306 . . . it's often the chronicity of neglect, a pattern of poor treatment, repeated day to day that creates the more lasting harm. Kagan, J. *The Nature of the Child*. New York: Basic Books, 1984.

311 Breakups have peaks at years five to seven, and years eighteen to twenty. Gottman, J. "Scientifically based marital therapy." Clinical presentation, King of Prussia, Penn.: May 7–8, 1999.

311 The earlier breakups most often represent volatile marriages that crash and burn from the sheer destructive energy of fighting. Gottman, J. with Silver, N. *Why Marriages Succeed or Fail: And How You Can Make Yours Last*. New York: Fireside (Simon & Schuster), 1994.

311 On average, there's a five-year interval between the emergence of a significant relationship problem and when a couple first seeks help for it. Gottman, J. "Scientifically-based marital therapy." Clinical presentation, King of Prussia, Penn.: May 7–8, 1999.

316 "Okay, we have the triggering event for 'a lost possible self.'" King, L. A., & Hicks, J. A. "Whatever happened to 'What might have been'?" *American Psychologist*, 62, No. 7, 2007, pp. 625–636.

317 "A soul is never sick alone, but always through a betweenness, a situation between it and another existing being." Cited in Friedman, M. *Martin Buber: The Life of Dialogue*. New York: Routledge Press, 2002, p. 224.

Chapter 10. Applying Your Fairness Toolbox

357 Despite the fact that expressing anger often leads to more aggression, people choose to be angry and stay angry for the same reason they eat chocolate. Carey, B. "Payback time: Why revenge tastes so sweet." *The New York Times*, July 27, 2004, pp. F1 and F6.

BIBLIOGRAPHY

Abrams Springs, J., with Michael Spring. *After the Affair: Healing the Pain and Rebuilding Trust When a Partner Has Been Unfaithful.* New York: Perennial, 1996.

Amato, P. "How You Interact with Your Kids Today Can Affect Their Future Romantic Lives." Cited by Sue Shellenbarger, WSJ online, Work and Family, July 13, 2006, p. F1.

Aristotle. Nicomachean Ethics. Trans. Martin Ostwalk. Englewood Cliffs, N.J.: Prenctice Hall, 1962.

Aron, A., Fischer, H., Mashek, D., Strong, G., Li, Haifang, Brown, L. L. "Reward, motivation, and emotion systems associated with early-stage intense romantic love." *Journal of Neurophysiology,* 94: pp. 327–337. First published May 31, 2005. Cited by B. Carey.

Begley, Sharon. "Vengeance Is Mine, Sayeth the Lord—But Scientists Differ." *The Wall Street Journal,* Science Journal, October 15, 2004, p. B1.

Bertalanffy, L. von. *General System Theory.* New York: George Braziller, 1969.

Böszörményi-Nagy, I., & Krasner, B. *Between Give & Take.* New York: Brunner/Mazel, 1986.

Böszörményi-Nagy, I., & Krasner, B. "Trust-based therapy: A contextual approach." *American Journal of Psychiatry,* 1980, pp. 137, 767–775.

Böszörményi-Nagy, I., & Spark, G. *Invisible Loyalties: Reciprocity in Intergenerational Family Therapy.* New York: Harper & Row, 1973.

Buhl, J. Personal communiqué, 2006.

Burns, D. *Feeling Good* (2nd ed.). New York: Avon, 1999.

Carey, B. "Watching new love as it sears the brain." *The New York Times,* May 31, 2005, pp. D1 and 6. Cites Aron.

Carey, B. "Payback time: Why revenge tastes so sweet." *The New York Times,* July 27, 2004, pp. F1 and F6. Cites Irwin Rosen.

Christensen, A., & Jacobson, N. S. *Reconcilable Differences.* New York: The Guilford Press, 2000.

Chu, K. *USA Today*. "Many marriages today are 'til debt do us part." Gallup Poll, March 2006, conducted in conjunction with *USA Today*/CNN, *USA Today*, pp. 1–2.

Collins, W. A. *How You Interact with Your Kids Today Can Affect Their Future Romantic Lives*. Cited by Sue Shellenbarger, WSJ online, Work and Family, July 13, 2006. http://online.wsj.com/article/SB115274479575305061.html

Cosomides, L., & Tooby, J. "Knowing thyself: The evolutionary psychology of moral reasoning and moral sentiments." *Business, Science, and Ethics*, 2002, pp. 99–127.

Cotroneo, M. "Women and Abuse in the Context of the Family." In *Journal of Psychotherapy and the Family* (Winter 1987), vol. 3, no. 4.

Eaker, E. (cited by Parker-Pope, T.) "Marital spats, taken to heart." *The New York Times*, Health Section, October 2, 2007, p. F1.

Eaker E., Sullivan, L., Kelly-Hayes, M., D'Agostino, R., Benjamin, E. "Marital Status, Marital Strain, and Risk of Coronary Heart Disease or Total Mortality: The Framingham Offspring Study." *Psychosomatic Medicine*, 69, July/August 2007, pp. 509–513, 2007.

Erikson, E. *Childhood and Society*. New York: Norton, 1963.

Friedman, M. *Martin Buber: The Life of Dialogue*. New York: Routledge Press, 2002, p. 224.

Fruzzetti, A. E. *The High Conflict Couple. A Dialectical Behavior Therapy Guide to Finding Peace, Intimacy & Validation*. Oakland, Calif.: New Harbinger Publications, 2006.

Gilbert, D. "He who cast the first stone probably didn't." *The New York Times*, July 24, 2006.

Gilligan, C. *Exit-voice dilemmas in adolescent development*. In A. Foxley, M. McPherson, and G. O'Donnell, eds. *Development, Democracy and the Art of Trespassing: Essays in Honor of Albert O. Hirschman*. Notre Dame, Ind.: University of Notre Dame Press, 1986, pp. 283–300.

Glick, P. "The future of the American family." In J. G. Wells (ed.), *Current Issues in Marriage and the Family* (3rd ed.). New York: Macmillan, 1983, pp. 289–301.

Gottman, J. *Clinical Manual for Marital Therapy*. The Gottman Institute, 2005.

Gottman, J. "Scientifically-based marital therapy." Clinical presentation, King of Prussia, Penn.: May 7–8, 1999.

Gottman, J., with Silver, N. *The Seven Principles for Making Marriage Work*. New York: Three Rivers Press, 1999.

Gottman, J., with Silver, N. *Why Marriages Succeed or Fail: And How You Can Make Yours Last*. New York: Fireside (Simon & Schuster), 1994.

Graham, S. ScientificAmerican.com. "Chimps sense of justice found similar to humans." January 26, 2005. From Sarah Brosnan & Frans, de Waal, Feb. 7, 2005, Proceedings of the Royal Society B: Biological Sciences.

Greenberg, L. *Emotion-Focused Therapy*. Washington, D.C.: American Psychological Association Press, 2002.

Haidt, J. *The Happiness Hypothesis*. New York: Basic Books, 2006.

Hibbs, B. Janet. "The context of growth: Relational ethics between parents and children." In L. Combrinck-Graham (ed.), *Family Contexts: Perspectives on Treatment*. New York: Guilford Publications, Inc., 1989.

Hibbs, B. Janet. "Intergenerational justice: An intergenerational approach to fathers who seek child custody." Dissertation: Bryn Mawr College, 1984, p. 42.

Hillel the Elder. *Pirkei avot (Ethics of the fathers)*: 1st century BCE.

Hochschild, A., & Machung, A. *The Second Shift*. New York: Penguin, 1989.

Hollis, J. *The Middle Passage: From Misery to Meaning in Midlife*. Toronto: Inner City Books, 1993, pp. 13, 47.

Hotz, R. "Scientists draw link between morality and brain's wiring." *The Wall Street Journal,* May 11, 2007, p. B1.

Jung, C. G. *Letters* (Bollingen Series XCV), 2 vols., vol. 1, p. 375. Trans. R.F.C. Hull. Ed. G. Adler, A. Jaffé. Princeton, N.J.: Princeton University Press, 1973.

Kabat-Zinn, J. *Full Catastrophe Living.* New York: Delta, 1990.

Kagan, J. *The Nature of the Child.* New York: Basic Books, 1984.

Kagan, J. *Three Seductive Ideas.* Cambridge, Mass.: Harvard University Press, 1998, p. 191.

Kegan, R. *The Evolving Self: Problem and Process in Human Development.* Cambridge, Mass.: Harvard University Press, 1983.

Karpel, M., and Strauss, E. S. *Family Evaluation.* New York: Gardner, 1983, pp. 34 and 186.

Kiley, D. *The Peter Pan Syndrome: Men Who Have Never Grown Up.* New York: Avon Books, 1995.

King, L. A., & Hicks, J. A. "Whatever happened to 'What might have been'?" *American Psychologist,* 62, No. 7, 2007, pp. 625–636.

Krasner, B., and Joyce, A. *Truth, Trust, and Relationships: Healing Interventions in Contextual Therapy.* New York: Brunner/Mazel, 1995, p. 18.

Krasner, B. "Towards a trustworthy context in family and community." Unpublished paper presented at Villanova University, Villanova, Penn., July 1983.

Lauer, M. "I know I'm a good mom" (MSNBC.com). *Dateline:* "Interview with Britney Spears," aired 9 p.m., June 15, 2006.

Marcus, Y. (Rabbi). *Pirkei avot: Ethics of the fathers.* Library Binding: 2005.

Nin, A. U.S. (French-born) author & diarist (1903–1977). Quote widely attributed but unsourced.

Parker-Pope, T. "Well: Marital Spats, taken to heart." *The New York Times,* October 2, 2007, p. F1.

Perel, E. *Mating in Captivity: Reconciling the Erotic and the Domestic.* New York: HarperCollins, 2006.

Pinker, S. "The moral instinct: Evolution has endowed us with ethical impulses. Do we know what to do with them?" *The New York Times Magazine,* January 13, 2008. Section 6, p. 32.

Rosen, I. "Payback time: Why revenge tastes so sweet." Cited by B. Carey. *The New York Times,* July 27, 2004, pp. F1 and F6.

Shainess, N. *Sweet Suffering: Woman as Victim.* New York: Bobbs-Merrill, 1984.

Shellenbarger, S. *How You Interact with Your Kids Today Can Affect Their Future Romantic Lives.* WSJ online, Work and Family, July 13, 2006, p. F1.

Stone, L. *The Family, Sex and Marriage in England 1500–1800.* London: Weidenfeld & Nicholson, 1977.

Tannen, D. *I Only Say This Because I Love You.* New York: Ballantine Books, 2001, p. 19.

Thompson, L. "Contextual and relational morality: Intergenerational responsibility in late life." In J. A. Mancini (ed.)., *Aging Parents and Adult Children.* Lexington, Mass.: Lexington Books, 1989, pp. 259–260.

Tolstoy, L. *Anna Karenina,* translated by Joel Carmichael. New York: Bantam Books, 1981.

Trivers, R. Cited by S. Pinker. "The moral instinct: Evolution has endowed us with ethical impulses. Do we know what to do with them?" *The New York Times Magazine,* January 13, 2008, Section 6, p. 32.

Wade, N. "Is 'Do unto others' written into our genes?" *The New York Times,* September 18, 2007, p. F1.

Winnicott, D. W. *The Maturational Process and the Facilitating Environment.* New York: International UP, 1965.

Zaslow, J. " 'It's All Your Fault': Why Americans Can't Stop Playing The Blame Game." *The Wall Street Journal,* September 14, 2006, Personal Section, Moving On, p. F1.

INDEX